Measurement in the social sciences

Measurement in the social sciences

The link between theory and data

RICHARD A. ZELLER
Department of Sociology
Bowling Green State University

EDWARD G. CARMINES
Department of Political Science
Indiana University

Cambridge University Press

Cambridge

LONDON · NEW YORK · NEW ROCHELLE
MELBOURNE · SYDNEY

Published by the Press Syndicate of the University of Cambridge
The Pitt Building, Trumpington Street, Cambridge CB2 1RP
32 East 57th Street, New York, NY 10022, USA
296 Beaconsfield Parade, Middle Park, Melbourne 3206, Australia

First published 1980

Printed in the United States of America
Printed and bound by BookCrafters, Chelsea, Michigan

Library of Congress Cataloging in Publication Data
Zeller, Richard A.
Measurement in the social sciences.
Bibliography: p.
Includes index.
1. Social sciences—Methodology. 2. Social
sciences – Statistical methods. I. Carmines, Edward G.,
joint author. II. Title.
H61.Z433   300'.1'82   79-15786
ISBN 0 521 22243 5 hard covers
ISBN 0 521 29941 1 paperback

To Joanie and Ett

Contents

Preface

The purpose of this book is to present a systematic and integrated approach to measurement in the social sciences. Unlike most treatments of this topic, however, we will not focus predominately on random measurement error and reliability estimation. Instead, our principal aim is to examine the fundamental structure and implications of nonrandom (that is, systematic) measurement error, especially its effects on the validity of empirical measures.

Nonrandom measurement error does not yield easily to statistical analysis. Indeed, it cannot be detected and estimated unless a series of simplifying assumptions are made about the theoretical structure underlying the empirical measurements. Thus, estimating the amount of nonrandom error in the measurement process – which lies at the very heart of validity assessment – depends more on one's theoretical understanding of the particular substantive area than it does on the mechanistic application of statistical formulas.

In order to assess the reliability and especially the validity of social measures, we formulate a strategy based on the integration of evidence from factor analysis and construct validation. We analyze data from a variety of substantive domains to illustrate the generalized applicability of this approach to assessing measurements in the social sciences. Yet, our basic objective is theoretical in character. Our ultimate purpose is to convey the *logic* underlying this measurement strategy and, more generally, to sensitize researchers to the multiple sources of nonrandom measurement error that probably influence data in the social sciences. Chapter 1 discusses the language and main principles of social measurement. Chapter 2 presents a nontechnical treatment of factor analysis, paying particular attention to the data reduction capabilities of this technique.

The remaining chapters formulate a general strategy for assessing the measurement characteristics of items and scales designed to measure theoretical concepts. Chapter 3 discusses reliability while Chapter 4 focuses on validity. Chapter 5 presents a strategy for evaluating systematic measurement error. Chapter 6 elaborates on this integrated approach to measurement, outlining in greater detail the sequential methodology for assessing the construct validity of empirically generated factors. Finally, this measurement strategy is compared to Costner's path-analytic approach and Jöreskog's analysis-of-covariance-structures approach in the appendix.

The writing of this volume was a collective effort; it depended upon the contributions of many. We appreciate their efforts. At the risk of leaving out many whose contributions are appreciated, we specifically thank each of the following: John P. McIver for his constructively critical comments on the manuscript; Art Neal and Ted Groat for their encouragement in the pursuit of this line of investigation, and the use of their data in this context; George W. Bohrnstedt for allowing us to see his forthcoming discussion of social science measurement; our reviewers for the painstaking care with which they read the manuscript; the many students in our classes, who not only tolerated less sophisticated versions of the material but also made contributions that improved it; and those to whom the book is dedicated.

Richard A. Zeller
Bowling Green, Ohio

Edward G. Carmines
Bloomington, Indiana

1 Introduction to measurement

The link between observation and formulation is one of the most difficult and crucial of the scientific enterprises. It is the process of interpreting our theory or, as some say, of "operationalizing our concepts." Our creations in the world of possibility must be fitted in the world of probability; in Kant's epigram, "Concepts without percepts are empty." It is also the process of relating our observations to theory; to finish the epigram, "Percepts without concepts are blind."

Scott Greer (1969: 160)

Is it useful, as Seeman (1959) and Neal and Rettig (1963) suggest, to think of alienation as an umbrella concept covering the related but distinguishable dimensions of powerlessness, normlessness, meaninglessness, and social isolation? [Groat and Neal (1967) choose not to operationalize self-estrangement, a fifth dimension of alienation. We will concur with this judgment in our discussion.] Is self-esteem, as Rosenberg (1965) argues, a unidimensional attitude toward oneself that mediates between background characteristics and current behaviors? Is it useful, as Schutz (1966) insists, to think of interpersonal needs in terms of either the expression of or desire for inclusion, control, and affection?

In large part, our capacity to answer these questions depends upon the power and robustness of our measurement procedures. The importance of measurement to social research is well stated in an observation by Hauser (1969:127–9): "I should like to venture the judgment that it is inadequate measurement, more than inadequate concept or hypothesis, that has plagued social researchers and prevented fuller explanations of the variances with which they are confounded."

But why are the social sciences characterized by "inadequate measurement"? Although the answer to this question is no doubt complex and multifaceted, we would suggest that a fundamental component of any complete answer must lie with the most popular definition of the term, that provided by Stevens more than 25 years ago. "Measurement," Stevens (1951:22) wrote, "is the assignment of numbers to objects or events according to rules." This definition implies that measurement is mainly an empirical, almost mechanistic process. In other words, Stevens' definition does not refer to the theoretical component of the measurement process. But measurement serves a vital theoretical purpose, as aptly described by Blalock (1970:88–9): "Measurement considerations often enable us to clarify our theoretical thinking and to suggest new variables that should be considered. It is often thought, prior to actual attempts at measurement, that we really understand the nature of a phenomenon because we have experienced it directly. . . . Careful attention to measurement may force a clarification of one's basic concepts and theories."

The purpose of this book is to explicate an approach to measurement that focuses on the theoretical as well as the empirical components of the measurement process. Stated more fully, our purpose is to introduce, justify, and illustrate a systematic and integrated approach to measurement in the social sciences. Our primary aim is not to review the vast methodological literature dealing with the general topic of measurement; this literature is readily available in a variety of psychometric texts and more specialized articles. Our purpose is to provide a general framework for answering questions about measurement found in the social sciences such as those posed in the opening paragraph of this chapter.

In attempting to describe the basic nature of measurement in the social sciences, Blalock (1968:12) has observed that "sociological theorists often use concepts that are formulated at rather high levels of abstraction. These are quite different from the variables that are the stock-in-trade of empirical sociologists. . . . The problem of bridging the gap between theory and research is then seen as one of measurement error." Following Blalock, we define *measurement* as the process of linking abstract concepts to empirical indicants. The implications of this definition will be dealt with throughout the book.

The purpose of this chapter is to develop the terminology and main principles that underlie the process of measurement in the social sciences. More specifically, this chapter has three aims. First, we discuss some of the main differences between concepts and indicants as exemplified in the theory construction process. Second, we demonstrate that reliability and validity provide the language of measurement. Finally, we outline the basic criteria for assessing the reliability and validity of empirical measurements.

Concepts and indicants

Measurement, as we have pointed out, concerns the process of linking abstract concepts to empirical indicants. Stated somewhat differently, measurement has been defined as "the process that permits the social scientist to move from the realm of abstract, indirectly observable concepts and theories into the world of sense experience" (McGaw and Watson, 1976:205). This definition takes on greater meaning and importance when we consider more fully the properties and characteristics of the key terms "abstract concepts" and "empirical indicants."

Abstract concepts, such as alienation, self-esteem, and interpersonal needs, are the most salient and substantively infused elements used in the explanation of social behavior. Abstract concepts do not have a one-to-one correspondence with empirical indicants; they can be operationalized and measured in an almost infinite variety of ways. For example, the concept "cross-pressures" has been measured by the degree to which persons hold conflicting political attitudes, the degree to which they are members of organizations that push or pull them in different political directions, and the degree to which they identify with groups that are in conflict politically. The point is that abstract concepts can only be approximated by empirical indicants. Indeed, it is the very vagueness, complexity, and suggestiveness of concepts that allow them to be empirically referenced with varying degrees of success at different times and places.

This fundamental openness of meaning that is characteristic of concepts has been insightfully described by Kaplan (1964:61–70). He notes that concepts can never be thought of as closed, fixed quantities. Rather, the specification of the meaning of concepts always leaves their usage uncertain to some degree. As Kaplan (1964:63) asserts: "As the theory is used – for scientific as well as practical purposes – its meaning is progressively more fixed; but some degree of openness always remains."

However, because concepts can be neither directly observed nor measured, the systematic exploration, testing, and evaluation of social theory requires social scientists to use empirical indicants, designed to represent given abstract concepts. Thus, in contrast to concepts, *empirical indicants* are designed to be as specific, as exact, and as bounded as theoretical formulations and research settings will allow. Indicants, in other words, are intended to approximate and locate concepts empirically. But it should be noted that indicants are never able to fully exhaust nor completely duplicate the meaning of theoretical concepts. Any particular set of empirical indicants that one chooses, therefore, is only a small subset of an almost infinite number of possible indicants that could be selected to represent a particular concept. For example, the concept of self-esteem has been represented empirically by numerous attitude scales. In addition, it has been measured by strictly behavioral indicants and manipulated within experimental settings. Even with all of this, however, the concept of self-esteem still has – and always will have – many meanings that are not represented by empirical indicants.

From this discussion, it is not difficult to see that *both* abstract concepts and empirical indicants are necessary if a worthwhile social science is to thrive and develop. Essentially, concepts provide a degree of generality and abstractness that theories require if they are to be relevant in different historical periods and in different research settings — that is, across time and space. Indeed, it would not be too much of an oversimplification to say that explanations of social phenomena represent nothing more than the final product of a process in which concepts are logically and plausibly linked to one another. Empirical indicants, for their part, must be precise as well as complete if they are to properly represent their respective concepts empirically, as those concepts are articulated in social science theories. By providing an accurate representation of concepts, empirical indicants contribute to the theoretical development of the social sciences by highlighting those gaps that exist between theoretical formulations and observed reality. Greer (1969:160) comments upon this essential interdependence between abstract concepts and their empirical indicants: "Our creations in the world of possibility must be fitted in the world of probability; in Kant's epigram, 'Concepts without percepts are empty' . . . Percepts without concepts are blind."

Measurement and theory construction

It is, of course, one thing to define measurement in terms of the relationship between abstract concepts and empirical indicants and quite another to design a general strategy for assessing the extent to which any set of indicants accurately represents given theoretical concepts. Nevertheless, this is precisely our intent. Our purpose is to establish a strategy for assessing measurements in the social sciences. As a first step toward this goal, we discuss briefly the crucial role of measurement in evaluating the empirical applicability of social science theories.

Figure 1.1 presents a schematic representation of the process of evaluating the empirical applicability of a theory. It graphically illustrates the key role of measurement in this complex process. Although the meaning and implication of this figure will become clearer as our discussion unfolds in succeeding chapters, essentially it shows that measurement involves a set of specific linkages that tie the theoretical and empirical components of theory evaluation together. Figure 1.1 also indicates that there are two basic inferences concerning measurement. The first focuses on the empirical meaning associated with specific theoretical concepts and the second inference relates to the correspondence between theoretically specified relationships and empirically generated relationships. Although these inferences are theoretically distinguishable, they are related from an empirical

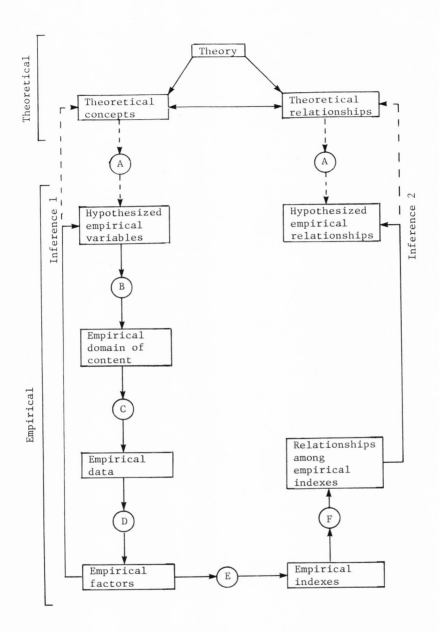

Figure 1.1. Schematic representation of the process of evaluating the empirical applicability of a theory. (A) Application of rules of correspondence (Kaplan calls this process "substruction"); (B) specification of operational definitions (Kaplan calls this "defining the property space"); (C) observation; (D) simplification of data (Kaplan calls this procedure "reduction"); (E) scaling; (F) analysis of index scores. Solid lines, direct inferences; dashed lines, indirect inferences between theoretical and empirical realms.

standpoint. That is, a successful measurement strategy will provide evidence relevant to both inferences.

Succeeding chapters will illustrate in great detail the critical role of measurement in evaluating the empirical applicability of theoretical propositions. Indeed, we will argue that the ultimate success of social science research depends strategically on how accurately theoretical concepts are measured. Viewed from this perspective, measurement is not an esoteric concern unrelated to the central issues of the social sciences but instead is woven into the very fabric of social research.

Language of measurement

Two key terms, reliability and validity, provide the essential language of measurement. A rather common definition of *reliability* is provided by Nunnally (1967:172): "Reliability concerns the extent to which measurements are *repeatable* – by the same individual using different measures of the same attribute or by different persons using the same measure of an attribute." From the vantage point of our definition of measurement, a highly reliable measure of self-esteem would imply, for example, that researchers using the same indicants to measure self-esteem – whether they be self-ratings, observer ratings, or whatever – would obtain the same results for a given set of individuals. Similarly, it would imply that a researcher would discover the same degree of self-esteem at two or more different times – assuming that the level of self-esteem itself did not change. Conversely, an unreliable measure is one that does not provide repeatable or consistent results. If several doctors use the same thermometer to measure the temperature of the same individual but obtain strikingly dissimilar results, the thermometer is unreliable. Thus, reliability is inversely related to the amount of random error in the measurement process.

Notice that in the preceding examples, it has not been indicated whether the indicants used to tap self-esteem do, in fact, reflect self-esteem or some other personality trait, such as anxiety or personal control. Nor has anything been said as to whether the thermometer actually measures temperature or some other physiological state, such as heartbeat or blood pressure. Strictly speaking, such considerations, despite their obvious importance, are not a part of reliability assessment because they do affect the consistency or repeatability of empirical measurements. Consequently, a set of indicants used to measure self-esteem can be perfectly reliable even if they have nothing to do with self-esteem, but measure alienation instead!

Thus, a highly reliable measure, in itself, does not ensure that one has obtained a good measure of a concept. What is also required is that the measure be valid. Nunnally (1967:75) has asserted: "In a very general sense, a measuring instrument is valid if it does what it is intended to do." Consequently, if a set of indicants were perfectly valid, it would represent the intended – and only the intended – concept. A less than perfectly valid measure, conversely, would imply that it does not fully represent the concept or that it represents something other than the concept.

From this discussion, it is easy to see that validity is more important than reliability. It is more important to have a set of indicants that corresponds to the concept for which one wants to obtain an empirical representation than it is to have a set of indicants that corresponds to some unspecified and theoretically uninteresting phenomenon. On the other hand, if a set of indicants does not represent anything systematic, it certainly cannot represent what it is intended to represent. Thus, to have a valid measure, one must have a reliable one; but simply because one has a reliable measure does not mean that it is valid as well. Reliability, then, becomes a necessary but not sufficient condition for validity. (We shall discuss a logical exception to this general statement later in this book.)

Classical test theory

The main body of statistical theory that has been used to estimate the reliability (and indirectly, the validity) of empirical measurements is classical test theory. Over the years, a vast and complex literature has developed on this topic. Fortunately, for our purposes, it is only necessary to discuss some of the underlying assumptions and basic results of this approach to measurement assessment.

Classical test theory begins with the basic formulation that an observed score, X, is equal to the true score, T, plus a measurement error, e. To state this idea as a formula:

$$X = T + e \qquad (1.1)$$

Lord and Novick (1968:36) make the following assumptions about measurement error:

1   The expected (mean) error score is zero,

$$E(e) = 0$$

2   The correlation between true and error scores is zero,

$$\rho_{(t,e)} = 0$$

3   The correlation between the error score on one measurement and the true score on a second is zero,

$$\rho_{(e_1,t_2)} = 0$$

4   The correlation between errors on distinct measurements is zero,

$$\rho_{(e_1,e_2)} = 0$$

From these assumptions, it follows that the expected (mean) value of the observed score is equal to the expected (mean) value of the true score. In formula form,

$$E(X) = E(T) \tag{1.2}$$

To derive the formula for reliability, we examine the consequences of the foregoing assumptions as follows [the Greek letter sigma (σ) with two subscripts refers to the covariance of the two subscripted variables]:

$$\sigma_x{}^2 = \sigma^2_{(t + e)}$$

By using algebraic expansion, we get

$$(t + e)^2 = t^2 + 2te + e^2$$

Hence,

$$\sigma_x{}^2 = \sigma_t{}^2 + \sigma_e{}^2 + 2\sigma_{te}$$

But by definition,

$$\sigma_{te} = 0$$

Hence, by dropping $2\sigma_{te}$, we get

$$\sigma_x{}^2 = \sigma_t{}^2 + \sigma_e{}^2 \tag{1.3}$$

In words, the observed score variance is equal to the sum of the true score variance and the error score variance. Reliability is then defined as the proportion of true variance to observed variance. In formula form,

$$\text{Reliability} = \rho_{xt}{}^2 = \sigma_t{}^2/\sigma_x{}^2 \tag{1.4}$$

The reliability of a measure varies between 0 and 1. If all observed variance is contaminated with error that is, by assumption, random, the reliability is 0. Conversely, if there is no random error involved in the measurement of some concept, the reliability equals 1.

To actually estimate reliability, it is necessary to obtain at least two distinct measurements of the phenomenon in question. These measurements must be either parallel, in which case they are assumed to have identical true scores and equal error variances, or they must be tau-equivalent, in which case only the former condition need hold. For convenience, let us assume that the two measures are parallel; symbolically, they can be expressed as follows:

$$X = T + e \quad \text{and} \quad X' = T + e'$$

where $\sigma_e{}^2 = \sigma_{e'}{}^2$ and $T = T$.

It may be useful to think of parallel measurements as being distinct from one another but similar and comparable in important respects. For example, examine the parallel measures of self-esteem from Rosenberg's (1965) self-esteem scale:

(a)   I feel that I have a number of good qualities.
(b)   I feel that I'm a person of worth, at least on an equal plane with others.

A respondent with high self-esteem will usually answer "often true" whereas a respondent with low self-esteem will usually answer "seldom true" to these statements, except, of course, for random fluctuations. However, this is precisely the point. If the responses to the items differ only with respect to random fluctuations, the items are considered to be parallel. Such items are distinct from one another but are similar and comparable in important respects.

Parallel measurements, such as the two items from Rosenberg's self-esteem scale, are assumed to have the following useful properties:

1   The expected (mean) values of parallel measures are equal,

$$E(X) = E(X')$$

2   The observed score variance of parallel measures are equal,

$$\sigma_x^2 = \sigma_{x'}^2$$

3   The intercorrelations among parallel measurements are equal from pair to pair,

$$\rho_{xx'} = \rho_{xx''} = \rho_{x'x''}$$

4   The correlations of parallel measures with other variables are equal,

$$\rho_{xy} = \rho_{x'y} = \rho_{x''y}$$

The correlation between parallel measures can be expressed in terms of error and true scores as follows:

$$\rho_{xx'} = \sigma_{xx'}/\sigma_x\sigma_{x'} = \frac{\sigma_{(t+e)}\sigma_{(t+e')}}{\sigma_x\sigma_{x'}}$$
$$= \frac{\sigma_t^2 + \sigma_{te} + \sigma_{te'} + \sigma_{ee'}}{\sigma_x\sigma_{x'}} \tag{1.5}$$

Because by assumption errors are uncorrelated with true scores and uncorrelated with each other and the standard deviations of parallel measures are equal, this expression reduces to

$$\rho_{xx'}^2 = \sigma_t^2/\sigma_x^2 \tag{1.6}$$

The correlation between parallel measures is equal to the true score variance divided by the observed variance.

The importance of this result is that it allows the unobservable true score variance to be expressed in terms of $\rho_{xx'}$ and $\rho_x{}^2$ – both of which are observable. In formula form,

$$\sigma_t{}^2 = \sigma_x{}^2 \rho_{xx'} \tag{1.7}$$

The true score variance is equal to the product of the observed variance and the correlation between parallel measures. Recalling from Formula 1.4 that reliability is $\rho_{xt}{}^2 = \sigma_t{}^2/\sigma_x{}^2$, it follows that the estimate of reliability is simply the correlation between parallel measures, because

$$\rho_{xt}{}^2 = \sigma_t{}^2/\sigma_x{}^2 = \sigma_x{}^2 \rho_{xx'}/\sigma_x{}^2 = \rho_{xx'} \tag{1.8}$$

Within classical test theory, validity is defined as the correlation between measurement X and measurement Y (Lord and Novick, 1968:61). That is,

$$\text{Validity} = \rho_{xy} = \sigma_{xy}/\sigma_x\sigma_y \tag{1.9}$$

If the two measures are parallel, then

$$X = T + e \quad \text{and} \quad Y = T + e'$$

Moreover,

$$\begin{aligned}
\sigma_{xy} &= \sigma_{[(t + e)(t + e')]} \\
&= \sigma_t{}^2 + \sigma_{te} + \sigma_{te'} + \sigma_{ee'} \\
&= \sigma_t{}^2
\end{aligned} \tag{1.10}$$

If the measures are parallel,

$$\sigma_{tt} = \sigma_t{}^2$$

Finally, validity is equal to

$$\rho_{xy} = \sigma_{xy}/\sigma_x\sigma_y = \sigma_t{}^2/\sigma_x{}^2 \tag{1.11}$$

It is thus seen that validity is equal to reliability – that "the reliability of a test is just its validity with respect to a parallel test" (Lord and Novick, 1968:63).

Although it is not proven here, it is also the case that the validity of a test with respect to any second measure cannot exceed the square root of its reliability (Nunnally, 1967:204; Lord and Novick, 1968:72). In formula form,

$$\rho_{xy} \leqslant \sqrt{\rho_{xt}{}^2}$$

or

$$\rho_{xy} \leqslant \sqrt{\rho_{xx'}} \tag{1.12}$$

There is no denying the importance of classical test theory in providing a sound statistical foundation for estimating the reliability and validity of empirical measures containing random error. Yet, it is crucially important to underline this qualification: that, by definition, classical test theory is only applicable if and when measurement error is entirely random. Stated simply, *in classical test theory, it is assumed that all measurement error is random*. Although this may be a tenable assumption with regard to research based on strict experimental designs, as in much of psychology, it is probably unjustified generally for data collected from sample surveys, field studies, or structured observations. Measurements based on data from these sources typically includes both random error and nonrandom or systematic error components. For example, systematic error includes yeasaying or naysaying (Sudman and Bradburn, 1974), social desirability (Crowne and Marlowe, 1964), and "memory effects." Moreover, systematic error is also present when a set of indicants measures more than the intended theoretical concept or represents a different theoretical concept entirely. By definition, these systematic errors do not conform to one or more of the basic statistical properties underlying random measurement errors. That is, with respect to systematic errors, one or more of the following occurs:

$$E(e) \neq 0$$
$$\rho_{te} \neq 0$$
$$\rho_{e_1 t_2} \neq 0$$
$$\rho_{e_1 e_2} \neq 0$$

For example, yeasaying and naysaying responses, which have been studied extensively under the general topic of response set, systematically inflate the relationship between items worded in the same direction, even if they would not be related otherwise. In this case, the correlation between errors on distinct measures is *not* zero and, consequently, the estimate of validity provided by classical test theory is inapplicable.

A second weakness of classical test theory is that it does not provide an adequate conceptualization of validity and the relationship between validity and reliability. It is simply not very useful or revealing to know merely that the validity of a measurement – its correlation with another variable – can never exceed the square root of its reliability. This posited relationship, as Bohrnstedt (1970:97) has observed, says nothing directly about validity – the degree to which a set of indicants measures what it is intended to measure. Nor does classical test theory provide an independent estimate of validity. On the contrary, its estimation occurs as a mere by-product of the assessment of reliability (Bohrnstedt, 1970:97).

Taken together, these two fundamental limitations of classical test theory – that it does not allow for the effects of systematic error and that it does not provide a compelling theoretical differentiation between reliability and validity – make it less than fully adequate as a general measurement model for the social sciences. Fortunately, these two limitations are logically related and can be solved simultaneously, which is demonstrated in the following section.

Reformulation of classical test theory

In our reformulation of classical test theory, an observed score, X, is equal to the true score, T, plus systematic measurement error, S, plus random measurement error, R. In formula form,

$$X = T + S + R \tag{1.13}$$

When some measurement error is systematic while other measurement error is random, the expected mean of the observed scores is equal to be expected mean of the true scores plus the expected mean of the systematic error. In formula form,

$$E(X) = E(T) + E(S) \tag{1.14}$$

For a finite number of observations, the mean of a variable becomes an unbiased estimate of the mean of the concept for which that item is an empirical indicant, plus the mean of the systematic error. In substantive terms, the observed mean estimates the mean of the concept plus systematic error.

Moreover, when measurement error is both systematic and random, the expected variance of the observed scores is equal to the expected variance of the true scores plus the expected variance of the systematic error plus the expected variance of the random error plus twice the covariance between the true and systematic scores. This important formula is derived as follows:

$$\sigma_x^2 = \sigma_{(t + s + r)}^2$$

Using algebraic expansion, we get

$$(t + s + r)^2 = t^2 + ts + tr + ts + s^2 + sr + tr + sr + r^2$$

Hence,

$$\sigma_x^2 = \sigma_t^2 + \sigma_{ts} + \sigma_{tr} + \sigma_{ts} + \sigma_s^2 + \sigma_{sr} + \sigma_{tr} + \sigma_{sr} + \sigma_r^2$$

But by definition,

$$\sigma_{tr} = \sigma_{sr} = 0$$

Hence, dropping the terms that equal zero and rearranging, we obtain

$$\sigma_x^2 = \sigma_t^2 + \sigma_s^2 + \sigma_r^2 + 2\sigma_{ts} \tag{1.15}$$

There are several matters of importance in Formula 1.15. First, since T and S may be correlated, the summing of the variances of T, S, and R will not invariably result in the variance of X. Instead, the sum of these variances plus twice the covariance of TS (acknowledging the possibility that T and S are correlated) sum to the variance of X. Within this context, it is not reasonable to think of partitioning the variance, as we did above. Instead, we can think of "describing components of the observed variance." Whereas the true, systematic, and random error variance components of the observed variance must be positive (or zero), the covariance TS may be either positive or negative. The implications of this will be discussed throughout this book.

Second, the observed variance and the random error variance can be estimated. However, from this information, we cannot estimate the true variance, the systematic error variance, or the covariance TS. Hence, without making additional substantive assumptions about the nature of the phenomenon under investigation, one cannot solve for the components of Formula 1.15. As Heise (1974:9) notes:

> There is no purely mechanical procedure for identifying latent variables with guaranteed theoretical validity. The definition of the latent variables underlying a set of indicators depends on two decisions that must be made in the course of the multivariate analysis – How many relevant latent variables are there? What is the proper pattern of correspondence between different latent variables and key indicators? – and these decisions always involve a subjective element.

Thus, although one cannot observe a concept, systematic error, or their covariance directly (because they are, in principle, unobservable), one can estimate these variances and covariances if one is willing to make informed, reasonable assumptions about the nature of the phenomena underlying a set of indicants. The criteria for making such informed, reasonable assumptions about the nature of the phenomena under investigation will be discussed throughout this book.

Within this context, one can meaningfully differentiate between reliability and validity. *Reliability* is the proportion of nonrandom variance; *validity* is the proportion of variance that the observed scores share with the true scores. In formula form,

$$\text{Reliability} = \frac{\sigma_t^2 + \sigma_s^2 + 2\sigma_{ts}}{\sigma_x^2} = \frac{\sigma_x^2 - \sigma_r^2}{\sigma_x^2} \qquad (1.16)$$

and

$$\text{Validity} = \sigma_t^2/\sigma_x^2 \qquad (1.17)$$

Formulas 1.16 and 1.17 are consistent with reliability and validity as defined earlier in this chapter. Reliability is the consistency or repeatability of measurements; validity is the degree to which a set of indicants measures the concept it is intended to measure. These formulations imply not only that systematic error is separable from true score variance but that these two components may be correlated with each other. Most important, these expressions make clear that the difference between reliability and validity is entirely dependent upon systematic error. If a set of indicants contains no systematic error – that is, it measures only the concept of interest with random fluctuations – then validity will equal reliability and both will differ from 1.00 by the amount of random error. Conversely, if measurements contain a substantial amount of systematic error, validity can be significantly less than reliability. In the unusual circumstance when *all* observed variance is represented by systematic error, reliability would be perfect but validity would be zero. Thus, systematic error produces reliable but invalid measurements. Althauser and Heberlein (1970:152) observe: "Matters of validity arise when other factors – more than one underlying construct or methods' factors or other unmeasured variables – are seen to affect the measures in addition to one underlying concept and random error."

Unfortunately, there is no established body of statistical theory that has been designed explicitly for dealing with systematic error-oriented measurement models, as classical test theory has been for the random error model. This means that the procedures for estimating reliability and validity in models containing both random and systematic errors are likely to be both less elegant and more complicated than in models containing only random errors. We believe, however, that these "costs" are well worth the benefits to be derived from a measurement model that is more isomorphic with the types of errors typically encountered in the social sciences.

This last point suggests that assessing reliability and especially validity under conditions of systematic error is as much a substantive, theoretical problem as it is a statistical one. As Alwin (1974:102–3) has observed: "The meaning one attaches to the results of these procedures [assessing reliability and validity] depends entirely on the veracity of the assumptions about nonrandom error on which the procedures themselves rest . . . The nature of nonrandom error depends on the particular set of measured variables; the correct model underlying the variable measures may well differ from situation to situation." Although Alwin's caveat must be taken seriously, it would defeat its own purpose if it were to leave the impression that efforts at empirically assessing reliability and validity were vacuous. On the other hand, it does correctly imply that an alternative measurement model – one useful for analyzing systematic as well as random errors – ultimately rests upon a series of assumptions about the nature of theory and the procedures by which data are obtained and analyzed. The implications of such a measurement model will be discussed throughout this book.

Criteria for assessing reliability and validity

At the most general level, there are two types of evidence that we believe are relevant to inferences concerning the degree to which indicants measure the concept they are designed to measure, other systematic nonrandom sources of variation, and random error.

1   *Internal association*: The pattern of interrelationships among the indicants designed to measure a concept.
2   *External association*: The pattern of relationships between indicants designed to measure a concept and other variables.

Internal association

The basic principle underlying internal association is that there should be positive intercorrelations among indicants designed to measure a concept. Selltiz et al. (1976:402) comment: "If all variables measure the same more general characteristics of an attitude . . . then we should be able to show that the variables are all highly intercorrelated."

The major technique for assessing clusters of items that intercorrelate among themselves is factor analysis. *Factor analysis* is primarily a data-reduction procedure; given a matrix of intercorrelations among a set of variables, factor analysis will describe those intercorrelations in terms of a smaller number of components or factors that may be interpreted as dimensions that underlie the matrix of correlations. Proponents of factor analysis argue that it is an adequate and appropriate method for bridging the gap between empirical measures and theoretical concepts. As Bohrnstedt (1970:96) notes: "Factor analysis . . . can be very useful in (a) determining the dimensionality of a domain and (b) selecting the items which fit best into the various strata of the domain . . . Items which correlate highly with a single factor are clearly to be preferred in construction of one's scales." Factor analysis can thus be used to describe the empirical dimensional structure that underlies a set of measured indicants. These empirical factors are, in turn, presumed to correspond to specific theoretical concepts.

As we discuss in detail in Chapter 3, factor analysis can be used to determine the main sources of variance underlying a set of indicants as well as their statistical characteristics. Stated somewhat differently, factor analysis can be used to estimate the systematic components of the observed variance – that is, the proportion of observed variance represented by true scores and by nonrandom or systematic errors – and is thus central to the empirical assessment of reliability.

Despite the usefulness of factor analysis for analyzing internal association, however, it does not always lead to unambiguous inferences concerning the theoretical structure that underlies a set of indicants designed to measure a specific concept. Simply stated, factor analysis itself provides no evidence for differentiating between factors that represent true score variance and those that represent systematic error. Because factor analysis provides a technical answer to the theoretical question of the correspondence between concepts and indicants, it is not directly relevant to the assessment of validity. Specifically, factor analysis provides no answer to the crucial question underlying validity estimation: Of the systematic factors, which correspond to the intended concepts? Which are theoretically meaningless, representing concepts other than the one the researcher is attempting to measure? These questions focus on the validity of empirical factors. It assumes that some factors are both reliable and valid, whereas others are reliable but are not valid.

External association
The kind of evidence needed to differentiate between valid factors (containing true score variance) and systematic error factors (containing reliable but invalid variance) is embedded within the theoretical and substantive context of the research. This evidence concerns the relationship between indicants designed to measure one concept and those designed to measure another concept, combined with the theoretical presumption that the two concepts of interest are correlated with one another. As Bohrnstedt (1970:94) says: "The researcher validates his scales by investigating whether they confirm or deny the hypotheses predicted from a theory which is based upon the constructs." That is, the pattern of external associations among indicants of different concepts provides evidence relevant to the following questions: Do the empirical factors represent the intended theoretical concepts? Do they represent artifacts of the method used in the research? Do they represent an irrelevant theoretical concept? In this sense, evidence concerning the pattern of external association is more sensitive to the theoretical question of validity than are the purely statistical criteria used in the application of factor scaling. Although a thorough discussion of this topic will be presented in Chapter 4, it will be useful here to describe briefly the logic underlying the idea of external association.

The notion of external association relates to the assumption that indicants of a theoretical concept should behave similarly toward theoretically relevant external variables (Lazarsfeld, 1958, 1959; Curtis and Jackson, 1962; Sullivan, 1971, 1974; Balch, 1974). For example, if a set of items represents a concept empirically, the relationship between these items and indicants of other theoretically relevant variables should be similar in terms of direction, strength, and consistency. Conversely, if the items hypothesized to measure the same concept relate differentially to other theoretically relevant variables, this is interpreted as evidence that all the items do not, in fact, reflect the same concept. Evidence of external consistency thus indicates that a set of items is measuring the same concept, whereas evidence of external inconsistency implies that the items are measuring different concepts. Their performance in terms of external variables thus provides evidence about the theoretical meaning that can be attributed to these items.

This approach is not, of course, without problems of its own. For example, as Bohrnstedt (1970:94) notes: "One of the limitations of this approach is, of course, that inability to predict according to the hypotheses can result either from a lack of construct validity or an incorrect theory." Indeed, contained with the context of the pattern of external relationships is the concept of internal association, for as Bohrnstedt (1970:95) concludes: "Because of the fallibility of any single [measure], we need to validate our measure of X by several *independent* measures, all of which supposedly measure X." This suggests that a successful measurement strategy must combine evidence based upon internal association with independent evidence revealed by the pattern of external associations.

Conclusion

This chapter has presented a theoretical framework within which a systematic and integrated approach to measurement can be developed. For purposes of this volume, measurement is defined broadly to include all aspects of the process by which abstract concepts are linked to empirical referents. This broad definition clearly implies that measurement is an integral element of theory construction and evaluation in the social sciences.

Two key terms, reliability and validity, provide the essential language of measurement. Reliability concerns the extent to which measurements are consistent or repeatable. Thus, a highly reliable measure is one that does not fluctuate greatly because of random error. Reliability can be assessed by observing the pattern of interrelationships among the indicants designed to measure a particular theoretical concept. Validity concerns the extent to which empirical indicants measure what they are intended to measure. Although random error reduces the validity of any measuring instrument, a far more important concern in validity assessment is nonrandom or systematic error. Systematic error does not yield easily to statistical solution. Indeed, as we will see, the detection, estimation, and elimination of systematic error depends far more on theoretical insight than on the blind application of statistical tools. Validity is most usefully approached through construct validation in which hypotheses specifying the relations among theoretical concepts are used to assess measures of those concepts. That is, in contrast to reliability, validity focuses on the relationships between indicants of a given theoretical concept and theoretically relevant, external variables.

Chapter 2 provides a nontechnical treatment of factor analysis, paying special attention to its use in measurement. Chapter 3 discusses reliability and Chapter 4 focuses on validity. Chapter 5 provides a systematic strategy for assessing systematic error in the social sciences. Finally, Chapter 6 formulates and illustrates on integrated approach to measurement, combining evidence based upon internal association with independent evidence revealed by the pattern of external associations.

2 Factor analysis

Chapter 1 presented the foundations of a general approach to measurement in the social sciences. It was argued that two complementary kinds of evidence – one focusing on internal association and the other on external association – are useful in assessing nonrandom (that is, systematic) and random sources of measurement error. It was also pointed out that factor analysis is the most widely used and appropriate statistical technique for assessing evidence concerning internal association. Its principal purpose in this regard is that it highlights and clarifies the pattern of association among a set of indicants designed to measure a particular theoretical concept. Thus, factor analysis plays a major role in measurement assessment. As we will show, factor analysis is primarily useful in the assessment of reliability.

Within this context, Chapter 2 provides a nontechnical discussion of this multivariate statistical technique. Since its introduction by Charles Spearman and Karl Pearson in the early 1900s, factor analysis has generated a huge and highly complex literature. For useful discussion of factor analysis, see Harman (1967) and Rummel (1970). It is not our purpose to review the literature. Instead, we will point out the logic and basic principles underlying factor analysis and indicate how the technique can be used to develop and assess empirical measures in the social sciences. This chapter focuses on a substantive example, the various psychological dimensions of alienation, to fulfill the former objective, and Chapter 3 discusses the uses of factor analysis in relation to reliability.

Factor analysis models

Factor analysis does not refer to a single statistical technique but to a variety of related techniques designed to make observed data more readily interpretable. It does so by analyzing interrelationships among variables in such a way that the variables can be described adequately and conveniently by a group of basic categories smaller in number than the original variables. These basic categories, called *factors*, are referenced by coordinates that geometrically define the location of each variable with respect to every other variable. Thus, the general purpose of factor analysis is parsimony; the factor analyst seeks to define the interrelationships among variables simply. The usual method for arriving at such a parsimonious structure is for the number of factors to be smaller than the number of variables in the factor analysis. The smaller the ratio of factors to items, the more parsimony has been achieved. Parsimony, however, comes at a price. The price of parsimony is diversity. The greater the number of factors one chooses to interpret in a factor analysis, the greater the diversity of dimensions one uses to define the content under investigation. Hence, the goal of parsimony and the goal of diversity are in conflict with one another. As we shall see, one of the most difficult questions that the factor analyst must answer concerns the number of factors to include in the analysis. The inclusion of too few factors results in an overly simplistic view of the content under investigation; the inclusion to too many factors results in an overly complicated view of the same content. Unfortunately, a factor analyst can commit both of these contradictory errors simultaneously.

There are a variety of different factor analysis models, including the image model, the canonical model, and the alpha model. Perhaps the most fundamental distinction is between the common factor analysis model and the principal component analysis model. Let us discuss these two models of factor analysis in turn.

Common factor analysis

Common factor analysis is based on the notion that there are two basic components of the variance of a variable: common variance and unique variance. *Common variance* is that proportion of the total variance that an item shares with the other variables in the analysis. The remainder of the variance in each item is considered to be "unique" variance. *Unique variance* consists both of variance that is specific to a particular variable and random error variance. The objective of common factor analysis is to define the factors that arise only from the common variance components of the variables. As noted above, the number of factors will ordinarily be less than the number of variables. Technically stated, the number of factors required to define this common factor space will be less than the number of items required for the full vector space.

Principal component analysis

In contrast to common factor analysis, *principal component analysis* is concerned with the total variance of a variable. Consequently, it makes no distinction between common and unique variance. All variance, in effect, is treated as common variance. Principal component analysis redescribes the interrelationships among the variables, transforming them into basic components. Although the number of principal components will almost always equal the number of variables, only the first few components – those accounting for most of the variance of the variables – are usually retained for further analysis. This aspect of principal component analysis is consistent with the goal of parsimony. From the perspective of common factor analysis, the components emerging from principal component analysis represent a combination of common, specific, and random error variances. But it is reasonable to presume that, in general, the first few components represent mostly common vector variance, whereas the last, minor components are primarily random error in nature. Statistically, the primary difference between these models is that principal components model factors a correlation matrix with unities in the main diagonal, whereas common factor analysis uses an estimate of "communality" in this diagonal. These terms will be discussed in greater detail later in this chapter. The fact that common factor analysis and principal components are based on different statistical/mathematical models is important for our purposes, because it means that they are associated with different composite reliability coefficients, a topic to be discussed in greater detail in Chapter 3.

Interpretation of factors

The interpretation of factors is facilitated by observing which variables define a particular factor and inferring what these variables have in common that is not shared by the variables not defined on that factor. A *dimension* is an interpretation attributed to a factor. Thus, factor-analytic procedures redescribe the interrelationships among variables in order that their underlying dimensional structure can be discovered.

As noted in Chapter 1, alienation has been conceptualized as containing four separate theoretical dimensions: Meaninglessness, Powerlessness, Normlessness, and Social Isolation. Neal and Groat (1974:550–2) constructed the conceptual definitions of these four dimensions of alienation as follows:

> The *meaninglessness* scale was designed to tap the perception of broader social and political events as overwhelmingly complex, without purpose, and lacking in predictability . . . *Powerlessness* was conceptualized as a low expectancy for control over the outcomes of events. The specific empirical reference for the present measure, however, was limited to the political and economic spheres . . . *Normlessness* was defined as a high expectancy that socially unapproved behavior is necessary in goal attainment. The content of the items emphasized the necessity of either coercion or deception in achieving socially desired political or economic goals . . . The *social isolation* scale . . . emphasized the view of social relations as impersonal, non-rewarding, and unfriendly . . .

The empirical referents for our alienation scales thus range from the broader political and economic spheres, in the cases of powerlessness and normlessness, to the more immediate and primary relationships in the social isolation scale. The variation in item content should facilitate our assessment of patterns of stability and change in kinds and degrees of alienation for our subjects.

The content of the items designed to measure these four conceptual dimensions of alienation are presented in Table 2.1. Neal and Groat

Table 2.1. *Item content for measures of dimensions of alienation*

Measures of Meaninglessness
1. The international situation is so complex that it just confuses a person to think about it.
2. One should live for today and let tomorrow take care of itself.
3. It's hard to sleep nights when you think about recurrent crises in the world and what would happen if they exploded.
4. With so many religions around, one really doesn't know which one to believe.
5. The only thing one can be sure of today is that he can be sure of nothing.
6. The tensions in the world today make one wonder whether he will be around in a few years or not.
7. Current political events have taken an unpredictable and destructive course.
8. Most people live lives of quiet desperation.
9. In spite of what some people say, the lot of the average person is getting worse, not better.

Measures of Powerlessness
1. A lasting world peace can be achieved by those of us who work toward it. (Reversed scoring)
2. This world is run by the few people in power, and there is not much the little guy can do about it.
3. There's very little that persons like myself can do to improve world opinion of the United States.
4. Wars between countries seem inevitable despite the efforts of men to prevent them.
5. The average citizen can have an influence on government decisions. (Reversed scoring)
6. People like me can change the course of world events if we make ourselves heard. (Reversed scoring)
7. More and more, I feel helpless in the face of what's happening in the world today.
8. I think each of us can do a great deal to improve world opinion of the United States. (Reverse scoring)
9. It is only wishful thinking to believe that one can really influence what happens in society at large.
10. There's very little we can do to keep prices from going higher.

Measures of Normlessness
1. In order to get elected to public office, a candidate must make promises he does not intend to keep.
2. Having "pull" is more important than ability in getting a government job.
3. Those running our government must hush up many things that go on behind the scene if they wish to stay in office.
4. In getting a good-paying job, it's necessary to exaggerate one's abilities (or personal merits).

5. In getting a job promotion, some degree of "apple polishing" is required.
6. Success in business can easily be achieved without taking advantage of gullible people. (Reversed scoring)
7. In order to have a good income, salesmen must use high-pressure salesmanship.
8. Those elected to public office have to serve special interests (e.g., big business or labor) as well as the public's interest.

Measures of Social Isolation
1. There are few dependable ties between people any more.
2. Sometimes I feel all alone in the world.
3. People are just naturally considerate and helpful. (Reversed scoring)
4. The world we live in is basically a friendly place. (Reversed scoring)
5. Most people are not really sincere in their relations with others.
6. The way things are now, a person has to look out pretty much for himself.
7. Most married people in our country lead trapped (frustrated) lives.
8. Real friends are as easy to find as ever. (Reversed scoring)
9. Most people seldom feel lonely. (Reversed scoring)

Note: The response format for each item consisted of a four-point continuum: strongly agree – agree – disagree – strongly disagree.

collected data on these 36 questionnaire items for 334 married women in the Toledo, Ohio, metropolitan area in 1971. For a more complete description of these procedures and the corresponding inferences, see Neal and Groat (1974). A common factor analysis of their data resulted in four interpretable factors, as presented in Table 2.2. The numerical values in this table are referred to as factor loadings. A *factor loading* indicates the correlation between a variable and a factor. The greater the absolute factor loading, the stronger is the relationship between the respective factor and item. Hence, a factor loading is analogous to a correlation coefficient, for just as a large correlation indicates a strong relationship, a large factor loading means that the variable is a strong definer of the factor. (For the present, ignore the column labeled "h^2.") Hence, factor 1 is defined by Meaninglessness items 1, 3, 5, 6, 7, 8, and 9, and by Powerlessness items 2 and 7; factor 2 is defined by Powerlessness items 1, 2, 3, 5, 6, 7, 8, 9, and 10, and by Normlessness item 4; factor 3 is defined by Normlessness items 1 through 7; and factor 4 is defined by Social Isolation items 1 through 9, and by Meaninglessness item 8. [Factors are denoted either by Arabic numbers (factor 1) or by Roman numerals (factor I).] On the whole, the factor structure in Table 2.2 corresponds with the way that the dimensions of alienation were differentiated theoretically. That is, with some exceptions, the items designed to measure Meaninglessness cluster together, the items designed to measure Powerlessness cluster together, and so forth. Moreover, these clusters of items are clearly distinguishable from one another, defining, as they do, separate factors.

This brief example illustrates, then, how factor analysis can be used in the measurement process. It shows that results from a factor analysis are useful in determining whether indicants supposedly mea-

Table 2.2 *Factor analysis of alienation indicants: rotated solution*

Indicant	Factor 1	2	3	4	h^2
Meaninglessness					
1	.430	.090	.107	.159	.230
2	.086	.132	.204	.042	.069
3	.618	.003	.079	.084	.395
4	.189	.169	.082	.201	.111
5	.362	.296	.163	.201	.286
6	.662	.090	.093	.202	.495
7	.474	.126	.155	.125	.280
8	.319	.135	.157	.310	.240
9	.439	.154	.151	.272	.313
Powerlessness					
1	−.103	.383	.062	.068	.166
2	.301	.684	.202	.090	.608
3	.160	.760	.163	.032	.631
4	.169	.270	−.009	.094	.111
5	.194	.682	.174	.171	.562
6	.045	.720	.157	.041	.547
7	.420	.469	.163	.244	.483
8	.012	.702	.214	.026	.539
9	.200	.656	.191	.176	.538
10	.131	.490	.129	.093	.283
Normlessness					
1	.209	.228	.616	.100	.485
2	.165	.221	.480	.054	.309
3	.200	.120	.508	.147	.334
4	.061	.309	.507	.092	.365
5	.012	.115	.558	.099	.334
6	−.050	.171	.446	.155	.255
7	.244	.174	.300	.108	.192
8	.090	−.029	.285	.029	.091
Social Isolation					
1	.261	.208	.138	.507	.388
2	.196	.056	.081	.567	.370
3	.093	.147	.032	.429	.216
4	.115	.144	−.039	.425	.217
5	.133	.024	.037	.565	.339
6	.250	.280	.193	.403	.341
7	.099	−.019	.275	.499	.335
8	.098	.084	.122	.630	.429
9	.003	−.041	.192	.303	.130

suring the same concept define the same factor; conversely, it shows whether indicants measuring different concepts define different factors. In order to explain the basic principles of factor analysis and demonstrate more fully how factor analysis can be used for purposes of measurement, this chapter includes a step-by-step application of factor analysis to measurement in the social sciences. The particular issues in factor analysis that are considered include extraction procedures, communality estimates, the number of factors problem, rotation, and factor interpretation.

Extraction of factors

Assume that a researcher is trying to measure two theoretical concepts, A and B, using three indicants of each concept: a_1, a_2, and a_3 (collectively referred to as a_i) and b_1, b_2, and b_3 (collectively, b_i). For simplicity, assume that all the intercorrelations among the $a_i = .6$; all the intercorrelations among the $b_i = .6$; and all the intercorrelations between the a_i and $b_i = .2$.

Factor analysis is usually based upon analysis of a correlation matrix. Table 2.3A presents a correlation matrix of these six indicants. A symmetrical correlation matrix can be divided into an upper right triangle, a lower left triangle, and a main diagonal, as shown in this table. Because the upper right triangle is a mirror image of the lower left triangle, no information is lost when just one of the two triangles is presented. (The value placed in the main diagonal will be discussed later.) An examination of Table 2.3A reveals that there are two basic dimensions underlying these data. More specifically, one can see, by inspection of the matrix, that the measures of A are distinguishable from the measures of B, for the intercorrelation of measures within concept (.6's) are greater than the correlation between measures of different concepts (.2). For a variety of reasons, however, inspection of correlation matrices is not ordinarily so straightforward. First, correlation matrices are usually much larger than the matrix presented in Table 2.3A. The correlation matrix of the 36 alienation measures discussed above includes 630 correlation coefficients. Moreover, it is often the case that some indicants do not provide a good representation of the concepts they are designed to measure. Finally, systematic error may affect the pattern of correlations, and random error will obscure that pattern. Consequently, although one can see the dimensions underlying the correlations in Table 2.3A, one will not ordinarily be able to discern this pattern by visual inspection.

Factor analysis has been developed so that the factors of a correlation matrix can be conveniently described when the more simple, visual procedures prove to be unsatisfactory. When factors are extracted from a correlation matrix, the original variables are transformed into

Table 2.3. *Extraction of factors*

A: Extraction of first factor

	a_1	a_2	a_3	b_1	b_2	b_3	$\Sigma\Sigma$
a_1	.6	.6	.6	.2	.2	.2	
a_2	.6	.6	.6	.2	.2	.2	
a_3	.6	.6	.6	.2	.2	.2	
b_1	.2	.2	.2	.6	.6	.6	
b_2	.2	.2	.2	.6	.6	.6	
b_3	.2	.2	.2	.6	.6	.6	
Σ	2.4	2.4	2.4	2.4	2.4	2.4	14.4
w_1	.2635	.2635	.2635	.2635	.2635	.2635	
f_1	.6324	.6324	.6324	.6324	.6324	.6324	

B: Residual matrix/extraction of second factor

	a_1	a_2	a_3	$(-)b_1$	$(-)b_2$	$(-)b_3$	$\Sigma\Sigma$
a_1	.2	.2	.2	-.2	-.2	-.2	
a_2	.2	.2	.2	-.2	-.2	-.2	
a_3	.2	.2	.2	-.2	-.2	-.2	
$(-)b_1$	-.2	-.2	-.2	.2	.2	.2	
$(-)b_2$	-.2	-.2	-.2	.2	.2	.2	
$(-)b_3$	-.2	-.2	-.2	.2	.2	.2	
Σ	.0	.0	.0	.0	.0	.0	
$\Sigma|\cdot|$	1.2	1.2	1.2	1.2	1.2	1.2	7.2
w_2	.3727	.3727	.3727	.3727	.3727	.3727	
f_2	.4472	.4472	.4472	$(-).4472$	$(-).4472$	$(-).4472$	

a new set of composite variables. These new composite variables (that is, factors) have a useful and unique property: they are *orthogonal* to (statistically independent of) one another. Thus, orthogonal factors are uncorrelated with one another and, therefore, they can be graphically represented on perpendicular axes. Given the correlations in Table 2.3A, a factor analysis of these data should produce one factor defined by the a_i and another defined by the b_i.

Before the matrix can be factored, the values to be placed in the main diagonal must be determined. For the principal components model, this is not a problem, for unities are placed in the main diagonal. However, when one is conducting a common factor analysis – that is, an analysis concerned only with the common factor variance – an appropriate estimate of the communality must be selected. Many different estimates have been suggested for the communality, including the average correlation of a variable, the highest correlation, and various estimates based on the rank of the correlation matrix. Probably the most widely used and generally recommended communality estimate, especially with a large number of variables (>30), is the *squared multiple correlation* (SMC) of a variable with all the others. Although this is considered a lower bound of the communality (the upper bound of a communality is unity), it is highly desirable as an actual estimate, for several reasons. First, the SMC does involve a relationship between a single variable and all the remaining variables in the analysis, thus providing an intuitively plausible way of operationalizing the common factor variance. Second, it has been shown to actually equal the communality in some cases (Guttman, 1940). Finally, the SMC increases in value as the number of variables increases; this is also consistent with the general notion of common factor variance.

However one arrives at an initial reliability estimate, most computer programs "iterate" the factor structure to "convergence." After the initial factor extraction, *iteration* is the process of substituting the initial communality as the reliability estimate and refactoring. Many computer programs will continue to iterate until convergence is reached. *Convergence* occurs when the new communality is, within certain limits, equal to the old one. The statement "15 iterations required for convergence" on a computer printout means that the computer iterated the extraction procedure (that is, substituted the new communalities and refactored) 15 times before the value of the new and old communalities was within the acceptable range. This range is usually set at a rather small value, ensuring that the reported factor structure is as accurate as is usually necessary in the social sciences.

Ordinarily, the particular values used as communality estimates will not have a significant effect on the factor analysis if there are a reasonably large number of variables in the analysis and if the diagonal values are not extreme compared to the off-diagonal correlations. If either of these conditions does not hold – that is, if the analysis is based on a small number of variables or if the communality estimates are extreme, then the choice of the initial communality is important because the diagonal estimates can alter the factor loadings and even the number of factors that underlie the data.

The *centroid technique*, with SMCs in the main diagonal, is a basic method for extracting factors from a correlation matrix. This technique, despite its historical popularity, should not generally be used if a computer is available, because its factors are not mathematically unique or completely orthogonal. Other, more efficient and mathematically elegant programs are available in most computer packages. The centroid technique is used here because it involves a small number of computationally easy steps (Harman, 1967:171–86; Rummel, 1970:335–7).

When doing a factor analysis by computer, the most widely used means of factor extraction is the *principal axes technique*. This technique has a number of desirable properties, which are thoroughly discussed in Harman (1967:137–71) and Rummel (1970:338–45). Roughly speaking, the centroid technique may be thought of as a mathematical approximation of the more precise but computationally difficult principal axes technique. The principal axes technique has been used for analyzing the data for the alienation example developed in this chapter.

When extracting a factor from a correlation matrix using the centroid technique, one proceeds as follows:

Step 1. *Add all correlations in the matrix.* Sum the correlations down the columns and then sum these sums across the rows. The sum of the correlations in Table 2.3A is 14.4.

Step 2. *Compute the square root of the sum of the correlations.* The sum of the correlations is 1,414. The square root of 14.4 is 3.7947.

Step 3. *Compute the reciprocal of the square root.* The reciprocal of X = $1/X$. In this example, $1/3.7947 = .2635$.

Step 4. *Multiply the sum of each variable (column) by the reciprocal (w_i) to obtain the factor loadings.* The reciprocal, $w_1 = .2635$. Because these are hypothetical data, the sum of each variable is equal to 2.4. (For real data, the sum of each variable will usually be different from variable to variable.) As 2.4 times .2635 = .6324, the factor loading for each variable on factor 1 is .6324. Roughly speaking, this factor loading can be interpreted as the correlation of the variable with the factor.

To extract a second factor, the variance associated with the first factor must be removed from the correlation matrix. This can be accomplished by computing, for each pair of variables, the product of their respective factor loadings, then subtracting this product from the observed correlation. For these data, variables a_1 and a_2 are correlated at a value of .6. The factor loading for each variable is .6324; $.6324^2 = .4$; $.6 - .4 = .2$. Thus, the residual correlation between a_1 and a_2 after the variance associated with factor 1 has been removed is .2. This same procedure is followed for every correlation in the matrix. The resulting matrix, presented in Table 2.3B, is called a *residual matrix*. Because we constructed the data in a particular way, all the factor loadings equal .6324. Consequently, the product of each pair of factor loadings is .4. Hence, to produce the residual matrix, it is only necessary to subtract .4 from each correlation in the original matrix. Within the limits of rounding error, the sum of each row and the sum of each column for any residual matrix will equal zero.

A *vector* is a set of numbers within a matrix. In Table 2.3B, vector a_1 refers to the correlation of a_1 with every other variable. When one *reflects a vector*, one changes all the algebraic signs of that vector from + to − or from − to +. The purpose of reflecting vectors is the removal of all minus signs from the matrix. There are 18 minus signs in Table 2.3B. Reflecting vectors b_i will produce a *positive manifold*, a matrix in which all correlations are positive (or zero).

Analyzing the positive manifold, a second factor is extracted from the residual matrix using the procedures as outlined above: sum the correlations, compute the square root of the sum, compute the reciprocal of the square root of the sum, and multiply the sum of each variable by the reciprocal to obtain the factor loadings. These procedures are followed until all useful factors have been extracted from the matrix.

But how does a researcher know when all the useful factors have been extracted from a correlation matrix? As factors are extracted from a matrix, they are not only uncorrelated with one another but they also account for decreasing proportions of variance. Thus, the first factor accounts for the largest proportion of variance in the matrix, the second factor accounts for the next largest proportion of variance *that is statistically independent of the first factor*, and so forth. Thus, the first several factors usually account for the major proportions of the variance in the data, leaving the last few factors to account for only minor proportions of variance.

It is difficult to determine precisely the number of important factors that underlie a set of data. Rummel (1970:349–67) discusses a variety of statistical and substantive criteria that are relevant to this decision. In the last analysis, perhaps the most important criterion is to retain the number of factors that is substantively meaningful and interpretable. Yet, as we shall see later, this criterion is difficult to implement in practice, especially if systematic error is distorting the measurement of theoretical concepts.

Characteristics of the unrotated factor matrix

Earlier, the results of a factor analysis of 36 items designed to measure four dimensions of alienation were discussed. The interpretation of that factor analysis was intuitively plausible. The items designed to measure the concept "Meaninglessness" defined (that is, loaded strongly on) factor 1; the items designed to measure "Powerlessness" defined factor 2; and so forth. Ordinarily, researchers will name factors for the concepts those factors represent. For example, it would be common practice to name factor 1 "Meaninglessness." In order to arrive at the factor structure displayed in Table 2.2, we performed the two major steps in factor analysis: extraction of factors and rotation of factors. One procedure for extracting factors – the centroid technique – was described above.

The extraction procedure itself did not result in the matrix of factor loadings presented in Table 2.2. Instead, this is the *rotated factor matrix*. The extracted but unrotated factor matrix, presented in Table 2.4, has several interesting properties. First, all the loadings on the first factor are positive and they have a mean value of .439. This factor could be considered a general "alienation" factor. Indeed, if one were to have extracted only this factor, one might argue that alienation is a uni-dimensional concept. Such an inference, however, is hardly consistent with the data contained in the remainder of Table 2.4. On factor 2, the Powerlessness items are all negative and average $-.273$, the Social Isolation items are all positive and average .290, most of the Mean-inglessness items are positive and average .167, and the Normlessness items are close to zero. Thus, this factor differentiates the Power-lessness items from the Social Isolation items, in that the Powerless-ness items define factor 2 in a strong negative fashion, whereas the Social Isolation items define it in a strong positive fashion. Factor 3 differentiates the Normlessness items from the other items, as the Normlessness items define this factor in a strong positive fashion, whereas the remaining items have only weak negative loadings. Fi-nally, factor 4 differentiates the Meaninglessness items from the Social Isolations items, in that the former have strong negative loadings, whereas the latter have strong positive loadings on this factor.

Although there seem to be four significant factors that underlie these data, the four factors do not correspond perfectly to the four theoretical dimensions of alienation discussed earlier. The reason for this relates directly to how the factors were extracted in the first place. Because the first factor is fitted to the data to account for the maximum variance and each successive factor is maximally fitted to the residual variance, the extraction technique *"often locates the first factor between independent clusters of interrelated variables"* (Rummel, 1970:373; italics in the original). That is, most of the variables usually have moderately strong positive loadings on the first factor because this factor is ex-

tracted so that it maximizes the variance of all the variables. Consequently, the different clusters of interrelated variables – like the four
dimensions of alienation – are undifferentiated on the first factor. The

Table 2.4. *Extracted but unrotated factors of alienation indicants*

Indicant	Factor 1	2	3	4	h^2
Meaninglessness					
1	.368	.197	−.078	−.222	.230
2	.232	−.036	.110	−.035	.069
3	.352	.277	−.120	−.424	.395
4	.318	.082	−.062	.003	.111
5	.513	.058	−.079	−.113	.286
6	.485	.310	−.164	−.370	.495
7	.418	.165	−.055	−.274	.280
8	.434	.221	−.035	−.041	.240
9	.482	.228	−.077	−.152	.313
Powerlessness					
1	.257	−.254	−.044	.182	.166
2	.704	−.297	−.135	−.070	.608
3	.647	−.436	−.145	.018	.631
4	.288	−.059	−.155	−.021	.111
5	.677	−.283	−.139	.064	.562
6	.571	−.446	−.106	.105	.547
7	.669	−.010	−.157	−.100	.483
8	.562	−.457	−.037	.112	.539
9	.673	−.260	−.118	.056	.538
10	.472	−.225	−.090	.033	.283
Normlessness					
1	.554	−.029	.405	−.114	.485
2	.450	−.066	.304	−.098	.309
3	.454	.073	.339	−.087	.334
4	.488	−.141	.326	.018	.365
5	.367	−.024	.446	.020	.334
6	.351	−.046	.339	.122	.255
7	.401	.034	.128	−.116	.192
8	.159	.063	.234	−.083	.091
Social Isolation					
1	.533	.277	−.084	.140	.388
2	.407	.395	−.075	.205	.370
3	.338	.209	−.101	.218	.216
4	.313	.219	−.169	.205	.217
5	.338	.393	−.086	.250	.339
6	.553	.156	−.041	.092	.341
7	.370	.362	.159	.205	.335
8	.426	.379	−.027	.320	.429
9	.191	.218	.145	.160	.130

different clusters will tend to have loadings different in sign on the second and subsequent factors, which can be observed in Table 2.4 for the alienation data.

There are several other interesting features of the unrotated (or extracted) factor matrix. *Communality*, symbolized as h^2, is the proportion of variance in each item that is associated with the factor structure. It is equal to the sum of the squared factor loadings for an item over all extracted factors. The procedure for computing h^2 is as follows: For each variable, square and sum the factor loadings across all factors. Thus, the communality for the item "Meaninglessness 1" $= .368^2 + .197^2 + (-.078)^2 + (-.222)^2 = .135 + .039 + .006 + .049 = .229$. Within the limits of rounding error, this is identical to the computer-generated value placed in the communality column in Table 2.4 for this item.

The *eigenvalue* equals the sum of the squared factor loadings for a factor over all items. The procedure for computing the eigenvalue is as follows: For each factor, square and sum the factor loadings over all items. For factor 1 in Table 2.4, the eigenvalue $= .368^2 + .232^2 + .352^2 + \cdots + .426^2 + .191^2 = .135 + .054 + .124 + \cdots + .181 + .036 = 7.632$.

There are a variety of interpretations for the eigenvalue. All of these interpretations involve proportions of variance attributable to the respective factor. The interpretations differ in that they make different assumptions about how much variance is in the matrix; that is, each uses a different denominator in the proportion. The three most widely used methods for evaluating the relative importance of factors using eigenvalues are as follows:

1. Proportion of the total variance. If 1.0's had been placed in the main diagonal (that is, if a principal component analysis had been conducted), the communality for each item based upon the extraction of all 36 facotrs would be 1.00. This value, summed over 36 items, would give us 36.00 as the total variance in the matrix. Following this procedure, the first unrotated factor in Table 2.4 accounts for $7.632/36 = .212$ of the total variance in the matrix. The various proportions of total variance associated with each factor plus the cumulation of these proportions across the four factors are presented under the "Total" variance columns in Table 2.5. Often, the decision about how many factors to interpret is based upon whether a factor removes more than the average amount of total variance from the matrix. Rotating factors with eigenvalues of 1.00 or higher while excluding from the rotation factors with eigenvalues of less than 1.00 accomplishes this purpose. It must be pointed out, however, that this decisional criterion is arbitrary; there will be circumstances in which one will want to rotate more or fewer factors than is indicated by the 1.00 criterion.

Table 2.5. *Information for alienation factor analysis*

Factor	Eigenvalue	Total variance		Common variance			Interpretable variance		
		Proportions	Cumulation	Proportions	Cumulation		Proportion	Cumulation	
1	7.632	.212	.212	.550	.550		.635	.635	
2	2.168	.060	.272	.156	.706		.181	.816	
3	1.193	.033	.305	.086	.792		.099	.915	
4	1.019	.028	.333	.073	.865		.085	1.000	
Sum	12.012								

2. Proportion of the common variance. Usually, the reliability of each item will be less than 1.00. When this is the case (using common factor analysis), the reliability estimate is placed in the main diagonal. Ordinarily, such a procedure will not result in 1.00 communalities; instead, they will ordinarily be less than 1.00. The sum of these communalities estimates how much common variance there is in the matrix. To compute the proportion of common variance that is due to each extracted factor, one divides the eigenvalue of that factor by the common variance. The computer printout that produced Tables 2.2 and 2.4 also reported the common variance that each item shares with the matrix. The sum of those common variance communalities for the 36 items in the matrix equals 13.886. Following this procedure, the first unrotated factor in Table 2.4 accounts for 7.632/13.886 = .550 of the common variance in the matrix. The various proportions of common variance associated with each factor, plus the cumulation of these proportions of the common variance, are presented in Table 2.5. These figures represent the proportion of variance accounted for by *all* common factors that is associated with *each* common factor. We note, parenthetically, that of the 36 common factors, the first four account for 86.5% of the common variance, and the remaining 32 account for the remaining 13.5%. This evidence is consistent with our assertion that the interpretable variance in the matrix was extracted in the first four factors and that the remaining 32 factors contained "statistically insignificant and substantively unimportant" variance.

3. Proportion of the interpreted variance. Another way to partition the variance of a factor matrix is to divide the eigenvalue of each factor by only that variance which is being rotated and interpreted in the analysis. For this example, the interpreted variance is equal to the sum of the eigenvalues for the first four factors. As shown in Table 2.5, this sum equals 12.012. The proportion of interpreted variance associated with factor 1 is 7.632/12.012 = .635. This figure, the remaining proportions of interpretable variance associated with factors 2, 3, and 4, and the cumulation of these proportions of the interpreted variance are presented in Table 2.5.

These different procedures for identifying the amount of variance in the matrix have different uses. The proportion of total variance measures the proportion of variance due to the factor as compared to the total possible variance in the matrix. The proportion of common variance indicates the proportion of variance due to that factor as compared to the best estimate of the actual common variance in the matrix. The proportion of interpreted variance measures the proportion of variance due to that factor as compared to all of the interpreted variance. The first two of these procedures provide a means of evaluating what proportion of variance one is choosing to interpret; the latter provides a method of evaluating how much of the interpreted variance is due to each of the respective factors. The cumulative proportions of variance measure the proportion of variance due to all of the extracted factors at or prior to the one under consideration. As shown in Table 2.5, one-third (.333) of the total variance is described by the first four factors. Seven-eighths (.865) of the common variance is described by these four factors. The cumulative proportion of variance in the first four factors, compared to the amount of variance that the researcher has chosen to rotate and interpret, is, by definition, 1.00.

Rotation of factors

Visual rotation of orthogonal factors
Figure 2.1 graphically presents the location of each of the 36 items on factors 1 and 2. The horizontal axis represents the factor loadings on factor 1; the right half represents the positive factor loadings; the left half (which is not presented) represents the negative factor loadings. The vertical axis represents the factor loadings on factor 2; the top half represents the positive factor loadings and the bottom half represents the negative factor loadings. Factors 1 and 2 are orthogonal to one another. This fact is represented graphically by the fact that the horizontal and vertical axes are 90° from one another.

Recall that a factor loading is the correlation of an item with a factor and that a correlation coefficient cannot be greater than 1.00. Therefore, the maximum distance any reference point can be from the origin is 1.00. Because of unreliability and/or because a variable may not share variance with the other items in the matrix, not all points are 1.00 unit away from the origin. Indeed, if a variable is totally unreliable and/or it shares no variance with the other variables in the matrix, its location on the graph will be at the origin.

Only two factors can be presented at a time because the page is only two-dimensional. It is not difficult, however, to visualize a third dimension. It must be perpendicular (that is, at a 90° angle) to both factors 1 and 2. To visualize that line, place your book down on the table with the page containing Figure 2.1 level with the floor. The line that would represent factor 3 passes through the origin and goes straight up and down. The up part represents the positive factor loadings on factor 3 and the down part (which goes through the table in the direction of the floor) represents the negative factor loadings on factor 3. In point of fact, there are n dimensions that make up the factor space. They are all independent of each other, which means that each reference axis is at a 90° angle from every other reference axis.

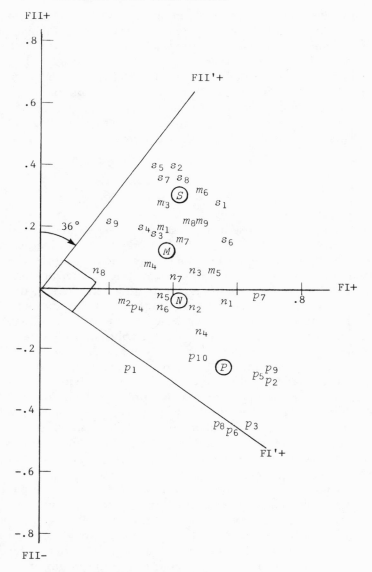

Figure 2.1. Graphic presentation of factors I and II.

Returning to Figure 2.1, each item is identified by the first letter of its name and its number. For example, m_1 is item "Meaninglessness 1." The circled capital letters represent the geometric center of all items designed to measure that dimension; for example, the circled *M* represents the geometric center of the Meaninglessness items. The purpose of rotation is to create, within the limits imposed by the data, a factor matrix that is meaningful and interpretable. In other words, the purpose of rotation is substantive; it depends upon theory. The present theory suggests that there are four dimensions of alienation: Meaninglessness, Powerlessness, Normlessness, and Social Isolation. An optimally interpretable factor structure, therefore, would be one in which the Meaninglessness items define one factor, the Powerlessness items define a second factor, the Normlessness items define a third factor, and the Social Isolation items define a fourth factor. Statistically, this implies that the Meaninglessness items load heavily on factor 1 and not on factors 2, 3, and 4; that the Powerlessness items load heavily on factor 2 and not on factors 1, 3, and 4; that the Normlessness items load heavily on factor 3 and not on factors 1, 2, and 4; and that the Social Isolation items load heavily on factor 4 and not on factors 1, 2, and 3. In other words, the purposes of extraction and rotation differ. The extraction technique is designed to maximize independent sources of variance in the matrix. The purpose of rotation is to delineate the factors so that they correspond to the clusters of interrelated variables. That is, the factors are rotated so that each defines a separate dimension of alienation.

As can be seen in Figure 2.1 and Table 2.4, the m_i and the s_i (that is, the measures of Meaninglessness and Social Isolation, respectively) have positive loadings on both factor 1 and factor 2; the n_i have positive loadings on factor 1 and approximately zero loadings on factor 2; and the p_i have positive loadings on factor 1 and negative loadings on factor 2. It appears that the s_i and m_i can be factorially differentiated from the p_i with a clockwise rotation of 36°. This angle was determined by visual inspection and was measured by an inexpensive plastic protractor.

Orthogonal rotation must follow certain rules. First, the origin cannot be moved. Second, after rotation, the factors must still be perpendicular to each other and to all other factors. Third, as we will demonstrate shortly, the communality for each variable before rotation must equal the communality after rotation. That is, the communality of a variable is invariant under orthogonal rotation.

There are standard formulas of rotation (Wilson and Tracy, 1937) that are usually more accurate than an estimate by inspection for computing the factor loadings on the rotated factors. For *clockwise* rotation, the formulas are

$$a'_{j1} = \cos \theta \, a_{j1} - \sin \theta \, a_{j2}$$
$$a'_{j2} = \sin \theta \, a_{j1} + \cos \theta \, a_{j2} \tag{2.1}$$

For *counterclockwise* rotation, the formulas are

$$a'_{j1} = \cos \theta \, a_{j1} + \sin \theta \, a_{j2}$$
$$a'_{j2} = - \sin \theta \, a_{j1} + \cos \theta \, a_{j2} \tag{2.2}$$

where

θ = the angle of rotation
a'_{j1} = factor loading of item j on rotated factor 1
a'_{j2} = factor loading of item j on rotated factor 2
a_{j1} = factor loading of item j on unrotated factor 1
a_{j2} = factor loading of item j on unrotated factor 2

In the preceding formulas, the terms "sin" and "cos" refer to properties of a right triangle. In a right triangle, one angle is 90°; the side opposite the 90° angle is called the hypotenuse. Because the angles of the triangle sum to 180°, the sum of the other two angles is 90°. Let one of those two remaining angles equal θ then the other angle equals $1 - \theta$. The side of the triangle opposite to θ is called the *opposite side*; the side of the triangle adjacent to θ is called the *adjacent side*. The *sine of θ* (symbolized "sin θ") is the length of the opposite side divided by the length of the hypotenuse. The *cosine of θ* (symbolized "cos θ") is the length of the adjacent side divided by the length of the hypotenuse. (The values for the sine and the cosine of θ are available in the table "Natural Trigonometric Functions for Angles in Degrees," the Appendix to this chapter.)

In order to compute the rotated factor loadings in Figure 2.1, one needs to find the sine of θ and the cosine of θ. (For angles from 0° to 45°, read down from the top; for angles from 45° to 90°, read up from the bottom.) The sine of 36° (symbolized: sin 36°) equals .5878; the cosine of 36° (symbolized: cos 36°) equals .8090. To simplify the presentation, only the geometric centers of each set of items, labeled M, P, N, S circled, are rotated. That is, the factor loadings in Table 2.6 represent the geometric centers of each of the clusters of items. The rotation of factors 1 and 2 proceeds as follows:

$$a'_{m1} = \cos 36° \, a_{m1} - \sin 36° \, a_{m2}$$
$$= (.8090)(.400) - (.5878)(.167)$$
$$= .323 - .098 = .225$$
$$a'_{m2} = \sin 36° \, a_{m1} + \cos 36° \, a_{m2}$$
$$= (.5878)(.400) + (.8090)(.167)$$
$$= .235 + .135 = .370$$

The remaining rotations were computed in a similar fashion. These rotated factors are presented as factors 1a and 2a in Table 2.6B. Notice that the communalities remain constant after rotation.

An examination of Table 2.6B reveals that the rotation had the desired effect in that the Social Isolation items now define factor 2a as the strongest, with the Meaninglessness items close behind. Conversely, the Powerlessness items define factor 1a as the strongest, with the Normlessness items a distant second. This is consistent with

Table 2.6 *Rotation of simplified extracted factors*

	A: Extracted factors				
	1	2	3	4	h^2
Meaninglessness	.400	.167	−.062	−.181	.224
Powerlessness	.552	−.273	−.113	.038	.393
Normlessness	.403	−.017	.316	−.042	.264
Social Isolation	.385	.290	−.031	.199	.273
	B: Factors 1 and 2 rotated 36° clockwise				
	1a	2a	3	4	h^2
Meaninglessness	.225	.370	−.062	−.181	.224
Powerlessness	.607	.104	−.113	.038	.393
Normlessness	.336	.223	.316	−.042	.264
Social Isolation	.141	.461	−.031	.199	.273
	C: Factors 2a and 4 rotated 45° clockwise				
	1a	2ab	3	4b	h^2
Meaninglessness	.225	.390	−.062	.134	.224
Powerlessness	.607	.047	−.113	.100	.393
Normlessness	.336	.187	.316	.128	.264
Social Isolation	.141	.185	−.031	.467	.273
	D: Factors 1a and 3 rotated 30° clockwise				
	1ac	2ab	3c	4b	h^2
Meaninglessness	.226	.390	.058	.134	.224
Powerlessness	.581	.047	.206	.100	.392
Normlessness	.133	.187	.442	.128	.264
Social Isolation	.138	.185	.044	.467	.273
	E: Factors 1ac and 2ab reversed				
	2ab	1ac	3c	4b	h^2
Meaninglessness	.390	.226	.058	.134	.224
Powerlessness	.047	.581	.206	.100	.393
Normlessness	.187	.133	.442	.128	.264
Social Isolation	.185	.138	.044	.467	.273
	F: Mean factor loadings in Table 2.2				
	1	2	3	4	h^2
Meaninglessness	.398	.133	.132	.177	.224
Powerlessness	.153	.582	.145	.104	.394
Normlessness	.116	.164	.463	.098	.264
Social Isolation	.139	.098	.115	.481	.274

the rotated structure, as visually projected in Figure 2.1. We have thus begun the process of differentiating the dimensions of alienation from one another. The process is only partially completed, however, because each cluster of interrelated variables does not define a separate factor. In other words, the process of rotation is not yet complete.

As can be seen in Table 2.6.B, both the Social Isolation items and the Meaninglessness items define factor 2a, but the latter load negatively while the former load positively on factor 4. Hence, a rotation of factor 2a against factor 4 might separate these two dimensions empirically. Specifically, it was determined that factors 2a and 4 should be rotated clockwise to 45°, as shown in Figure 2.2A:

$$a'_{m2a} = \cos 45° \, a_{m2a} - \sin 45° \, a_{m4}$$
$$= (.7071) \, (.370) - (.7071) \, (-.181)$$
$$= .262 + .128 = .390$$
$$a'_{m4} = \sin 45° \, a_{m2a} + \cos 45° \, a_{m4}$$
$$= (.7071) \, (.370) + (.7071) \, (-.181)$$
$$= .262 - .128 = .134$$

The remaining rotations were computed in a similar fashion. These rotated factors, 4b and 2ab, are presented in Table 2.6C. Again, the communalities were unaffected by the rotational procedure.

Table 2.6C shows that the rotation increased the interpretability of the factors since the Powerlessness items define factor 1a, the Meaninglessness items define factor 2ab, the Normlessness items define factor 3, and the Social Isolation items define factor 4. Indeed, the process of differentiating the dimensions of alienation from one another is now almost complete. The lone remaining difficulty is that the Normlessness items define factor 1a somewhat more strongly than they define factor 3. In other words, the Normlessness items are not defined on a separate factor. Figure 2.2B presents these two factors graphically and indicates that a rotation of these factors clockwise to 30° would accomplish the desired alteration in the factor matrix.

$$a'_{m1a} = \cos 30° \, a_{m1a} - \sin 30° \, a_{m3}$$
$$= (.866) \, (.225) - (.5) \, (-.062)$$
$$= .195 + .031 = .226$$
$$a'_{m3} = \sin 30° \, a_{m1a} + \cos 30° \, a_{m3}$$
$$= (.5) \, (.225) + (.866) \, (-.062)$$
$$= .112 - .054 = .058$$

The remaining rotations were computed in a similar fashion. These rotated factors, 1ac and 3c, are presented in Table 2.6D. Finally, in Table 2.6E, factors 1ac and 2ab are reversed and the highest loading on each factor is shown in italic. This table reveals that the rotational structure is now complete, because each cluster of interrelated variables now defines one and only one factor. Stated somewhat differ-

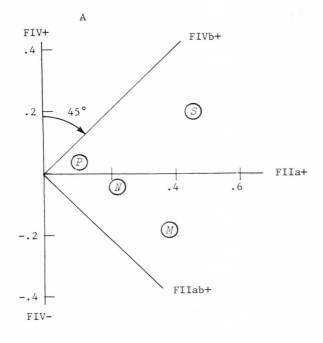

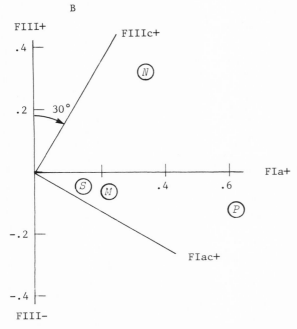

Figure 2.2. Graphic presentation of factors. (A) Factors IIa and IV; (B) factors Ia and III.

ently, the four factors are now properly aligned with the items measuring the four dimensions of alienation.

As a final step, we calculated the mean factor loadings for the rotated factor matrix in Table 2.2; these figures are presented in Table 2.6F. A comparison of Table 2.6E and 2.6F reveals a striking similarity in the pattern of the factor loadings that define each factor. In fact, the purposive rotation completed by hand and the computer rotation specified by a mathematical minimization function differ only trivially on the major loadings for the four dimensions of alienation. So it is quite possible to rotate a factor matrix graphically through visual inspection. But as the factor matrix increases in terms of the number of variables and factors, it becomes much more efficient to rotate according to mathematical functions, a topic that we now address.

Mathematical rotation of orthogonal factors
There is no unique orthogonal rotation solution to a factor analysis. There are, however, some rotational techniques that usually operate to increase both simplicity and interpretability. In general, there are two strategies for simplification of a factor matrix. On the one hand, one can attempt, as much as possible, to simplify the columns; on the other, one can attempt, as much as possible, to simplify the rows. The varimax rotation is designed to do the former; quartimax the latter. Both of these rotational systems maintain the orthogonality of factor loadings.

Quartimax rotation is a mathematical procedure designed to rotate the extracted factors in such a way that each variable will load high on one (the first) factor and low on all other factors. In mathematical terms, quartimax rotation minimizes the cross-products of the factor loadings for each variable. If one of the two terms in a cross-product is zero, the cross-product is zero. Therefore, this criterion is maximized when as much of the variance of an item as possible loads on the first factor with no variance loading on the other factors. Quartimax rotation rotates in this direction as much as it can within the constraints of the data. In the process of simplifying the rows, much of the variance in the matrix gets rotated onto the first factor. This first factor is often called a *G* or *general factor*.

Varimax rotation is a mathematical procedure designed to rotate the extracted factors in such a way that the factor loadings on any one factor are as high or as low as possible. In mathematical terms, varimax rotation minimizes the cross-products of the factor loadings for each factor. If one of the factor loadings on a particular factor is zero, the cross-product of those two factor loadings on that factor will also be zero. Therefore, this criterion is maximized when as much of the variance of a factor as possible loads on a few number of items, with as little of the variance as possible loading on the other items. The criterion is met when all of the variance of a factor loads on a small number of items with no variance loading on the other items. Varimax rotation rotates in this direction as much as it can within the constraints of the data. In the process of simplifying the columns, less of the variance in the matrix of factor loadings gets rotated on the first factor than is the case with quartimax rotation. Varimax rotation also leads to factor invariance, whereby factors define the same cluster of variables irrespective of the other variables in the analysis.

Oblique rotation

If reference axes are not at a 90° angle from each other, one no longer has orthogonal factors, but instead has established an oblique rotational scheme. Because oblique factors are not perpendicular to each other, the factors themselves are correlated. Oblique rotation has two attractive features. The first is that with an oblique rotation, the factors can pinpoint more accurately clusters of interrelated variables. The reason for this increased accuracy is that the factors no longer need to be perpendicular to each other but can individually delineate the clusters. Thus, if the clusters themselves are related, the factors in an oblique rotation can be established directly in the center of the clusters, whereas this would not be possible with an orthogonal rotation. The second attractive feature of oblique rotation is that if dimensions in the real world are correlated with each other, the oblique factors will be more consonant with reality.

Nevertheless, there are some very real disadvantages to oblique rotation. First, not only does one have to describe the factor loadings of each item with each factor, one also has to specify the degree to which each factor is correlated with every other factor. Second, there are two sets of factor loadings, referred to as pattern and structure factor matrices, which adds substantially to the interpretational complexity of the factor structure. Third, communalities of variables cannot be computed directly from the oblique loadings because the sum of the squared factor loadings can exceed 1.00. Finally, it is difficult to devise criteria for setting the minimum angle to be demanded from an oblique factor rotation.

It is not ordinarily necessary to choose arbitrarily between orthogonal and oblique rotational systems. Instead, Rummel (1970:388) observes that "with computer facilities now widely available, the researcher can try both options and with oblique and orthogonal results at hand, he can then commit himself to one of them." Moreover, it frequently occurs that the interpretation of the results will not differ substantively regardless of whether an orthogonal or oblique rotational system is used. We demonstrated this to ourselves by performing an oblique rotation on Table 2.4. This procedure resulted in one factor for each dimension of alienation, with the same items clustering on the same factors as we observed in Table 2.2. This being the case, two criteria, interpretational ease and correlated factors, are relevant to the decision about using orthogonally or obliquely rotated factor structures.

Interpretational ease

In orthogonal rotation, the factor loadings can be interpreted as correlation coefficients between items and factors; in oblique rotation, this interpretation is not legitimate. As Harman (1976:275) comments, while the term "factor loading"

> may be perfectly acceptable in the case of an orthogonal solution, it lacks precision of meaning in an oblique solution. Factor "loading" is not a mathematical or statistical term meaning either "correlation" or "coefficient," and hence has been used inconsistently in both senses. [Hence, the factor matrix for an oblique rotation contains] the projections of the test vectors on a set on oblique reference axes.

The damage done by yielding the correlation-of-an-item-with-a-factor interpretation of a factor loading is considerable. Not only does the term "factor loading" lapse into ambiguity, but eigenvalues and communalities lose their integrity as well. Indeed, both factor loadings and communalities can exceed a maximum value of 1 in this situation. These considerations favor use of orthogonal rather than oblique rotation.

Correlated factors

Oblique rotation allows factors to be correlated with one another; orthogonal rotation does not. Presumably, many of the phenomena in the real world are related to one another. Therefore, since oblique rotation allows for correlated factors whereas orthogonal rotation does not, it would appear that oblique rotation would be preferred to orthogonal rotation on this basis. Such a preference, however, is based upon what Rudner (1966:69) calls the "reproductive" fallacy: "The mistake involved consists in assuming that it is the function of science to *reproduce* 'reality' and concluding that science is defective from the fact that it accomplishes no such thing. Basically, this error rests on a confusion between a description and what is described." Just as we can acknowledge that a tornado twists and tears without being twisted and torn by it, so we can acknowledge that clusters of items in a factor analysis are correlated without making the factors correlated. When clusters of items are highly correlated (as they sometimes are) oblique rotation is recommended in order that the results of the analysis will reproduce "reality." However, the researcher's concern is the parsimonious, interpretable identification of distinct, separable clusters of items. This purpose is frequently better served by orthogonal than by oblique rotation.

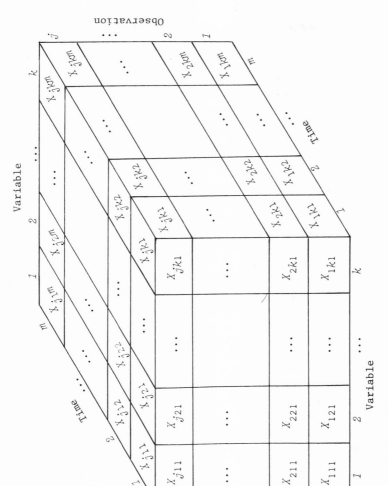

Figure 2.3. The data cube.

General factor-analytic framework

Typically, factor analysis has been used to clarify the intercorrelations among variables, such as test scores, questionnaire responses, and so forth, at a given point in time. The usual procedure is to compute the correlation matrix among the variables for a given number of observations at one point in time. The ensuing factor analysis and associated interpretation completes the analysis. The classic use of factor analysis in this regard is in achievement tests.

In fact, there are six kinds of factor analysis. They can be most easily described by examining the data cube in Figure 2.3. In Figure 2.3, the observations are represented by 1 through j, the variables are represented by 1 through k, and time is represented by 1 through m. We can see three surfaces; each surface can be factored in two directions. The six types of factor analysis on the data cube are as follows:

1   Factor the interrelationships among variables across observations in one time period.
2   Factor the interrelationships among observations across variables in one time period.
3   Factor the interrelationships among time periods across observations for one variable.
4   Factor the interrelationships among observations across time periods for one variable.
5   Factor the interrelationships among variables across time periods for one observation.
6   Factor the interrelationships among time periods across variables for one observation.

The remaining chapters in this book will show how factor-analytic type 2, in particular, provides a useful way of analyzing measurements containing systematic error.

Appendix: Natural trigonometric functions for angles in degrees

Degree	Sine	Cosine	Degree
0	.00000	1.0000	90
1	.01745	.9998	89
2	.03490	.9994	88
3	.05234	.9986	87
4	.06976	.9976	86
5	.08716	.9962	85
6	.10453	.9945	84
7	.12187	.9925	83
8	.13917	.9903	82
9	.15643	.9877	81
10	.1736	.9848	80
11	.1908	.9816	79
12	.2079	.9781	78
13	.2250	.9744	77
14	.2419	.9703	76
15	.2588	.9659	75
16	.2756	.9613	74
17	.2924	.9563	73
18	.3090	.9511	72
19	.3256	.9455	71
20	.3420	.9397	70
21	.3584	.9336	69
22	.3746	.9272	68
23	.3907	.9205	67
24	.4067	.9135	66
25	.4226	.9063	65
26	.4384	.8988	64
27	.4540	.8910	63
28	.4695	8829	62
29	.4848	.8746	61
30	.5000	.8660	60
31	.5150	.8572	59
32	.5299	.8480	58
33	.5446	.8387	57
34	.5592	.8290	56
35	.5736	.8192	55
36	.5878	.8090	54
37	.6018	.7986	53
38	.6157	.7880	52
39	.6293	.7771	51
40	.6428	.7660	50
41	.6561	.7547	49
42	.6691	.7431	48
43	.6820	.7314	47
44	.6947	.7193	46
45	.7071	.7071	45
Degree	Cosine	Sine	Degree

3 Reliability

Reliability concerns the degree of repeatability and consistency of empirical measurements. A *reliable measure* is one that is repeatable and consistent, whereas an *unreliable measure* provides results that are unrepeatable and inconsistent. If a well-anchored rifle is fired but the shots are widely scattered about a target, the rifle is unreliable. But if the shots are closely concentrated around the target, the rifle is considered reliable.

It was shown in Chapter 1 that, from a statistical standpoint, reliability is equal to the nonrandom components of the observed variance. These nonrandom components are made up of true score variance and systematic error variance as well as the covariance between these elements. In estimating reliability, it is not necessary to separate systematic error variance from true score variance. For systematic error does not detract from a measure's reliability, because it does not reduce consistency and repeatability. Moreover, as we will show later, systematic error may increase or decrease the reliability of a composite measure of a concept.

The focus of attention in reliability assessment is on random error. If there is no random error involved in the measurement of some particular concept, the reliability will equal 1.00. But as the amount of random error increases, the reliability is reduced until in the unusual circumstance when all observed variance is random, reliability would be zero. Thus, reliability is inversely related to the amount of random error in the measurement process.

Composites versus single indicants

Many studies in the social sciences use a single indicant to approximate a theoretical concept. From a measurement perspective, this approach is highly undesirable, for unless there is a priori information available (and such information is not usually available), it is impossible to estimate the reliability of a single indicant. Moreover, even if the reliability of single indicants can be obtained, it is usually inferior to combined multiple indicants (that is, a composite) because it is more affected by random error. Blalock (1970:111) comments:

With a single measure of each variable, one can remain blissfully unaware of the possibility of measurement [error], but in no sense will this make his inferences more valid. Though there is always the danger of becoming so hypersensitive to the possibility of measurement error that one becomes immobilized in the process, present practice seems to err in the opposite direction. Methodological studies on the implications of measurement errors can help us see more clearly the nature of the steps we must take if we are to become increasingly precise. In the absence of better theory about our measurement procedures, I see no substitute for the use of multiple measures of our most important variables.

The following section empirically demonstrates the superiority of multiple indicant composites in comparison to a single indicant in providing an empirical approximation of a theoretical concept and also illustrates the general logic underlying reliability estimation.

Figure 3.1A presents an example of a structural/measurement model containing two theoretical concepts, X_t and Y_t, and 12 indicants, X_1 through X_6 measuring X_t and Y_1 through Y_6 measuring Y_t. For the theoretical model – that is, the structural model measured without error – the relevant population parameters are as follows:

$$\mu_{x_t} = \mu_{y_t} = 0 \qquad \sigma_{x_t}^2 = \sigma_{y_t}^2 = 1.684 \qquad \rho_{x_t y_t} = .5$$

A scattergram of X_t and Y_t showing the locations of the 19 observations making up the theoretical model is presented in Figure 3.2. If random error is now added to the theoretical model, it is possible to solve for the parameters of the full structural/measurement model. Specifically, if the random error is chosen from the set of values -2, -1, 0, 1, and 2, the random error variance equals 2.00. Thus, using formula 1.15, we obtain

$$\sigma_{x_1}^2 = \sigma_t^2 + \sigma_s^2 + \sigma_r^2 + 2\sigma_{ts}$$
$$= 1.684 + 0 + 2.00 + 0$$
$$= 3.684$$

Reliability then equals (from Formula 1.16)

$$\frac{\sigma_x^2 - \sigma_r^2}{\sigma_x^2} = \frac{3.684 - 2.00}{3.684} = .457$$

Thus, 45.7% of the observed variance in each indicant is reliable. (This statement refers to the special case in which there is no systematic error. We will introduce systematic error into the structural measurement model and discuss its effects in Chapters 4 to 6.) Alternatively stated, each indicant of X (or Y) shares 45.7% of its variance with X_t (or Y_t). Since

$$\rho_{x_i x_t}^2 = .457$$
$$\rho_{x_i x_t} = \sqrt{.457} = .676$$

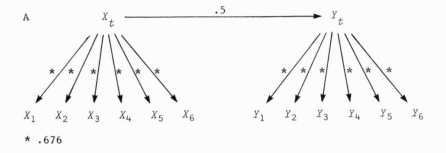

A

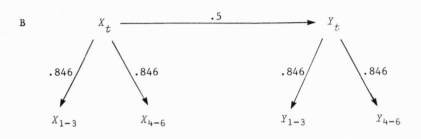

B

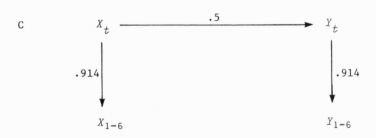

C

Figure 3.1. Structural measurement model of X and Y. Causal relationships between X and Y concepts and (A) X and Y indicants; (B) three-item X and Y composites; (C) six-item X and Y composites.

This value is referred to as an *epistemic correlation* – the correlation between the observed indicator and the unobserved theoretical concept. In other words, the reliability of an indicator equals the square of the epistemic correlation in the measurement model. The structural parameter, in this case the correlation between the theoretical concepts X_t and Y_t, equals .5.

This information can be used to compute the intercorrelations

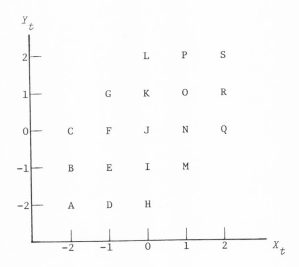

Figure 3.2. Scattergram of X_t and Y_t.

among the X indicants and the Y indicants as well as the cross-indicant correlations. The correlations among the X indicants are equal to the products of the correlations of each X indicant with X_t. That is, $\rho_{x_i x_j} = \rho_{x_i x_t} \rho_{x_j x_t}$ where $i \neq j$. Using the data in Figure 3.1A, we obtain

$$\rho_{x_i x_j} = (.676)(.676) = .457$$

The correlation between each X indicant and each Y indicant equals

$$\rho_{x_i y_j} = \rho_{x_i x_t} \rho_{x_t y_t} \rho_{y_t y_j}$$

where $i \neq j$. Thus,

$$\rho_{x_i y_j} = (.676)(.5)(.676) = .2285$$

Figure 3.1B presents a structural/measurement model of the relationships between the X and Y concepts and the sets of three-indicant X and Y composites, respectively. In the structural model, the causal effect between X_t and Y_t remains at .5. Moreover, X_t causes each respective three-indicant X composite; and Y_t causes each respective three-indicant Y composite. The reliability for each three-item composite is .716, and the epistemic correlations equal $\sqrt{.716} = .846$.

Comparing Figure 3.1A and 3.1B, it is clear that the reliabilities (and epistemic correlations) for the indicants are higher for the latter than for the former. That is, the three-item composite shares more of its variance with the underlying concept than does the single indicant. Finally, as indicated in Figure 3.1C, the reliabilities and epistemic correlations for a six-item composite equals .835 and .914, respectively.

Therefore, just as a three-indicant composite is a better approximation of the underlying concept than is a single indicant, so a six-indicant composite is a better approximation than is a three-indicant composite.

These results clearly indicate that composites formed by simply adding together individual indicants are less affected by random error than are single indicants. Moreover, in general, the greater the number of proper indicants in the composite, the more reliable is the resulting composite.

Types of reliability

The definition of *reliability* centers on the degree of *repeatability* and *consistency* of empirical measurements. The two key terms "repeatability" and "consistency" correspond to the two basic strategies used to assess reliability. These strategies are referred to as "stability" and "equivalence," respectively.

Stability
On the one hand, reliability can be assessed by analyzing the same measure for the same population at more than one point in time. The most typical method used to evaluate the *stability* of measurements is the test–retest reliability correlation. In such analysis, one correlates the same measures at different points in time. If one obtains exactly the same measurements across time, the test–retest reliability would be 1.00. But, generally, the correlation of measurements across time will be less than perfect because of the instability of measurements taken at multiple points in time. For example, a person may respond differently to a set of indicants used to measure alienation from one time to another because "[t]he respondent may be temporarily distracted, misunderstand the meaning of an item," feel uncomfortable because of someone else being present, and so forth (Bohrnstedt, 1970:85). All of these conditions reduce the reliability of empirical measurements.

While test–retest correlations represent an intuitively appealing procedure by which to assess reliability, they are not without serious problems and limitations. Perhaps most important, researchers are often only able to obtain a measure of a phenomenon at a single point in time. Not only can it be unduly expensive to obtain measurements at various points in time, but it can be impractical as well. Even if test–retest correlations can be computed, their interpretation is not necessarily straightforward. A low test–retest correlation, for example, may not be an indication that the reliability of the measure is low but may, instead, signify that the theoretical concept itself has changed. But true change is interpreted as measurement instability in the assessment of test–retest reliability. Moreover, the longer the time interval between measurements, the more likely it is that the concept has actually changed. Heise (1969) has shown that true change can be distinguished from unreliability if one has a single variable measured at three points in time and is willing to make a series of simplifying assumptions. One of these assumptions is that the true score variance be constant across time. Wiley and Wiley (1970) have noted, however, that it is sufficient if the error variances are identical, thus allowing the effects of the true score on the observed score to vary across time. In any case, the key point is that the naive interpretation of test–retest correlations can drastically underestimate the degree of reliability in the measurement of some concepts.

A second problem that affects test–retest correlations and also leads to deflated reliability estimates is reactivity. *Reactivity* refers to the fact that sometimes the very process of measuring a phenomenon can induce change in the phenomenon itself. Thus, in measuring a person's attitude at time 1, the person can be sensitized to the subject under investigation and demonstrate a change at time 2 which is due solely to the earlier measurement. For example, if a person is interviewed about the likelihood of voting in an approaching election at time 1, the person might decide to vote (at time 2) and actually cast a ballot (at time 3) merely because he or she has been sensitized to the election. In this case, the test–retest correlation will be lower than it would be otherwise because of reactivity.

But the problems encountered in assessing stability with test–retest correlations do not always lead to deflated reliability estimates. If the time interval between measurements is too short, respondents can remember their earlier responses and will appear more consistent than they actually are. Such "memory" effects lead to inflated reliability estimates.

In summary, there are several serious problems that affect measures of stability. These problems have seemed so severe that, as Bohrnstedt (1970:86) reported, "many researchers have abandoned measures of stability. . . ." But interest in the estimation of over-time reliability and stability has increased in the last several years (Pelz and Andrews, 1964; Yee and Gage, 1968; Duncan, 1969, 1972, 1975; Rozelle and Campbell, 1969; Blalock, 1970; Heise, 1970; Kenny, 1973; Beck, 1975; Kimberly, 1976; Hannan and Young, 1977; and Wheaton et al., 1977). This has occurred, in part, because of the greater availability of multiple time point data. Moreover, more powerful techniques for analyzing such data have been developed in recent years. For a review of this literature, see Wheaton et al., 1977. While these developments are quite interesting and important, they go beyond the scope of our present discussion. In our judgment, this literature is excessively complex mathematically. A simpler, more useful style of analysis, appropriate for data of this type, is presented in Carmines and Zeller (in preparation).

Equivalence

The second broad strategy for assessing reliability focuses on multiple indicators of a concept measured at a single point in time. Each indicator is considered a separate but equivalent measure of the underlying concept. The earliest measures of equivalence focused on *split-half methods*. In these methods, the total number of indicants is divided into two halves and the correlation between the two halves used to provide an estimate of the reliability of the full set of indicants. For example, referring to Table 3.1, let items X_{1-3} represent one of the split halves and items X_{4-6} the other split half. The correlation between X_{1-3} and X_{4-6} can be computed using the following formula:

$$\rho = \frac{e}{\sqrt{(a = 2b)\,(c + 2d)}} \tag{3.1}$$

where a = number of indicants in the X_{1-3} composite
$\quad\quad b$ = sum of the correlations in the upper right triangle of the X_{1-3} indicants
$\quad\quad c$ = number of indicants in the X_{4-6} composite
$\quad\quad d$ = sum of the correlations in the upper right triangle of the X_{4-6} indicants
$\quad\quad e$ = sum of the intercorrelations between the X_{1-3} indicants and the X_{4-6} indicants

Given the data in Table 3.1, $a = 3$, $b = 1.371$, $c = 3$, $d = 1.371$, and $e = 4.113$. Consequently,

$$\rho_{xx'} = \frac{4.113}{\sqrt{3 + (2)\,(1.371)}\,\sqrt{3 + (2)\,(1.371)}} = \frac{4.113}{5.742} = .716$$

The Spearman–Brown prophecy formula, derived independently by Spearman (1910) and Brown (1910), uses this correlation to estimate the reliability of the six-item scale. In particular, since the six-item scale is twice as long as each of the three-item scales, the appropriate Spearman–Brown prophecy formula is

$$\rho_{xx''} = \frac{2\rho_{xx'}}{1 + \rho_{xx'}} \tag{3.2}$$

where $\rho_{xx''}$ = reliability coefficient for the whole test
$\quad\quad \rho_{xx'}$ = split-half correlation
Therefore,

$$\rho_{xx''} = \frac{(2)\,(.716)}{1 + .716} = \frac{1.432}{1.716} = .835$$

The estimated reliability of the six-item scale is .835. It is not difficult to see that the split-half reliability varies between 0 and 1, taking on these limits if the correlation between the halves is .00 or 1.00, respectively.

The more general version of the Spearman–Brown prophecy formula (of which Formula 3.2 is a special case) is

$$\rho_{x_n x_n''} = \frac{N\rho_{xx'}}{1 + (N - 1)\rho_{xx'}} \qquad (3.3)$$

As illustrated by Stanley (1971:395–6), this formula is quite useful. For example, if a five-item split half form of a test correlates .22 with another five-item split half form, the estimated reliability for a scale or composite four times that long would equal .53, as follows:

$$\rho_{x_n x_n''} = \frac{(4)\,(.22)}{1 + (4-1)\,(.22)} = \frac{.88}{1.66} = .53$$

"This means that, if one form of a test composed of 5 items correlates .22 with a parallel form of that test that also has 5 items, then a form composed of 20 items similar to the initial 5 should correlate .53 with a parallel form containing 20 items" (Stanley, 1971:395). The same reasoning can be employed to determine the number of items that would be needed to attain a given reliability or what the split-half correlation must be, given a desired reliability and test length.

There is a certain indeterminancy with respect to the use of split-half methods for assessing reliability due to the different ways that the items can be grouped into halves. The most typical way to divide the items is to place the even-numbered items in one group and the odd-numbered items in the other group. But other ways to partition the total item set are also used, including separately scoring the first and second halves of the items and randomly dividing the items into two groups. Indeed, as Bohrnstedt (1970:86) has noted, for a composite $2N$ items long, the number of possible partitions of items is $2N!/2(N!)(N!)$. Hence, for a six-item composite, there are

$$\frac{2N!}{2(N!)\,(N!)} = \frac{(6)\,(5)\,(4)\,(3)\,(2)\,(1)}{(2)\,(3)\,(2)\,(1)\,(3)\,(2)\,(1)} = 10$$

possible item groups. For a 10-item composite, there are

$$\frac{2N!}{2(N!)\,(N!)} = \frac{(10)\,(9)\,(8)\,(7)\,(6)\,(5)\,(4)\,(3)\,(2)\,(1)}{(2)\,(5)\,(4)\,(3)\,(2)\,(1)\,(5)\,(4)\,(3)\,(2)\,(1)} = 126$$

possible item groups. The point is that each split will probably result in a different correlation between the halves, which, in turn, leads to a different reliability estimate. Thus, it is quite possible to obtain different reliability estimates even if the same items are administered to the same individuals.

Cronbach's alpha

In response to the arbitrariness inherent in estimating reliability by use of split-half methods, several psychometricians have developed reliability coefficients that do not require the splitting or repeating of items. These procedures were developed to make use of all the variance and covariance information of the items and thus provide a unique estimate of reliability. As a group, these coefficients are referred to as *measures of internal consistency* or *equivalence*. By far the most popular of these coefficients is *Cronbach's alpha* (Cronbach, 1951), which can be expressed as follows:

$$\alpha = \frac{N}{N-1}\left[1 - \frac{\Sigma\,\sigma^2(Y_i)}{\sigma_x^2}\right] \tag{3.4}$$

where N = number of indicants or items
$\Sigma\,\sigma^2(Y_i)$ = sum of indicant variances
σ_x^2 = variance of the total composite
If one is working with the correlation matrix rather than the variance–covariance matrix, alpha reduces to the following formula:

$$\alpha = \frac{a}{a-1}\left[1 - \frac{a}{a+2b}\right] \tag{3.5}$$

where a = number of indicants in the composite
b = sum of the correlations among the indicants
Solving for alpha for the six-indicant X composite in Table 3.1,

$$\alpha = \frac{6}{6-1}\left[1 - \frac{6}{6+(2)(6.855)}\right] = (1.2)(.696) = .835$$

Cronbach's alpha is equal to the average of all possible split-half correlations for a composite scale $2N$ items long. Alternatively stated, Cronbach's alpha is equal to the application of the Spearman-Brown prophecy formula 3.2 to the average of all possible split-half correlations. Implications of this definition will be explored in greater detail later in this chapter. Cronbach's alpha varies between .00 and 1.00, taking on these extremes when the item intercorrelations are equal to zero and unity, respectively.

In general, as the average correlation among the items increases and as the number of items increases, alpha takes on a larger value. This can be seen by observing Table 3.2A, which shows the value of

Table 3.1. *Correlation matrix of x and y indicants (conceptual)*

	X_1	X_2	X_3	X_4	X_5	X_6	Y_1	Y_2	Y_3	Y_4	Y_5	Y_6
X_1	—	.457	.457	.457	.457	.457	.2285	.2285	.2285	.2285	.2285	.2285
X_2		—	.457	.457	.457	.457	.2285	.2285	.2285	.2285	.2285	.2285
X_3			—	.457	.457	.457	.2285	.2285	.2285	.2285	.2285	.2285
X_4				—	.457	.457	.2285	.2285	.2285	.2285	.2285	.2285
X_5					—	.457	.2285	.2285	.2285	.2285	.2285	.2285
X_6						—	.2285	.2285	.2285	.2285	.2285	.2285
Y_1							—	.457	.457	.457	.457	.457
Y_2								—	.457	.457	.457	.457
Y_3									—	.457	.457	.457
Y_4										—	.457	.457
Y_5											—	.457
Y_6												—

Table 3.2. *Values of Cronbach's alpha*

A: Value of Cronbach's alpha given an average interindicant correlation and the number of items included in the scale

No. of indicants	Average interindicant correlation								
	.1	.2	.3	.4	.5	.6	.7	.8	.9
2	.182	.333	.462	.572	.667	.750	.824	.889	.947
3	.250	.428	.563	.667	.750	.818	.875	.922	.965
4	.308	.500	.632	.727	.800	.857	.903	.941	.973
5	.358	.556	.682	.769	.833	.883	.921	.953	.979
6	.400	.600	.720	.800	.858	.900	.933	.960	.982
7	.437	.636	.750	.824	.875	.914	.943	.966	.985
8	.471	.666	.774	.842	.889	.924	.949	.970	.9864
9	.500	.692	.794	.857	.900	.932	.954	.973	.9877
10	.526	.714	.811	.870	.909	.938	.959	.976	—

B: Increase in the size of Cronbach's alpha given the addition of an indicant

Added indicant	.1	.2	.3	.4	.5	.6	.7	.8	.9
Second	.082	.133	.162	.172	.167	.150	.124	.089	.047
Third	.068	.095	.101	.09£	.083	.068	.051	.033	.018
Fourth	.058	.072	.069	.060	.050	.039	.028	.019	.008
Fifth	.050	.056	.050	.042	.033	.026	.018	.012	.006
Sixth	.042	.044	.038	.031	.025	.017	.012	.007	.003
Seventh	.037	.036	.030	.024	.017	.014	.010	.006	.003
Eighth	.034	.030	.024	.018	.014	.010	.006	.004	.0014
Nineth	.029	.026	.020	.015	.011	.008	.006	.003	.0013
Tenth	.026	.022	.017	.013	.009	.006	.005	.003	—

alpha given a range in the number of indicants from 2 to 10 and a range in the average interindicant correlation from .1 to .9. For example, a three-item composite with an average interitem correlation of .10 has an alpha of .250, but with 10 items, the alpha increases to .526. Similarly, an eight-item composite with an average interitem correlation of .20 has an alpha of .666, whereas if the eight items have an average interitem correlation of .80, the composite's alpha would be .970. Thus, the addition of more indicants to a composite – if they do not result in a reduction in the average interitem correlation – will increase the reliability of one's measuring instrument. There are, however, some severe limitations to this procedure. First, as can be seen in Table 3.2B, the adding of indicants indefinitely makes progressively less impact on the reliability. Thus, given an average interindicant correlation of .5, the adding of the fourth indicant increases the alpha for the composite by .05, but the addition of the tenth indicant only increases the alpha by .009. Second, the greater the number of indicants, the more time and resources are spent on constructing the instrument. Third, and most important, as one adds different, independently measured indicants to a composite, the likelihood is that not all of those indicants will be an empirical representation of the same theoretical concept. These indicants may represent more than one concept (which is, in this context, systematic error); they may represent some methodological artifact (which also is systematic error); and/or they may fluctuate to a greater degree as a result of random error.

It is also possible for the addition of indicants to a composite to lower the composite reliability. If the sum of the correlations in the upper right rectangle of Table 3.1 were equal to zero (as they would be if X_t and Y_t were uncorrelated), the reliability of the 12-item composite would be .68, substantially lower than the .835 alpha for the six-item X composite and the six-item Y composite. Thus, if the addition of items reduces the average intercorrelation, then alpha will be reduced as well.

The use of dichotomous indicants in composites
The discussion of Cronbach's alpha is applicable to scaled multichotomous indicants. In such indicants, a higher numerical value is attached to each succeeding response category that represents a greater degree to which the respondent possesses the characteristic under investigation. The development of Cronbach's alpha was a generalization of a procedure developed by Kuder and Richardson (1937) designed to provide reliability information applicable to scaled dichotomous indicants. Dichotomous indicants in a composite are scored one or zero, depending upon whether the respondent does or does not possess the characteristic under investigation. The Kuder–

Richardson equivalency formula (symbolized KR20) takes the following form:

$$KR20 = \frac{N}{N-1}\left[1 - \frac{\Sigma p_i q_i}{\sigma_x^2}\right] \qquad (3.6)$$

where N = number of dichotomous items
$\quad p_i$ = proportion responding "positively" to the ith item
$\quad q_i = 1 - p_i$
$\quad \sigma_x^2$ = variance of the total composite

If the items have identical p_i values – that is, if the proportion responding positively is the same for all the items–KR20 can be reduced to KR21, which is expressed as follows:

$$KR21 = \frac{N}{N-1}\left[1 - \frac{N\bar{p}\bar{q}}{\sigma_x^2}\right] \qquad (3.7)$$

where $\bar{p} = \Sigma\, p_i/N$
$\quad \bar{q} = 1 - \bar{p}$
It is not difficult to see that KR20 $\geqslant$ KR21. Moreover, KR20 is the more general and useful reliability coefficient for dichotomous items, because it does not make any special assumptions about the distribution of the items. Thus, it is the recommended reliability coefficient for composites formed by adding together dichotomously scored items. Finally, because it is a generalization of KR20, Cronbach's alpha can be applied to dichotomous as well as to multichotomous indicants.

In summary, Cronbach's alpha has a number of desirable properties as a reliability estimate. First, it is a very general reliability coefficient, encompassing both the Spearman–Brown prophecy formula and the Kuder–Richardson 20 and 21. Although not discussed here, it also is equivalent to Hoyt's coefficient (1941), which is developed by use of analysis-of-variance procedures. It also makes use of all the information contained in the items (that is, their number, variances, and covariances). Finally, alpha is easy to compute and has a straightforward, compelling theoretical interpretation.

Factor analysis and reliability

Although Cronbach's alpha does have several desirable properties that make it a widely used estimate of reliability for linear composites, it is not without certain shortcomings and limitations. Perhaps most important, it has been shown by Novick and Lewis (1967) that alpha equals reliability only if the items are strictly parallel or, at least, essentially tau-equivalent. (Parallel items have identical true scores, whereas tau-equivalent items have true scores that differ pairwise by no more than an additive constant.) Otherwise, the value of alpha merely sets a lower bound on the reliability. Stated more precisely,

Cronbach's alpha is a maximum likelihood estimator of a parameter; the reliability of the composite cannot be less than the value of this parameter. From a practical estimation standpoint, this means that alpha does not provide an optimal estimate of reliability when the items that make up the composite are heterogeneous in their relation to one another (and when N is small). In these conditions, Cronbach's alpha is smaller than the internal consistency of the composite. Thus, the more the interitem correlations diverge from one another, the more the value given by alpha understates the true reliability. As noted by Armor (1974:24–5), this suggests that there are two conditions under which alpha may not provide a good estimate of reliability: if the items measure a single concept unequally or if the items measure more than one concept equally or unequally. If the number of items in the composite is fairly small and if the pattern of interitem correlations is reasonably clear and distinct, both of these conditions can be detected by examining the items' correlation matrix. However, as Armor (1974:26) argues, "[A]s the number of items increases (say, over ten), as the number of dimensions increases, and as items contribute differentially to each dimension, none but the most patient and diligent analyst would be able to produce optimum scaling with the usual alpha reliability and covariance scaling techniques."

The very conditions that limit the usefulness of alpha as a reliability estimate suggest that reliability estimation based on factor analysis would be relevant and appropriate. In other words, as we have seen in Chapter 2, factor analysis is quite useful in identifying and describing the number of separate dimensions underlying a set of data, and the factor loadings for each item provide a convenient and meaningful indication of the contribution of each item to a given factor. Thus, reliability coefficients based on factor analysis have the potential for overcoming the limitations associated with alpha reliability. Of these we shall discuss two popular coefficients: theta and omega.

Theta

Coefficient *theta* can be easily understood once we consider in greater detail principal components, the factor analysis model on which this reliability coefficient is based. Given a set of items in which there are no perfect intercorrelations, a principal component analysis will yield as many components as there are items. The components are extracted in decreasing order of importance in terms of the amount of variance associated with each component. That is, the first component accounts for the largest proportion of variance among the items, the second component for the second largest proportion that is independent of the first component, and so on. Corresponding to each of these components is a series of loadings. The size of these loadings gives an indication of the contribution that the item makes to each component.

Since the components are extracted in decreasing order of importance, it follows that the sum of (and average of) the loadings will be higher for the first components than for the last extracted components. Thus, there is a negative relationship between the eigenvalue of a component and when that component was extracted. For example, the third extracted component always has an eigenvalue that is less than the second component and greater than the fourth component.

Given these properties of principal components, what should one expect if a set of indicants is measuring a single theoretical concept? Several aspects of the extracted (that is, unrotated) factor matrix could support this hypothesis: (1) the first extracted component should explain a large proportion of the variance in the items (say, >40%); (2) subsequent components should explain fairly equal proportions of the remaining variance except for a gradual decrease; (3) all or most of the items should have substantial loadings on the first component (say, >.3); and (4) all or most of the items should have higher loadings on the first component than on subsequent components.

Now consider the alternative situation in which the researcher has hypothesized that a set of items taps more than a single theoretical concept (as was done in Table 2.2). In this case, a principal component analysis of the items should meet the following conditions:

1   The number of statistically meaningful components should equal the number of hypothesized theoretical concepts. As Armor (1974:37) notes, the pattern of the eigenvalues gives a rough indication of when the last meaningful component has been extracted. Specifically, "[A] large drop from one root to another followed by slightly decreasing roots [eigenvalues] usually marks the end of meaningful factors and the beginning of error or specific variance components." A more exact criterion will be discussed later.

2   After rotation, specific items should have higher factor loadings on the hypothesized relevant component than on other components.

3   Components extracted subsequent to the number of hypothesized concepts should be statistically unimportant and substantively uninterpretable. We observed such a factor structure of the alienation items in Table 2.2.

When a set of items is measuring more than a single underlying concept, it is often necessary to rotate the extracted components in order for them to be optimally interpretable. At this point, the researcher has two options in constructing composites. First, composites can be computed directly from the rotated factor structure. Alternatively, subsets of items defining each of the rotated components can be refactored according to the principal-component procedure.

However the items and their corresponding weights are chosen, the reliability of the resulting composite can be estimated using the following formula for theta:

$$\theta = \frac{N}{N-1}\left(1 - \frac{1}{\lambda_1}\right) \tag{3.8}$$

where N = number of items
λ_1 = largest (i.e., the first) eigenvalue
For the data in Table 3.1,

$$\theta = \frac{6}{5}\left(1 - \frac{1}{3.285}\right) = (1.2)(.696) = .835$$

Theta lends itself to many different interpretations, but it is understood most simply as being a special case of Cronbach's alpha. Specifically, theta is the alpha coefficient for a composite in which the weighting vector has been chosen so as to make alpha a maximum. In other words, theta may be considered a maximized alpha coefficient (Greene and Carmines, 1979).

Omega
Another estimate of reliability for linear composites that has gained widespread use is *omega*, a reliability coefficient introduced by Heise and Bohrnstedt (1970). Omega is based on the common factor analysis model and takes the general form

$$\Omega = 1 - \frac{\Sigma \sigma_i^2 - \Sigma \sigma_i^2 h_i^2}{\Sigma\Sigma \sigma_{x_i x_j}} \tag{3.9}$$

where σ_i^2 = variance of the ith item
h_i^2 = communality of the ith item
$\Sigma\Sigma \sigma_{x_i x_j}$ = sum of the covariances among the items
If one is working with correlations, the formula for omega reduces to

$$\Omega = 1 - \frac{a - \Sigma h_i^2}{a + 2b} \tag{3.10}$$

where a = number of indicants
b = sum of the correlations among the indicants
Solving for omega for the six-indicant X composite in Table 3.1,

$$\Omega = 1 - \frac{6 - 2.742}{19.71} = 1 - .165 = .835$$

There are three important differences between omega and theta (Armor, 1974:46–8). First, they are based on different factor-analytic models. Theta is grounded in the principal components model, whereas omega is based on the common factor analysis model. This means that one always uses 1.0's in the main diagonal to compute the eigenvalues on which theta is based, but the value of omega depends, in part, on communalities, which are estimated quantities, not fixed ones. This is another way of saying that because omega is based on estimated communalities, there is an element of indeterminancy in its calculation that is not present in theta. Finally, unlike theta, "omega does not assess the reliability of separate scales in the event of multiple dimensions" (Armor, 1974:47). Rather, omega provides a coefficient that estimates the reliability of all the common factors in a given item set.

Notice that for the data in Table 3.1, all three of these internal consistency reliability coefficients – alpha, theta, and omega – are equal to the same value (.835). These coefficients will always be equal to one another if the interitem correlations are equal (and all item variances are equal). In other words, if the items are essentially tau-equivalent, these coefficients provide an identical estimate of reliability. Otherwise, the following order should hold:

$$\alpha < \theta < \Omega$$

Thus, even though omega is usually a lower bound to reliability, it is the "best" lower bound among these three coefficients (see Greene and Carmines, 1979). A final point needs to be emphasized: if the items making up a composite have highly heterogeneous intercorrelations, the difference between theta and omega on the one hand and alpha on the other can be sizable. In effect, alpha assumes that the items should be weighted equally, whereas omega and theta weight them unequally according to their correlation with the other items, which is expressed in their factor loading. But if the weaker items are eliminated, resulting in interitem correlations that are fairly homogeneous, the three coefficients are generally comparable, with variations usually less than .02.

Correction for attenuation

However a reliability estimate is obtained, one of its important uses is to "correct" correlations for unreliability due to random measurement error. Referring to the earlier discussion of Figure 3.1, it was shown that whereas $\rho_{x_t y_t} = .5$, the correlations between an X indicant and a Y indicant is only .2285. The reason for this difference is that each X indicant is imperfectly correlated with X_t and each Y indicant is imperfectly correlated with Y_t. The fact that the theoretical correlation is greater than the correlation between the respective indicants due to random error is called *attenuation* of the correlation. If a researcher observes a correlation between the indicants of two different concepts and is able to obtain an estimate of the reliability of the respective indicants, he can estimate the value of the theoretical correlation. This procedure is called *correction for attenuation*. The formula for the correction for attenuation is as follows:

$$\rho_{x_t y_t} = \frac{\rho_{x_i y_j}}{\sqrt{\rho_{xx'} \rho_{yy'}}} \tag{3.11}$$

where $\rho_{x_t y_t}$ = correlation corrected for attenuation

$\quad \rho_{xx'}$ = reliability of X

$\quad \rho_{yy'}$ = reliability of Y

Substituting the between-indicant correlations within concepts and across concepts into Formula 3.11, we get

$$\rho_{x_t y_t} = \frac{.2285}{\sqrt{(.457)(.457)}} = .5$$

Thus, correction of a correlation between indicants for attenuation due to unreliability results in the correlation between the concepts. In research situations, the observed correlation and the reliabilities are estimates, so the corrected correlation is also an estimate. The conditions under which it is advisable to correct an empirical correlation for attenuation will be discussed in Chapter 5.

Table 3.3 provides a set of examples of the behavior of the correlation coefficient under varying conditions of correction for attenuation. Table 3.3A shows the value of the correlation corrected for attenuation given that the observed correlation is .3 with varying reliabilities of X and Y. As an example, when the reliabilities of both X and Y are .4, the corrected correlation is .75. When the reliabilities of both X and Y are 1.0, the corrected correlation is equal to the observed correlation of .3. Table 3.3B presents similar calculations when the observed correlation is .5. Examining Tables 3.3A and B, it is clear that the higher the reliabilities of the variables, the less the corrected correlation differs from the observed correlation.

Table 3.3C presents the value of the correlation that one will observe when the correlation between X_t and Y_t is .5 under varying conditions of reliability. If the reliabilities of X and Y are .8, the observed value of a theoretical .5 correlation is .4. Table 3.3D presents similar calculations when the correlation between X_t and Y_t is .7. For example, even if the theoretical correlation between X_t and Y_t is .7, the observed correlation will be only .14 if the reliabilities are quite low (.2). Thus, one must be careful not to conclude that the theoretical correlations are low simply because their observed counterparts are low; it may instead be the case that the measures are quite unreliable.

Table 3.3. *Examples of correction for attenuation*

A: $\rho_{x_t y_t} = .3/\sqrt{\rho_{xx'}\rho_{yy'}}$

$\rho_{yy'}$	$\rho_{xx'}$ .2	.4	.6	.8	1.0
.2	—	—	.87	.75	.67
.4	—	.75	.61	.53	.47
.6	.87	.61	.50	.43	.39
.8	.75	.53	.43	.38	.33
1.0	.67	.47	.39	.33	.30

B: $\rho_{x_t y_t} = .5/\sqrt{\rho_{xx'}\rho_{yy'}}$

$\rho_{yy'}$	$\rho_{xx'}$ .2	.4	.6	.8	1.0
.2	—	—	—	—	—
.4	—	—	—	.88	.79
.6	—	—	.83	.72	.65
.8	—	.88	.72	.63	.56
1.0	—	.79	.65	.56	.50

C: $.5 = \rho_{xy}/\sqrt{\rho_{xx'}\rho_{yy'}}$

$\rho_{yy'}$	$\rho_{yy'}$ .2	.4	.6	.8	1.0
.2	.10	.14	.17	.20	.22
.4	.14	.20	.24	.28	.32
.6	.17	.24	.30	.35	.39
.8	.20	.28	.35	.40	.45
1.0	.22	.32	.39	.45	.50

D: $.7 = \rho_{xy}/\sqrt{\rho_{xx'}\rho_{yy'}}$

$\rho_{yy'}$	$\rho_{xx'}$ .2	.4	.6	.8	1.0
.2	.14	.20	.24	.28	.31
.4	.20	.28	.34	.40	.44
.6	.24	.34	.42	.48	.54
.8	.28	.40	.48	.56	.63
1.0	.31	.44	.54	.63	.70

Application of the principles of reliability to the measurement of alienation

Let us apply the principles of reliability estimation to the alienation items presented in Table 2.1. First, we factor-analyzed the set of measures of each dimension of alienation separately. The results of these four factor analyses are presented in Table 3.4. A comparison of Tables 2.2 and 3.4 illustrates the differences and similarities in factoring these 36 items together or separately. There is slight shifting in the factor loadings; this may be attributed to the altered definition of the location of the factor given the different number of items included in the matrix and the constraint of orthogonal rotation in Table 2.2. In general, however, there is a similar pattern of factor loadings across the two analyses.

The alpha and omega reliability coefficients are presented in Table 3.4 for each of the four dimensions of alienation. Theta requires principal component analysis rather than common factor analysis. Hence, we do not present theta in this context. For Meaninglessness, these coefficients are computed as follows:

$$a = 9$$
$$a + 2b = 25.39194$$
$$\Sigma\,h^2 = 2.297$$

Table 3.4. *Factor analysis of alienation indicants within dimension*

Item	1	h^2	Item	1	h^2
Meaninglessness			*Powerlessness*		
1	.411	.169	1	.351	.123
2	.205	.042	2	.766	.587
3	.563	.317	3	.781	.610
4	.325	.106	4	.312	.097
5	.608	.370	5	.750	.563
6	.690	.476	6	.714	.510
7	.499	.249	7	.611	.373
8	.513	.263	8	.761	.579
9	.552	.305	9	.717	.514
		$\Sigma = 2.297$	10	.528	.279
$\alpha =. 726; \Omega = .736$			$\alpha = .864; \Omega = .872$		
Normlessness			*Social Isolation*		
1	.684	.468	1	.616	.379
2	.570	.325	2	.583	.340
3	.607	.368	3	.459	.211
4	.606	.367	4	.441	.194
5	.557	.310	5	.566	.320
6	.467	.218	6	.530	.281
7	.410	.168	7	.523	.274
8	.276	.076	8	.644	.415
			9	.399	.159
$\alpha = .740; \Omega = .749$			$\alpha = .769; \Omega = .774$		

Using these values, we get

$$\alpha = \frac{9}{9-1}\left(1 - \frac{9}{25.39194}\right) = \frac{9}{8}(.64557) = .726$$

$$\Omega = 1 - \frac{9 - 2.297}{25.39194} = 1 - .264 = .736$$

Notice that all of the composites have reliability estimates above .7 and that the Powerlessness dimension is particularly reliable for an attitude scale (>.85), reflecting the higher interitem correlations among these particular items. Notice, in addition, that the more heterogeneous the interitem correlations, the greater the difference between alpha and omega; thus, one can add approximately .01 to the reliability of the Meaninglessness dimension by using a reliability coefficient that assumes differential weighting. Such a gain in reliability is marginal at best and may not warrant the additional effort required to get it. This assertion is consistent with both recent (Alwin, 1973) and not-so-recent (Sewell, 1941) statements on the creation of composites. On the other hand, if the items have homogeneous interitem correlations, as with the social isolation items, the differences between the coefficients are minimal.

A Monte Carlo study

Earlier in this chapter, we outlined a theoretical model with known parameters (see Figure 3.1). An analysis of this model showed how and to what extent random error obscures estimation of the underlying theoretical model. Attention focused on a variety of ways to assess the reliability of the measuring instrument and how a researcher could estimate the theoretical relationship from the empirical one by correcting the observed correlation for attenuation.

With all its uses, this model suffers from the limitation of being strictly theoretical, being based on a series of assumptions that may not be appropriate in actual research settings. The purpose of this section is to discuss a Monte Carlo simulation in which an actual research situation is more closely approximated.

Instead of assuming an infinite number of observations, the Monte Carlo simulation will operate with 19 observations, one at each location in Figure 3.2. From this basic structure, we will create six measures of X and six measures of Y. Hence, the Monte Carlo analysis will consist of 12 measures per observation for 19 observations. In Table 3.5, the columns labeled e_i include the numbers -2, -1, 0, 1, and 2, which are taken from a table of random numbers with equal probabilities. When the value in column e_i is added to the value of X_t, the variable X_i is created. Each X_i is an empirical indicant of X_t. X_1 and

Table 3.5. *Observations relevant to reliability simulation*

Obs.	X_t	e_1	X_1	e_2	$X_2 \cdots$	ΣX_i	$\Sigma X_i/N$	Y_t	e_7	Y_1	e_8	$Y_2 \cdots$	ΣY_i	$\Sigma Y_i/N$
A	-2	-1	-3	0	-2	-13	-2.2	-2	2	0	-2	-4	-13	-2.2
B	-2	-1	-3	2	0	-8	-1.3	-1	1	0	-1	-2	0	0.0
C	-2	2	0	2	0	-6	-1.0	0	1	1	2	2	2	0.3
D	-1	2	1	0	-1	-7	-1.2	-2	0	-2	0	-2	-14	-2.3
E	-1	0	-1	-1	-2	-7	-1.2	-1	1	0	-2	-3	-4	-0.7
F	-1	1	0	-2	-3	-9	-1.5	0	2	2	1	1	-1	-0.2
G	-1	2	1	1	0	-3	-0.5	1	1	2	1	2	14	2.3
H	0	2	2	1	1	8	1.2	-2	0	-2	2	0	-11	-1.8
I	0	2	2	2	2	2	0.3	-1	-1	-2	-2	-3	-7	-1.2
J	0	-1	-1	-1	-1	-7	-1.2	0	-2	-2	-1	-1	-7	-1.2
K	0	0	0	0	0	-3	-0.5	1	2	3	1	2	9	1.5
L	0	-1	-1	-2	-2	-2	-0.3	2	1	3	2	4	19	3.2
M	1	-1	0	0	1	4	0.7	-1	0	-1	-2	-3	-9	-1.5
N	1	2	3	1	2	9	1.5	0	1	1	-2	-2	2	.3
O	1	-2	-1	2	3	7	1.2	1	0	1	-2	-1	5	.8
P	1	-1	0	0	1	3	0.5	2	2	4	1	3	14	2.3
Q	2	-1	1	2	4	13	2.2	0	1	1	-2	-2	2	.3
R	2	-1	1	2	4	11	1.8	1	0	1	-2	-1	3	.5
S	2	1	3	2	4	12	2.0	2	0	2	1	3	20	3.3
Σ	0	4	4	11	11	4	0.5	0	12	12	-7	-7	24	3.7
Σ/N	0	0.21	0.21	0.58	0.58	0.21	0.03	0	0.63	0.63	-0.37	-0.37	1.26	.19
σ^2	1.7		2.7		4.5	61.8	1.72	1.7		3.2		5.6	101.6	2.81
σ	1.3		1.6		2.1	7.9	1.31	1.3		1.8		2.4	10.1	1.68

X_t are correlated .568. The correlation between X_1 and X_t is not perfect because of the presence of random error. Six indicants of X_t, labeled $X_1, X_2 \ldots, X_6$, were created as were six indicants of Y_t, labeled $Y_1, Y_2, \ldots, Y_6$. A correlation matrix of these 12 measures is presented in the upper right triangle of Table 3.6. With this information, all the parameters of the structural/measurement model as described above can be estimated.

As noted earlier, one approach to reliability estimation is based upon the split-half procedure. Table 3.7 demonstrates the assets and liabilities of the split-half approach to reliability with the six X indicants and the six Y indicants. Column (a) in Table 3.7 presents all the possible split-half combinations of six indicants. Column (b) presents the correlation between the respective X split-half subscales; column (d) presents the correlation between the respective Y split-half subscales. An examination of the split-half correlations indicates considerable range in the values, depending upon which items are split into which half. In column (b), the values range from .587 to .811; in column (d), the values range from .643 to .863. We can, of course, compute the average of these coefficients; these averages are .706 and .802, respectively. As shown above, these values estimate the reliability coefficient, .716.

The split-half correlation coefficient reports what the reliability of the six-item scale would be if it were three items long. To find out how reliable the six-item composite is, the Spearman–Brown prophecy formula 3.2 is applied to each split-half correlation, as shown in columns (c) and (e) of Table 3.7. Again, there is a range in these reliability estimates, depending on which items are included in which half of the scale. The mean Spearman–Brown reliability coefficient for X is .826 and for Y is .889. Applying Formula 3.2 to the average split-half correlation coefficients [Σ col. (b)/N and Σ col. (d)/N, respectively] gives a Spearman–Brown reliability coefficient for X of .828 and for Y of .890.

Cronbach's alpha is an approximation of the average of all possible split-half reliabilities adjusted by the Spearman–Brown prophecy formula. Applying Formula 3.5 to the X indicants shows that

$$\alpha_x = \frac{6}{5}\left[1 - \frac{6}{6 + (2)(6.44)}\right] = (1.2)(.682) = .818$$

Similar calculations for the Y indicants result in a Cronbach's alpha of .883. Within the limits of rounding error and approximations built into the computational formula for Cronbach's alpha, these values are identical to the average of all possible split-half correlation coefficients after application of the Spearman–Brown prophecy formula. This, then, is the interpretation of Cronbach's alpha. It uses most of the

Table 3.6. Correlation matrix of X and Y indicants (empirical and residual)

	X_1	X_2	X_3	X_4	X_5	X_6	Y_1	Y_2	Y_3	Y_4	Y_5	Y_6
X_1		.558	.519	.501	.300	.194	-.027	.196	.130	.113	.357	.097
X_2	-.076		.435	.712	.616	.590	.043	-.031	.083	.308	.525	.350
X_3	.143	-.108		.333	.272	.437	.331	.430	.324	.234	.395	.378
X_4	.060	.076	-.044		.253	.314	-.211	-.223	.044	-.012	.085	.068
X_5	-.073	.078	-.047	-.121		.406	-.021	-.079	-.006	.109	.681	.136
X_6	-.202	.019	.099	-.083	.070		.315	.094	.093	.324	.455	.467
Y_1	-.230	-.250	.157	-.415	-.193	.132		.716	.607	.647	.330	.758
Y_2	.004	-.308	.266	-.415	-.241	-.079	.059		.700	.574	.312	.523
Y_3	-.038	-.160	.180	-.213	-.149	-.059	.030	.155		.545	.306	.410
Y_4	-.097	.005	.054	-.223	-.069	.135	.073	-.106	-.052		.607	.788
Y_5	.223	.332	.281	-.049	.568	.335	-.128	-.121	-.074	.133		.552
Y_6	-.108	.054	.202	-.138	-.038	.282	.054	-.142	-.174	.060	.089	

Table 3.7. Split-half reliability coefficients for indicants of X and Y

(a) A–B	(b) $\rho_{xx'}$	(c) $\rho_{xx''}$	(d) $\rho_{yy'}$	(e) $\rho_{yy''}$
123-456	.728	.843	.643	.783
124-356	.630	.773	.851	.920
125-346	.694	.819	.863	.926
126-345	.811	.896	.787	.881
134-256	.587	.740	.858	.924
135-246	.665	.799	.826	.905
136-245	.654	.791	.843	.915
145-236	.719	.837	.831	.908
146-235	.793	.885	.745	.854
156-234	.776	.874	.770	.870
Σ	7.057	8.257	8.017	8.886
Σ/N	.706	.826	.802	.889
Corrected	.828		.890	

information that one has about a set of indicants, it is easy to compute, and it has a very convincing and forceful interpretation. As shown in the structural/measurement model above, these values estimate .835.

As described above, factor analysis can be useful in estimating reliability. Accordingly, the X indicants and Y indicants were factored separately using both the principal components and the common factor analysis methods. Table 3.8 presents the results of these analyses which are consistent with the presumption that the X indicants measure X_t and the Y indicants measure Y_t. Specifically, the first extracted factor explains a large proportion of the variance in the items; subsequent factors explain fairly equal proportions of the remaining variance; all items have substantial loadings on the first factor; and all items have higher loadings on the first factor than on subsequent ones. Moreover, as discussed in Figure 3.1, the theoretical factor loadings are .676 for each item. The factor loadings in Table 3.8 appear to hover around a value of .676.

From this information, theta and omega reliability coefficients can be computed using Formulas 3.8 and 3.10, respectively, as follows:

$$\theta_x = \frac{6}{5}\left(1 - \frac{1}{3.154}\right) = .820 \qquad \theta_y = \frac{6}{5}\left(1 - \frac{1}{3.833}\right) = .887$$

$$\Omega_x = 1 - \frac{6 - 2.791}{18.88} = .830 \qquad \Omega_y = 1 - \frac{6 - 3.554}{22.75} = .892$$

A comparison of theta and omega with alpha indicates that there is

Table 3.8. *Factors extracted from X and Y indicants*

Item	Principal components		Common factors	
	Loading	Squared	Loading	Squared
A: X indicants				
X_1	.708	.501	.663	.440
X_2	.914	.835	.957	.916
X_3	.674	.419	.567	.321
X_4	.732	.536	.665	.442
X_5	.646	.417	.562	.316
X_6	.668	.446	.597	.356
		$\Sigma = 3.154$		$\Sigma = 2.791$
B: Y indicants				
Y_1	.864	.746	.834	.696
Y_2	.806	.650	.788	.621
Y_3	.744	.554	.692	.479
Y_4	.875	.766	.863	.745
Y_5	.624	.389	.549	.301
Y_6	.853	.728	.844	.712
		$\Sigma = 3.833$		$\Sigma = 3.554$

very little difference among these reliability estimates. For X, the estimates range from .818 to .830; for Y, the estimates range from .883 to .892. Moreover, the pattern of these results is consistent with the assertion that $\alpha \leq \theta \leq \Omega$, as shown above.

The upper right triangle of Table 3.7 can be used to compute the correlation between the X scale and the Y scale using Formula 3.1 as follows.

$$r = \frac{6.47}{\sqrt{[6 + (2)(6.44)][6 + (2)(8.40)]}} = \frac{6.47}{20.75} = .312$$

Within the limits of rounding error and approximations built into this computational formula for the correlation coefficient, this value is equal to the correlation between the X and Y composites created in Table 3.5.

Using any of the reliability estimates, the observed correlation can be corrected for attenuation due to unreliability using Formula 3.11 as follows:

$$\hat{\rho}_\alpha = \frac{r}{\sqrt{\alpha_x \alpha_y}} \quad \hat{\rho}_\theta = \frac{r}{\sqrt{\theta_x \theta_y}} \quad \hat{\rho}_\Omega = \frac{r}{\sqrt{\Omega_x \Omega_y}}$$

Substituting the calculated values given above into these formulas gives the following:

$$\hat{\rho}_\alpha = \frac{.312}{\sqrt{(.818)(.883)}} = .367$$

$$\hat{\rho}_\theta = \frac{.312}{\sqrt{(.820)(.887)}} = .366$$

$$\hat{\rho}_\Omega = \frac{.312}{\sqrt{(.830)(.892)}} = .363$$

The correlation corrected for attenuation is approximately the same regardless of the reliability estimate used. Moreover, as shown in Figure 3.1, this corrected correlation estimates .5.

From this information and the model specification made earlier, the parameters of the model can be estimated, as presented in Figure 3.3. The effect of each concept on its respective measures is estimated using the common factor loading (as presented in Table 3.8). The effect of X_t on Y_t is estimated using the correlation between the X composite and the Y composite corrected for attenuation, as presented above. How accurate is the estimation of the model? This question can be answered by comparing the estimated model (in Figure 3.3) with the theoretical model (in Figure 3.1A). In general, the correspondence between the two models is fairly close, especially considering that the estimated model was based on an analysis of only 19 observations.

Before concluding this chapter, we would like to take up a question that was raised but not answered in our foregoing discussion: when does a researcher know that the systematic variance – that is, the reliable variance – has been accounted for in the measurement/structural model? Information that is obtained by residualizing the original correlation matrix on the causal model is useful in answering this question. In particular, if only random error remains in the matrix after residualization, then there is strong evidence that the causal model contains all of the reliable variance.

Only random error remains in a correlation matrix when the following conditions are met: (1) the mean residual correlation is equal to zero, (2) there is no systematic pattern of correlations in the residual matrix, (3) the shape of the residual correlation matrix approximates the appropriate sampling distribution, and (4) the standard deviation of the residual correlations in the matrix is equal to or less than the standard deviation of the appropriate sampling distribution.

The procedures for residualizing the correlation matrix on the es-

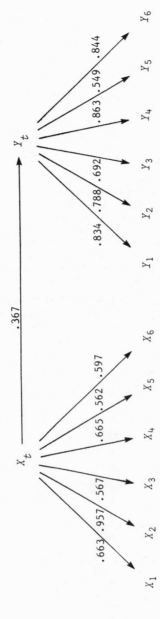

Figure 3.3. Empirical estimation of causal measurement model of X and Y.

timated model are as follows. For each indicant pair, the product of the paths connecting those indicants is subtracted from the correlation between them. For measures of the same concept, one subtracts the product of the respective factor loadings from the observed correlation. For X_1 and X_2, this is

$$.558 - (.663)(.957) = .558 - .634 = -.076$$

For measures of different concepts, one subtracts the product of the respective factor loadings times the structural effect from the observed correlation. For X_1 and Y_1, this is

$$-.027 - (.663)(.367)(.834) = -.027 - .203 = -.230$$

The full set of residuals are placed in the lower left triangle of Table 3.6. We will now evaluate this residual matrix according to the preceding criteria.

In general, the following analysis of the residual matrix will show that it contains only random error. The evidence in support of this conclusion is as follows. First, the mean residual correlation is $-.014$ for the X indicants, $-.010$ for the Y indicants, and $-.009$ across the $X-Y$ indicants. Second, a visual inspection of the residual matrix reveals that, with some qualifications, there is no consistent pattern of either positive or negative residuals for a single item with every other item. Third, the distribution of residuals is symmetrical and bell-shaped. Finally, the standard deviation of the residuals, both within and across indicant sets, is less than the standard deviation of the t distribution with 17 df, the appropriate sampling distribution for these data. Only 1 of the 66 residual correlations exceeds the critical value of t at the .05 level. Hence, analysis of the empirical observations leads to the conclusion that, by and large, the estimated model in Figure 3.3 accounts for all of the systematic variance in the matrix. The use of this procedure on the alienation indicants described above will be discussed later in this volume.

Conclusion

Reliability concerns the extent of repeatability or consistency of measurements. The greater the repeatability or consistency of measurements, indicating minimal effects of random error, the higher the reliability of the measurement. The converse is also true. Thus, in reliability assessment, one is concerned with estimating the amount of random error rather than the amount of systematic error. In general, composites are preferable to single indicants precisely because they are less affected by random error (that is, they have higher reliability).

There are two basic approaches to reliability assessment. Measures of stability focus on the analysis of the same measure at multiple time points. Measures of equivalence focus on multiple indicators of a theoretical concept measured at a single point in time. The indicators are considered separate but equivalent measures of the underlying concept. Cronbach's alpha is undoubtably the most popular coefficient of internal consistency. However, coefficient theta, based on principal components, and coefficient omega, based on the common factor analysis model, have recently gained attention.

Reliability coefficients not only allow the researcher to estimate the amount of random error in empirical measurements, but they can also be used to "correct" correlations for unreliability due to random error. This procedure is called "correction for attenuation."

Finally, a Monte Carlo study was presented showing how reliability can be estimated in actual research situations. This study also suggested a set of conditions indicating the presence of only random error in a correlation matrix. The evidence that only random error remains in the matrix is consistent with the assertion that the causal model contains all of the reliable variance.

4 Validity

In Chapter 3, we considered several well-known, alternative approaches to the estimation of the reliability of empirical measurements. That is, these alternative methods and procedures are used to assess the degree of repeatability or consistency of empirical measurements. If a measure fluctuates widely because of random disturbances, it will not be highly repeatable or highly consistent. Consequently, the particular measure will have a low reliability. Reliability is thus concerned with the amount of random error in the observed scores. If all the observed variance is random-error-filled, the reliability of the measure will be zero (0.00). Conversely, if the measure is completely unaffected by random error, its reliability will be perfect (1.00).

Notice that in our discussion of reliability, no reference was made to systematic error. The omission was deliberate; systematic error, in contrast to random error, does not detract from a measure's reliability. On the contrary, as we pointed out in Chapter 1, all of the observed variance could represent systematic error variance and the reliability of the measure would still be perfect! This is because systematic error does not reduce the repeatability or consistency of a measure, as this source of error is uniform or constant rather than stochastic in nature. For example, if the shots from a well-anchored rifle hit exactly the same location but not the proper target, the targeting of the rifle is consistent (and hence reliable) but it did not hit the location that it was supposed to hit (and hence it is not valid). Similarly, a thermometer that gives exactly the same reading for an individual on 10 different occasions is reliable even if it is later discovered that the instrument provided a temperature of 103.2° F for a patient whose actual temperature was 98.6° F. Moreover, such an instrument is reliable but not valid if it is designed to measure blood pressure but it measures body temperature instead. To repeat, systematic error, strictly speaking, does not affect the reliability of an empirical measure.

Systematic error, of course, does confound the measurement process; however, it affects a measure's validity rather than its reliability. Thus, the rifle and the thermometer in the examples above may be reliable, but they are clearly not valid: they do not measure what they were intended to measure. More generally, it is not difficult to see that repeatability and consistency alone do not ensure that a measure is valid. On the contrary, as we will show, it is quite possible for a set of indicants to represent the "wrong" concept but do so in a consistent and/or repeatable manner.

Types of validity

Although the definition of validity, that an instrument measures exactly what it is supposed to measure and nothing else, seems simple and straightforward, there exist many different types of validity within this broad definition. We now consider briefly some of the more prominent types of validity, pointing out their meaning, assumptions, possible uses, and relative limitations.

Content validity

Content validity has played a major role in the development of tests in psychology and education, but has not been widely used by political scientists or sociologists. Fundamentally, content validity concerns the extent to which a set of items taps the content of some domain of interest. To the degree that the items reflect the full domain of content, they can be said to be content-valid. Thus, a test in arithmetical operations would not have content validity if the test problems focused only on addition, neglecting subtraction, multiplication, and division. By the same token, a content-valid measure of Seeman's concept of alienation should include items representing powerlessness, normlessness, and meaninglessness as well as social isolation.

From the foregoing discussion, it should be clear that obtaining content validity involves two interrelated steps: (1) specifying the domain of content, and (2) construction and/or selecting items associated with the domain of content. While it may seem straightforward to specify the domain of content for various psychological and educational tests, the process is considerably more complex when dealing with the abstract concepts typically found in the social sciences. To continue our earlier example, what is the domain of content relevant to alienation? To pose the question is to begin to appreciate the complexity of an adequate answer to it. Presumably, one would begin by thoroughly exploring the available literature on alienation, hoping thereby to come to a general understanding of the phenomenon. A thorough search and examination of the literature may suggest that alienation is properly conceived of in terms of the four basic dimensions discussed by Seeman (1959): powerlessness, normlessness, meaninglessness, and social isolation. It may be useful to examine Seeman's fifth alienation dimension: self-estrangement. In addition, it may be useful to further subdivide these dimensions. For example, one may wish to subdivide powerlessness into its political, social, and economic aspects.

It is then necessary to construct items that reflect the meaning associated with each dimension and each subdimension of alienation. It is impossible to specify exactly how many items need to be developed for any particular domain of content. But one point can be stated with confidence: it is almost always preferable to construct too many items rather than too few; inadequate items can always be eliminated, but one is rarely in a position to add "good" items at a later stage in the research when the original pool of such items is inadequate. What should emerge from this process is a measure – in the form of sets of items – whose content clearly reflects the domain of content under consideration.

The major problem associated with this type of validity is that there are no agreed-upon criteria for establishing whether, in fact, a measure has attained content validity. In the absence of well-defined, objective criteria, Nunnally (1967:82) has noted: "Inevitably content validity rests mainly on appeals to reason regarding the adequacy with which important content has been sampled and on the adequacy with which the content has been cast in the form of test items." This problem is associated with another, more fundamental problem: that in content validation, "*acceptance* of the universe of content as defining the variable to be measured is essential" (Cronbach and Meehl, 1955:282). However easy this may be to achieve with regard to the domains involving reading or arithmetic, it has proved to be exceedingly difficult with respect to the more abstract phenomena that characterize the social sciences. These interrelated problems have prevented content validation from becoming fully satisfactory as a means of assessing the validity of social science measures.

Criterion-related validity
A second type of validity and one that perhaps has a closer association to what is normally meant by "valid" is criterion-related validity. Simply stated, criterion-related validity concerns the correlation between a measure and some criterion variable on interest. For example, one could "validate" a written driving test by demonstrating that for some well-defined group of subjects, there is a high correlation between their scores on the test and their actual ability to drive a car. Similarly, viewed from this perspective, college board exams would only be valid to the extent that they correlated with performance in college instruction. Notice that criterion-related validity is solely determined by the degree of correspondence between the measure and its criterion(s). If the correlation is high, the measure is considered

to be valid *for that criterion*. Thus, as Nunnally (1967:77) has observed: "If it were found that accuracy in horseshoe pitching correlated highly with success in college, horseshoe pitching would be a valid measure for predicting success in college." Notice, further, that there is no single criterion-related validity coefficient. Instead, there are as many coefficients as there are criterions for a particular measure.

Technically, one can differentiate between two types of criterion-related validity. If the criterion exists in the present, *concurrent validity* is assessed by correlating a measure and the criterion at the same point in time. For example, a verbal report of voting behavior could be correlated with actual participation in an election, as revealed by official voting records. *Predictive validity*, on the other hand, concerns a future criterion that is correlated with the relevant measure. Tests used for selection purposes in different occupations are, by nature, concerned with predictive validity. Thus, a test used to screen applicants for police work could be validated by correlating their test scores with future perfomance in fulfilling the duties and responsibilities associated with police work. Notice that the logic and procedures are the same for both concurrent and predictive validity; the only difference between them concerns the current or future existence of the criterion variable.

While the logic underlying criterion-related validity is straightforward and its use often compelling in certain practical situations, this type of validity has severe limitations for the social sciences. Most important, for many if not most of the measures used in the social sciences, there simply do not exist any relevant criterion variables. For example, what would be an appropriate criterion variable for a measure of self-esteem? We know of no particular group in society that has clear and undeniably high (or low) self-esteem such that it could be used to validate a measure of this personality trait. In other words, the use of the known group technique for assessing concurrent validity would be inapplicable to self-esteem. More generally, as indicated, it is not difficult to see that criterion-related validity has very limited usefulness in the social sciences, for the simple reason that with respect to many variables, there are no criteria against which the measure can be reasonably evaluated. Moreover, it is clear that the more abstract the concept, the less likely one is to be able to discover appropriate criteria for assessing a measure of it (Nunnally, 1967:84). In sum, however desirable it may be to evaluate the criterion-related validity of social science measures, it is simply inapplicable to many of the abstract concepts used in the social sciences.

Construct validity
We have suggested that both content validity and criterion-related validity have limited usefulness for the social sciences. It is partly for

this reason that this volume focuses on construct validity. As Cronbach and Meehl (1955:282) note: "Construct validity must be investigated whenever no criterion or universe of content is accepted as entirely adequate to define the quality to be measured." In formulating the underlying logic of construct validation, Cronbach and Meehl (1955:290) observe that: "Construct validation takes place when an investigator believes his instrument reflects a particular construct, to which are attached certain meanings. The proposed interpretation generates specific testable hypotheses, which are a means of confirming or disconfirming the claim." In other words, construct validity is assessed within a given theoretical context. Specifically, construct validity focuses on the assessment of whether a particular measure relates to other measures consistent with theoretically derived hypotheses concerning the concepts (or constructs) that are being measured.

Although the logic of construct validation may at first seem complicated, it is actually quite simple and straightforward, as the following example illustrates. Suppose that a researcher wanted to evaluate the construct validity of a particular measure of self-esteem – say, Rosenberg's self-esteem scale. Theoretically, it has been argued that a student's level of self-esteem is positively related to participation in school activities (Rosenberg, 1965). Thus, the theoretical prediction is that the higher the level of self-esteem, the more active the student will be in school-related activities. One then administers Rosenberg's self-esteem scale to a group of students and also determines the extent of their involvement in school activities. These two measures are then correlated, thus obtaining a numerical estimate of the relationship. If the correlation is positive and substantial, *one piece of evidence* has been adduced to support the construct validity of Rosenberg's self-esteem scale.

Construct validation involves three distinct steps. First, the theoretical relationship between the concepts themselves must be specified. Second, the empirical relationship between the measures of the concepts must be examined. Finally, the empirical evidence must be interpreted in terms of how it clarifies the construct validity of the particular measure. From this discussion, it should be clear that the process of construct validation is, by necessity, theory-laden. Indeed, strictly speaking, it is impossible to "validate" a measure of a concept in this sense unless there exists a theoretical network that surrounds the concept. For without this network, it is impossible to generate theoretical predictions, which, in turn, lead directly to empirical tests involving measures of the concept. This should not lead to the erroneous conclusion that only formal, fully developed theories are relevant to construct validation. On the contrary, Cronbach and Meehl (1955:284) note: "The logic of construct validation is involved whether the construct is highly systematized or loose, used in ramified theory or a few simple propositions, used in absolute propositions or probability statements." What is required is only that one be able to state several theoretically derived hypotheses involving the particular concept.

Notice that in the self-esteem example discussed above, we concluded that the positive association between Rosenberg's self-esteem scale and participation in school activities provided one piece of evidence supporting the construct validity of this measure. Greater confidence in the construct validity of this measure of self-esteem would be justified if subsequent analysis revealed numerous successful predictions involving diverse, theoretically related variables. Thus, construct validity is not established by confirming a single prediction on different occasions or confirming many predictions in a single study. Instead, construct validation ideally requires a pattern of consistent findings involving different researchers across a significant portion of time and with regard to a variety of diverse but theoretically relevant variables. Only if and when these conditions are met can one speak with confidence about the construct validity of a particular measure.

But what is a researcher to conclude if the evidence relevant to content validity is negative? That is, if the theoretically derived predictions and the data are inconsistent with each other, what is the appropriate inference? Four different interpretations are possible (Cronbach and Meehl, 1955:295). The most typical interpretation of such negative evidence is that the measure lacks construct validity. Within this interpretation, it is concluded that the set of indicants does not measure what it purports to measure. This does not mean, of course, that the set of indicants does not measure some other theoretical construct, but only that it does not measure the construct of interest. In other words, as negative evidence accumulates, the proper inference to be drawn is that the measure lacks construct validity *for a particular construct*. Consequently, it should not be used as an empirical referent for that concept in future research. Moreover, previous research employing *that* measure is also called into question.

Unfortunately, however, this is not the only conclusion that is consistent with negative evidence. Negative evidence may also support one or more of the following inferences:

1. The theoretical network used to generate the empirical predictions is incorrect. To continue with the earlier example, it may be the case that, from a theoretical perspective, self-esteem should not be positively related to participation in school activities. Therefore, a nonpositive relationship between these variables would not undermine the construct validity of Rosenberg's self-esteem scale but rather cast doubt on the underlying theoretical perspective.

2. The method or procedure used to test the theoretically derived hypotheses is faulty or inappropriate. Perhaps it is the case that theoretically, self-esteem should be positively associated with participation in school activities, and that the researcher has used a "good" measure of self-esteem. Under these circumstances, the hypothesis will still not be confirmed unless it is tested properly. To take a simple example, the negative evidence could be due to the use of an inappropriate statistical technique or using the proper technique incorrectly.

3. The final interpretation that can be made with respect to negative evidence is that it is due to the lack of construct validity of some other variable(s) in the analysis. In a very real sense, whenever one assesses the construct validity of the measure of interest, one is also evaluating simultaneously the construct validity of at least one other measure. In the self-esteem example, it could be the case that Rosenberg's self-esteem scale has perfect construct validity but that the measure of "participation in school activities" is quite poor.

Unfortunately, there is no foolproof procedure for determining which one (or more) of these interpretations of negative evidence is correct in any given instance. The first interpretation, that the measure lacks construct validity, becomes increasingly compelling as grounds for accepting the latter interpretations become untenable. In other words, to the degree possible, one should assess the construct validity of a particular measure in situations characterized by the use of strong theory, appropriate methodological procedures, and other well-measured variables. Only in these situations can one confidently conclude that negative evidence is due to the absence of construct validity for a particular measure.

From this discussion, it is not difficult to see that construct validity is the most appropriate and generally applicable type of validity used to assess measures in the social sciences. However, it can only be assessed within a particular theoretical context, for construct validity focuses on the pattern of external evidence – associations external to the sets of indicants designed to measure a given concept (Curtis and Jackson, 1962; Sullivan, 1971, 1974; Balch, 1974). Following the logic of construct validity, it is reasoned that if concept A and concept B should be related from a theoretical standpoint, the indicants that are designed to reflect these concepts should be related empirically. More specifically, it is argued that if the indicants of concept A do, in fact, accurately reflect concept A, the correlations between each of these indicants and the indicants of concept B should be similar in terms of direction, strength, and consistency. Conversely, if the indicants of concept A relate differentially to the indicants of concept B, this is interpreted as evidence that the indicants do not reflect a single concept. Moreover, if, theoretically, concept A is strongly related to concept B but weakly related to concept C, the indicants of A should consistently be strongly related to the indicants of B but the indicants of A should consistently be weakly related to the indicants of C. In other words, construct validation assesses the validity of a set of items indirectly by focusing on the pattern of relationships between indicants making up different concepts, whereas the assessment of reliability focuses on the relationships among indicants of a single concept. Moreover, just as the results of a factor analysis are quite useful in evaluating the reliability of measures, so patterns of external associations are crucial to the assessment of their construct validity.

The purpose of this chapter is to show that evidence concerning construct validity – that is, evidence focusing on the external associations of items designed to measure a given concept – can be used to evaluate the theoretical content and relevance of empirically generated factors. It will also be shown that this external, theoretically relevant evidence concerning validity can be joined with the purely statistical, factor-analytic evidence concerning reliability to foster a more comprehensive strategy for assessing the connection between concepts and indicants. The next section of this chapter will show how certain classes of systematic error can contaminate the factor structure of indicants used to measure concepts. The final section of the chapter will illustrate the way in which evidence concerning external associations can be used in conjunction with factor analysis to evaluate both the validity and reliability of sets of indicants as approximations of their respective concepts.

Effects of systematic error on factor analysis

Despite the attractiveness of factor analysis, the use of this technique does not always lead to unambiguous inferences about the underlying theoretically relevant dimensionality of a set of indicants used to measure specified concepts. That is, the empirical factor emerging from a factor analysis are not always isomorphic with given theoretical constructs.

The major problem with relying solely on factor analysis to establish the underlying dimensionality of indicants representing concepts can be illustrated using the following hypothetical data. Figure 4.1 presents two possible path models which describe the causal effects of theoretical concepts and, in the case of Figure 4.1B, systematic error in the form of a method artifact on a set of indicants designed to measure the underlying concept. For purposes of this discussion, a *method artifact* may be considered any systematic alteration of empirical scores that arises from efforts to measure a particular concept. For a

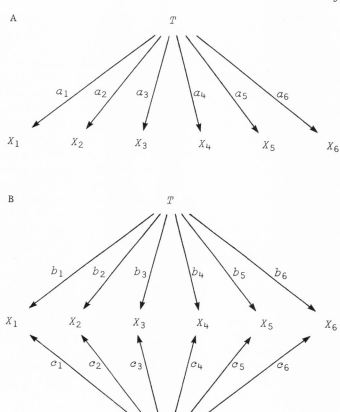

Figure 4.1. Path diagram underlying unidimensional factor structure.

set of empirical indicators, a method artifact thus represents a systematic but theoretically irrelevant source of variance. In Figure 4.1A, the set of indicants is caused by the theoretical concept, T, and by error. If the epistemic correlations (a_i) are high, these can be considered good indicants. In Figure 4.1B, the set of indicants is caused by the theoretical concept, T, by a method artifact, M, and by error. These should not be considered good indicants, for there is a systematic source of variance other than the theoretical concept which causes variance in the indicants. If the values of c_i are low and the values of b_i are high, these indicators are better than if the values of c_i are high and the values of b_i are low. If the values of a_i are equal to .8, the correlation matrix that would result from Figure 4.1A is presented

Table 4.1. *Correlation matrix among indicators in Figure 4.1A when* $a_i = .8$, *and in Figure 4.1B when* $b_i = .7$ *and* $c_i = .39$

	1	2	3	4	5	6
1	—	.64	.64	.64	.64	.64
2		—	.64	.64	.64	.64
3			—	.64	.64	.64
4				—	.64	.64
5					—	.64
6						—

in Table 4.1. This is the case because all the off-diagonal values are equal to the product of the path coefficients $[(.8)\ (.8) = .64]$. If the values of b_i are equal to .7 and the values of c_i are equal to .39, the correlation matrix that would result from Figure 4.1B is also presented in Table 4.1 $[(.7)\ (.7) + (.39)\ (.39) = .64]$.

A factor analysis of these interitem correlations provides a single dominant factor with factor loadings of .8 for each item. From our perspective, the importance of this factor analysis is as follows: *a factor analysis of these items will produce an identical factor structure regardless of whether Figure 4.1A or B is the actual measurement model underlying the data.*

Figure 4.2 presents a second pair of path models, which, when the path coefficients take on certain values, will produce identical interitem correlation matrices. In Figure 4.2A, theoretical concept T_1 causes theoretical concept T_2. T_1 also causes indicants 1, 2, 3, and 4, and T_2 causes indicants 5, 6, 7, and 8. If all d_i are equal to .8 and e is equal to .5, the resulting correlation matrix would be given in Table 4.2. In Figure 4.2B, a single theoretical concept, T, causes all eight indicants. At the same time, a method artifact, M, is also influencing these indicants. The effect of M is positive on indicants 1, 2, 3, and 4 and negative on indicants 5, 6, 7, and 8. If all f_i in Figure 4.2B are equal to .7 and all g_i are equal to .39 (with the appropriate algebraic sign), the correlation matrix presented in Table 4.2 is also consistent with this measurement model.

A factor analysis of this correlation matrix is presented in Table 4.3 and is shown graphically in Figure 4.3. If Figure 4.2A is the appropriate underlying model, the rotated factor structure displayed in Figure 4.3 should be considered the terminal one. This structure reveals two substantively interpretable factors. Factor 1 roughly corresponds to the indicants of T_1 and factor 2 roughly corresponds to the indicants of T_2. The angle intersecting the two clusters of indicants is 60°. The cosine of 60° is .5, which is the causal effect that T_1 has on T_2 (the value of e in Figure 4.2A).

Table 4.2. *Correlation matrix among indicators in Figure 4.2A when* $d_i = .8$ *and* $e = .5$ *and in Figure 4.2B when* $f_i = .7$ *and* $g_i = .39$

	1	2	3	4	5	6	7	8
1	—	.64	.64	.64	.32	.32	.32	.32
2		—	.64	.64	.32	.32	.32	.32
3			—	.64	.32	.32	.32	.32
4				—	.32	.32	.32	.32
5					—	.64	.64	.64
6						—	.64	.64
7							—	.64
8								—

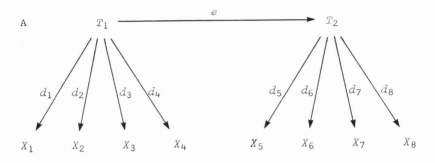

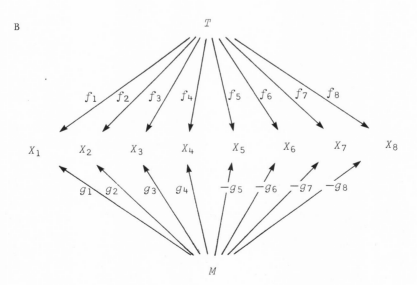

Figure 4.2. Path diagram underlying bidimensional factor structure.

Table 4.3. *Factor analysis of correlation matrix presented in Table 4.2*

	Unrotated		Rotated		
	1	2	1'	2'	h^2
1	.693	.400	.773	.207	.64
2	.693	.400	.773	.207	.64
3	.693	.400	.773	.207	.64
4	.693	.400	.773	.207	.64
5	.693	−.400	.207	.773	.64
6	.693	−.400	.207	.773	.64
7	.693	−.400	.207	.773	.64
8	.693	−.400	.207	.773	.64
Eigenvalue	3.84	1.28	2.56	2.56	
Percent of common variance	48%	16%	32%	32%	
Percent of interpretable variance	75%	25%	50%	50%	

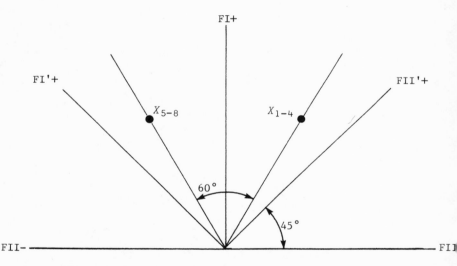

Figure 4.3. Graphic plot of factor loadings in Table 4.3.

On the other hand, if Figure 4.2B is the actual underlying model, the unrotated factor structure shown in Figure 4.3 should be considered the terminal one. This structure also reveals two underlying factors. However, factor 1 is the only theoretically interpretable factor; factor 2 is purely a method artifact. Again, the factor analysis is inconclusive as to whether Figure 4.2A is the actual measurement model underlying the data. Thus, factor analysis does not provide definitive evidence concerning the theoretical status of the empirical factors. It is for this reason that factor analysis cannot be used alone to assess the validity of empirical measures.

Detecting method artifacts through construct validation

Figures 4.1 to 4.3 and Tables 4.1 to 4.3 show that some method artifacts can be detected by factor analysis, whereas others cannot. The method artifact in Figure 4.1B is not detectable but the method artifact in Figure 4.2B is detectable through factor analysis. If, for example, all b_i's are equal and all c_i's are equal in Figure 4.1B, we could not detect the method artifact. Consequently, one could not apportion the observed variance into that part due to T, S, and Cov TS as required by Formula 1.15. If the b_i's $= .8$ and the c_i's $= 0$, then $.8^2 = .64$ of the variance is both reliable and valid (that is, $\sigma_t^2 = .64$; $\sigma_s^2 +$ Cov $TS = 0$). If the b_i's $= .7$ and the c_i's $= .39$, then $.7^2 = .49$ of the variance is valid but $.7^2 + .39^2 = .64$ of the variance is reliable (that is, $\sigma_t^2 = .49$; $\sigma_s^2 +$ Cov $TS = .15$). If the b_i's $= .39$ and the c_i's $= .7$, then $.39^2 = .15$ of the variance is valid but $.39^2 + .7^2 = .64$ of the variance is reliable (that is, $\sigma_t^2 = .15$; $\sigma_s^2 +$ Cov $TS = .49$). Regardless of which of the above is the case, a factor analysis will yield factor loadings of .8 on the first factor, accounting for 64% of the item variance, and the other factors will have zero loadings.

On the other hand, if one can establish that Figure 4.2B is the structure that underlies the data, one will be able to solve for the values of f_i and g_i. In Figure 4.2B, $f_i = .7$ and $g_i = .39$. In the unrotated factor structure presented in Table 4.3, the factor loadings on factor 1 are quite close to the values of f_i and the factor loadings on factor 2 are quite close to the values of g_i.

Moreover, even when factors have attractive statistical properties and do not represent systematic method error variance, factor analysis does not provide information about the theoretical meaning to be attributed to these factors. An example of such a theoretically misspecified model is given in Figure 4.4. In Figure 4.4, indicants 1, 2, 3, and 4 are intended to measure concept T_i. Hence, if the h_i are high and the i_i are 0, a factor analysis will provide us with a single primary factor where the h_i are the epistemic correlations. However, although it may have been the researcher's intention that indicants 1 to 4 measure T_1, they might be empirical approximations of T_2 nevertheless. In this case, the h_i could equal zero and the i_i could be high. Moreover, any relationship that these indicants might have with T_1 would be a product of the respective i_i and j. In this case, the indicants do not measure a method artifact but rather some theoretical concept other than what they were intended to measure.

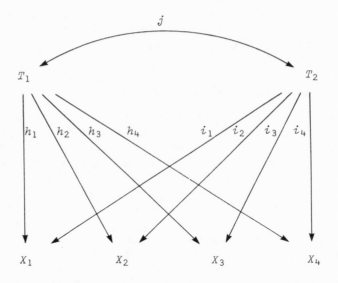

Figure 4.4. Path diagram underlying a theoretically misspecified model.

Let us provide a substantive illustration of how one could create indicants of T_1 which inadvertently tapped T_2 instead. Suppose that a researcher wanted to measure the degree of discrimination; we will label degree of discrimination as T_1. The researcher constructs a questionnaire asking individuals about how much they are discriminated against, how much discrimination there is against others that they have known, and so on. Although these indicants are intended to measure T_1, in fact they measure *perceived* degree of discrimination; we will label perceived degree of discrimination as T_2. Now the relationship between T_1 and T_2 is problematic (and is described by the value j in Figure 4.4). On the one hand, a good case could be made that T_1 and T_2 are positively correlated; on the other hand, it could be the case that T_1 and T_2 are negatively correlated; finally, T_1 might be uncorrelated with T_2. The point is that the same factor structure will emerge irrespective of which interpretation is correct.

We have shown that systematic error can have a deleterious effect on factor analysis when it is used as a statistical technique to assess the underlying theoretical dimensionality represented by a set of measured indicants. As we have seen, one of the most troublesome issues revolves around being able to specify the number of meaningful empirical factors that are measured by a given set of items. From a theoretical perspective, however, there is a second and more important question: Of the meaningful empirical factors, which are theoretically relevant and meaningful, and which are theoretically irrelevant, representing no more than method artifacts? Moreover, even if the factors do represent theoretical concepts, are they the intended concepts? In other words, even when empirical factors have desirable statistical properties, that in itself does not establish the theoretical appropriateness of each of those factors.

Evidence concerning construct validity provides a solution to this problem, for it allows the social researcher to determine whether empirical factors represent the intended theoretical concept. In this sense, evidence concerning construct validity is more sensitive to the theoretical question of validity than is the purely statistical criteria that are used in the application of factor analysis. First, we will describe briefly the logic underlying construct validity as it relates to external association. Then we will demonstrate how this logic can be integrated with factor-analytic evidence to provide a more comprehensive strategy for assessing the theoretical dimensionality of items used to measure concepts.

As discussed earlier, construct validation implies that indicants of a single concept should behave similarly toward theoretically relevant external variables. That is, if a set of items does reflect a given concept, the relationship between these items and indicants of other theoretically relevant variables should be similar in terms of direction, strength, and consistency. But construct validation also implies that if the items hypothesized to measure a single concept relate differentially to other theoretically relevant variables, not all of the items are reflecting the intended theoretical construct. Positive evidence concerning external associations thus indicates that the set of items is measuring the appropriate concept, whereas negative evidence implies that the items are measuring an inappropriate concept or a method artifact.

In contrast to factor analysis, then, construct validity focuses on the performance of items as they relate to outside variables. Their performance via external variables provides evidence about the theoretical meaning that can be attributed to the set of items.

Measuring self-esteem

We will now illustrate how evidence concerning construct validity can be used to detect and estimate systematic error by an examination of the concept of self-esteem. Rosenberg (1965) defines self-esteem as the overall attitude that a person maintains with regard to his own worth and importance. Rosenberg conceptualized self-esteem as a unitary personal predisposition, and he constructed 10 items designed to measure this unidimensional concept. As evidence for the unidimensionality of the self-esteem scale, Rosenberg reports its repro-

Table 4.4. *Correlation matrix of self-esteem items* (N = 340)

Items[a]	1[b]	2[c]	3	4[c]	5	6[c]	7[c]	8	9[c]	10
1	—	.185	.451	.399	.413	.263	.394	.352	.361	.204
2		—	.048*	.209	.248	.246	.230	.050*	.277	.270
3			—	.350	.399	.209	.381	.427	.276	.332
4				—	.369	.415	.469	.280	.358	.221
5					—	.338	.446	.457	.317	.425
6						—	.474	.214	.502	.189
7							—	.315	.577	.311
8								—	.229	.374
9									—	.233
10										—

[a]Definition of items:
 1. I feel that I have a number of good qualities.
 2. I wish I could have more respect for myself.
 3. I feel that I'm a person of worth, at least on an equal plane with others.
 4. I feel I do not have much to be proud of.
 5. I take a positive attitude toward myself.
 6. I certainly feel useless at times.
 7. All in all, I'm inclined to feel that I am a failure.
 8. I am able to do things as well as most other people.
 9. At times I think I am no good at all.
 10. On the whole, I am satisfied with myself.
[b]Response categories for items are: (1) never true, (2) seldom true, (3) sometimes true, (4) often true, (5) almost always true.
[c]Items 2, 4, 6, 7, and 9 have been reflected such that higher scores indicate higher self-esteem.
*$p < .05$. For all other correlations in the table, $p < .001$.

ducibility of .93 and its scalability of .72. That is, Rosenberg apparently conceptualizes the items as forming a Guttman scale in which the items tap the domain of content in differential degrees of difficulty and in which, therefore, the demands on the respondent form steps (Wallace and Zeller, 1974b). However, since Rosenberg did not discuss the self-esteem scale in these terms, we will consider the scale to be unidimensional if the items measure a single domain of content, whether the items are Guttman-ordered or not. The data for this analysis come from a study of the relationship between personality traits and political attitudes among high school students (Carmines, 1978).

A correlation matrix of the 10 items used to measure self-esteem is presented in Table 4.4. On the whole, the items intercorrelate positively, significantly, and consistently. But do the items form a single dimension of self-esteem?

A common factor (principal axes) analysis (using SMCs in the main

Table 4.5. *Factor loadings of the self-esteem items*

Items[a]	Extracted			Rotated		
	I	II	h	I	II	h
1	.590	.109	.360	.495[b]	.339	.360
2	.328	−.176	.138	.109	.356	.138
3	.581	.314	.436	.633	.187	.436
4	.600	−.085	.367	.365	.483	.367
5	.669	.198	.487	.614	.332	.487
6	.577	−.346	.453	.165	.653	.453
7	.731	−.202	.575	.376	.659	.575
8	.549	.387	.451	.662	.113	.451
9	.640	−.359	.539	.200	.706	.539
10	.480	.196	.269	.478	.200	.269
Eigenvalue	3.410	.666		2.043	2.032	
Percent of variance	.341	.067	.408	.204	.203	.407

[a]For an exposition of items, see Table 4.4.
[b]The italicized factor loading indicates which of the factors each item loads higher on.

diagonal) of the items is shown in Table 4.5. Within a strict factor-analytic framework, Rosenberg's conceptualization implies that we should observe a unifactorial structure. However, the results of the factor analysis do not support this presumption. Rather, the factor solution indicates that there are two substantial empirical factors. Further, when these two factors are rotated to a varimax solution, as shown in Table 4.5, they show a fairly distinct clustering of items. Factor 1 is defined principally by items 1, 3, 5, 8, and 10, whereas items 2, 4, 6, 7, and 9 most clearly define factor II. We may refer to factor I as the *positive self-esteem factor*, because those items that load most strongly on it are reflective of a positive, favorable attitude toward the self. For example, one of these items states, "I feel that I'm a person of worth, at least on an equal place with others." By contrast, those items that most clearly define factor II have in common a negative, unfavorable reference to the self. For example, the item that loads highest on factor II states, "At times I think I am no good at all." We may refer to factor II, therefore, as the *negative self-esteem factor*. These empirical factors of self-esteem are not polar opposites of one another. Rather, the results of the factor analysis indicate that the dimensions are definitely distinguishable from one another, forming, as they do, separate identifiable factors.

Moreover, when we factor-analyze the two sets of items separately,

Table 4.6. *Factor loadings of positive and negative self-esteem items factored separately*

Item	Factor loading	h^2
Positive self-esteem items		
1	.568	.323
3	.651	.424
5	.699	.489
8	.658	.433
10	.524	.275
Negative self-esteem items		
2	.351	.123
4	.577	.333
6	.674	.454
7	.757	.573
9	.727	.528

one and only one substantial factor emerges for each dimension of self-esteem. Further, the items forming these factors show fairly strong loadings on their respective factors. That is, the positive self-esteem items have loadings ranging from .524 to .699 on their principal factor, whereas the negative self-esteem items have loadings ranging from .351 to .757 on their principal factor, as shown in Table 4.6. This analysis offers strong support for the bidimensionality of self-esteem.

An alternative interpretation of the two-factor solution
The factor analysis of Rosenberg's self-esteem scale has indicated that the items do not form a single empirical dimension of self-esteem but rather that they reflect two distinct components of the self-image. Because of the items that tended to define each factor, we labeled one of these components the positive self-esteem factor and referred to the other as the negative self-esteem factor. We now want to consider an alternative interpretation of the two-factor solution. Specifically, we want to consider the possibility that the dual dimensionality of self-esteem is a function of systematic error: namely, response set among the two sets of scale items.

Response set may be defined as the general tendency to respond to interview or questionnaire items in a particular manner, irrespective of their content. Clearly, this is a very real possibility in the present case, for the items forming each of the dimensions of self-esteem are worded in a similar manner. That is, the items that load higher on the positive self-esteem factor are all worded in a positive direction, and those loading higher on the negative self-esteem factor are all worded in a negative direction. Given this situation, it is not unusual to find somewhat higher correlations among items that are worded in the same direction than among items that differ in the direction of their wording. This, of course, is precisely what we observed in the intercorrelations among the self-esteem items. Notice also that the positive and negative signs of the factor loadings on the second principal factor in the unrotated structure are representative of the positive and negative wording of the items.

In addition, since factor analysis does nothing more than redefine and simplify the correlation matrix, we would also expect that response set among items would contaminate the factor structure of those items. A two-factor empirical solution, in other words, does not invariably indicate that the two factors measure two separate theoretical concepts. It may also be an indication that the items are an empirical representation of a single concept, self-esteem, with the second factor due to a method artifact such as response set. Let us assume, for the moment, that the underlying unidimensional structure with response set producing the second factor is the appropriate interpretation. In this case, the first factor obtained from the principal factor unrotated solution represents valid variance while the second factor represents systematic error variance. The point is that a factor analysis itself cannot differentiate between these two interpretations, because it only reflects the differential pattern of correlations among the scale items.

In summary, the factor analysis of the scale items does not provide unambiguous, and even less unimpeachable, evidence of the theoretical dimensionality underlying these self-esteem items. On the contrary, since the bifactorial structure can be a function of a single theoretical dimension that is contaminated by a method artifact as well as being indicative of two separate, substantive dimensions, the factor analysis leaves the theoretical structure of self-esteem indeterminate.

Resolving the alternative interpretations of the two-factor solution
Factor analysis does not resolve the issue of the conceptual/theoretical structure of Rosenbero's self-esteem scale. Following the logic of construct validation, the appropriate procedure is to compare the correlations of each empirical dimension of self-esteem with a set of theoretically relevant external variables. If the positive and negative self-esteem factors measure different components of the self-image, they should relate differentially to at least some of these external variables. If, on the other hand, the factors measure a single dimension of self-esteem with the bifactorial structure being due to a method artifact, the two factors should relate similarly to these theoretically relevant variables. By following this procedure, we will be able to evaluate the theoretical structure of self-esteem.

Table 4.7. *Correlations between positive and negative self-esteem scales and external variables*

Criterion variable	N	Positive self-esteem factor[a]	Negative self-esteem factor[b]	Difference between correlations
Socioeconomic background factors				
Father's education	198	.17**	.15**	.02
Mother's education	208	.11***	.08	.03
Father's occupation	198	.12***	.08	.04
Psychological predispositions				
Personal control	334	.31*	.33*	−.02
Anomia	340	−.54*	−.49*	.05
Trust in people	340	.24*	.25*	−.01
Self-anchoring scale:				
Present	216	.16**	.14***	.02
Future	216	.18**	.14***	.04
Intelligence	272	.22*	.24*	−.02
Social and political attitudes				
Participation in school activities	338	.14**	.11***	.03
Participation in community activities	228	.05	.02	.03
Political efficacy	334	.18*	.22*	−.04
Political cynicism	331	−.09***	−.13**	.04
Knowledge of political authorities	331	.14**	.09***	.05
Knowledge of government services	333	.12***	.10***	.02
Understanding of democratic principles	334	.16**	.13**	.03

[a]The positive self-esteem items were unit-weighted to form a composite scale.
[b]The negative self-esteem items were unit-weighted to form a composite scale. These items were reflected such that higher scores indicate higher self-esteem.
$*p < .001$, $**p < .01$, $***p < .05$.

Table 4.7 presents the correlations between each dimension of self-esteem and 16 external variables. These variables cover three broad substantive areas: socioeconomic background factors, other psychological predispositions, and social and political attitudes. Almost all of the correlations are statistically significant (at the .05 level), and a majority of them seem to be substantively important as well. The positive and negative self-esteem scales, in other words, seem to capture a salient dimension of the adolescent's self-image. But these factors seem to tap the same, rather than different, dimensions, for their correlations with these theoretically relevant external variables are almost identical to one another in terms of direction, strength, and consistency. Indeed, the average difference between correlations across all 16 variables is approximately .03, with the highest difference being .05. None of these differences is statistically significant (at even the .25 level), and it would be extremely difficult to attach theoretical importance to the differences as well.

In summary, while the factor analysis left the theoretical structure of the self-esteem items indeterminate, the evidence provided by an analysis of their construct validity leads to a definitive conclusion: that the items measure a single dimension of self-esteem. The two-factor solution, therefore, offers only spurious evidence for the dual dimensionality of self-esteem. The more appropriate interpretation is that the bifactorial structure of the items is a function of a single theoretical dimension of self-esteem that is contaminated by a method artifact, response set.

We have now established that the preferred interpretation of the two-factor structure underlying the self-esteem items is that of one theoretical concept, self-esteem, and one method artifact, response set. With this information, we can now compute the estimates of reliability and validity using Formulas 1.13 to 1.15, and the eigenvalues for the extracted factor matrix in Table 4.5. According to Formula 1.15,

$$\hat{\sigma}_x^2 = \hat{\sigma}_t^2 + (\hat{\sigma}_s^2 + 2\text{ Cov } TS) + \hat{\sigma}_r^2$$

Given the foregoing interpretation of our measurement model, the variance associated with the first extracted factor in Table 4.5 is valid variance, and the variance associated with both the first and second factors is reliable variance. Setting the variance of each item to 1, we can describe each of those components of the variance as follows:

$\hat{\sigma}_t^2 = .341$
$\hat{\sigma}_s^2 + 2\text{ Cov } TS = .067$
$\hat{\sigma}_r^2 = 1 - .341 - .067 = .592$

where $\hat{\sigma}_t^2$ = mean squared factor loading on factor 1 of Table 4.5

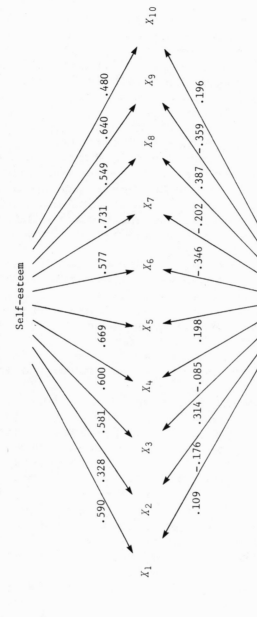

Figure 4.5. Causal measurement model of self-esteem.

$\hat{\sigma}_s^2 + 2 \text{ Cov } TS = $ mean squared factor loading on factor 2 of Table 4.5

$\hat{\sigma}_r^2 = $ remaining proportion of variance

Consequently, the mean reliability and validity on a per item basis is as follows:

$$\hat{R}\text{eliability} = \frac{\hat{\sigma}_x^2 - \hat{\sigma}_r^2}{\hat{\sigma}_x^2} = \frac{1 - .592}{1} = .408$$

and

$$\hat{V}\text{alidity} = \frac{\hat{\sigma}_t^2}{\hat{\sigma}_x^2} = \frac{.341}{1} = .341$$

These are mean squared values. The specific unsquared values for each item are placed in a causal measurement model in Figure 4.5. These values correspond to the appropriate factor loadings in Table 4.5.

The reliability of the 10-item self-esteem scale can be assessed by computing alpha, and omega. We do not calculate theta for we have not conceptualized the problem from a principal components perspective. Using Formula 3.5 and Table 4.4, the alpha coefficient is computed as follows:

$a = 10$
$b = 14.487$

Substituting these values into Formula 3.5, we get

$$\alpha = \left(\frac{10}{9}\right)\left(1 - \frac{10}{38.974}\right) = .826$$

The omega coefficient can be computed on the basis of either one or two factors. We will compute it both ways; we will postpone discussion of the interpretation of these two statistics until Chapter 6.

Using one factor and Formula 3.10, we get

$$\Omega = 1 - \frac{a - \Sigma h_i^2}{a + 2b} = 1 - \frac{10 - 3.41}{38.974} = .831$$

Using two factors and Formula 3.10, we get

$$\Omega = 1 - \frac{10 - (3.41 + .67)}{38.974} = .848$$

This example graphically illustrates the key point that we have tried to make in this chapter: that in spite of the usefulness of factor analysis,

it does not always lead to unambiguous inferences about the theoretical dimensionality of concepts and that, therefore, it cannot be
used as the *sole* criterion for establishing the adequacy of the concept-
indicant linkage. Substantive interpretation of factor structures can
be misleading in terms of determining the dimensional nature of the
content area. Issues governing the extraction and rotation of factors
cannot be completely answered within the factor-analytic framework.
Rather, decisions in the extraction and rotation of factors must be
made through a series of steps in which the empirical factors are
adjusted in such a way that they more accurately reflect their respective concept(s). We have shown how response set can artificially
produce an inference of two underlying concepts when there is, in
fact, only one. Any methodological artifact that can systematically
alter the correlations among indicants may produce this kind of faulty
inference.

Conclusion

In this chapter, we have considered several different types of validity,
concluding that construct validation is most appropriate for the social
sciences. It not only has generalized applicability for assessing the
validity of social science measures, but it can also be used to differentiate between theoretically relevant and theoretically meaningless
empirical factors. This is a crucially important contribution to measurement because reliability assessment in general and factor analysis
in particular are insensitive to this problem. For as Heise (1974:12) has
observed: "The meaningfulness of a factor does not depend on the
statistical characteristics of its indicators but on their theoretical content, and in ordinary analytic procedures these considerations are not
entered as constraints on the numerical analysis." Thus, however
useful factor analysis may be for assessing the reliability of a measure,
it is not directly relevant to assessing its validity. Viewed from this
perspective, efforts to assess validity within a strictly factor-analytic
approach – as with Heise and Bohrnstedt's validity coefficient (ρ_{ts})
– have the important limitation that they *assume* what we want to test
in validity assessment – whether the set of items measure what they
are intended to measure (Heise and Bohrnstedt, 1970). Thus, we
obviously concur with Smith's (1974b:177) observation that: "There
should be no question that an internal index of validity is not a
complete substitute for an external check on the validity of a composite
scale." Indeed, we believe it can, in principle, never be an adequate
substitute for a theoretically oriented assessment of a measure's
validity.

Moreover, it is clear that the key question underlying validity – deciding which of the empirical factors represents the appropriate theoretical concept – is not so much a technical as a theoretical question. Thus, in assessing validity, one must go beyond the statistical criteria used in factor analysis to the more explicit theoretically relevant criteria used in construct validation. Only in this way can the social researcher ensure that his measures are valid as well as reliable.

5 Evaluating systematic error

In Chapter 4, we considered several different types of validity, defined, at the most general level, as the extent to which a set of empirical indicants measures what it purports to measure. In contrast to the limited usefulness and specialized applications of content and criterion-related validity, construct validation, we argued, has generalized applicability for assessing the validity of measures used in the social sciences. Construct validation focuses on the extent to which a measure of a given concept performs according to theoretical expectations. That is, instead of focusing on the internal behavior among the indicants measuring a particular concept, as is the concern of reliability assessment, construct validity concentrates on the pattern of external associations between the indicants and other theoretically relevant variables. Thus, viewed from this perspective, the validity of a measure can only be assessed within a given theoretical context.

Chapter 4 developed a general measurement strategy that is based on the logic of construct validation. Specifically, it applies the logic of construct validation to factor analysis. Thus, instead of focusing on the theoretically relevant performance of the individual items measuring a particular concept, this approach to measurement examines the external behavior of the factor-generated scales (that is, the linear composites). In other words, evidence relating to external associations is used to evaluate the theoretical content and appropriateness of the empirically determined factor-based composites. Through this means, the analyst can determine whether empirical factors represent the intended theoretical concepts, some other theoretical concepts, or method artifacts.

This approach to measurement, then, combines and integrates the empirically based evidence provided by factor analysis with the theoretically relevant evidence concerning construct validity to foster a comprehensive strategy for assessing the reliability and validity of social science measures. Applying this methodology to self-esteem, we discovered that whereas a factor analysis of 10 items measuring this personality trait yielded two empirical factors, there was only one theoretical dimension underlying these items. The second factor represented a systematic source of measurement error – the method artifact, response set.

This chapter extends the approach to measurement introduced and developed in Chapter 4, showing that it is capable of being used to analyze a wide variety of specific sources of systematic error. In fulfilling this objective, the chapter also outlines a general measurement model for the detection and estimation of method artifacts – probably the most prevalent form of systematic measurement error found in the social sciences.

Factor analysis, method artifacts, and construct validation

Consider a simple causal relationship between two theoretical concepts as follows:

$$X \rightarrow Y$$

Let us suppose that an error has been made in the conceptualization of X. Although it is assumed that X is a single, unidimensional concept, in fact, it is made up of two correlated but definitely distinguishable theoretical dimensions. We will refer to these dimensions as Xa and Xb, respectively. Given that the actual dimensionality of X does not correspond with the conceptualization of X, the causal relations among the concepts must now be formulated to coincide with their actual state. In actuality, Xa causes Y. Although we do not know and cannot infer the causal relationship between Xa and Xb, we do know that they are correlated. Moreover, Xb and Y share no variance apart from their common association with Xa. A model of the actual causal relationship underlying the analysis is as follows:

$$Xb \quad Xa \rightarrow Y$$

However, since the theoretical differentiation between Xa and Xb was not known when the research design was formulated, indicants were selected to measure only X and Y. In point of fact, eight indicants were selected to measure Y and eight indicants were selected to measure X. Four of the X indicants actually represent Xa and the other four actually represent Xb. The appropriate causal model with the paths designating the effect of the concepts on the empirical indicants is presented in Figure 5.1.

The arrows from Xb to Xb_i in Figure 5.1 represent the causal effect of Xb on the indicants that are hypothesized to measure X but in fact measure Xb; the arrows from Xa to Xa_i represent the causal effect of Xa on the indicators that are hypothesized to measure X but in fact measure Xa. The arrows from Y to Y_i represent the causal effect of Y on Y_i.

Finally, the causal diagram presented in Figure 5.1 specifies the effects of a method artifact. Specifically, the method artifact (labeled

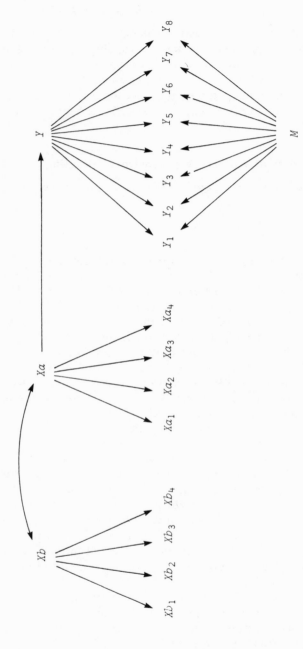

Figure 5.1. Structural measurement model illustrating specification error and a method artifact.

M) is influencing the measures of Y. As shown in Figure 5.1, the method artifact has a positive causal effect on Y_1, Y_3, Y_5, and Y_7 but a negative causal effect on Y_2, Y_4, Y_6, and Y_8.

It will be convenient to conceptualize the method artifact as response set. As pointed out earlier, response set is the tendency of subjects to respond systematically to a set of questionnaire or interview items regardless of the content of the items (for details, see Sudman and Bradburn, 1974). For example, an elementary type of response set is provided by the respondent who systematically marks down the right or left side of a questionnaire irrespective of the content of the item. If all of the items are stated in a similar fashion (with, for example, a positive response on the right side and a negative response on the left side of the questionnaire), response set is indistinguishable from a meaningful response to a single underlying theoretical dimension. This situation is causally illustrated in Figure 4.1B. However, if some of the items are stated positively and some negatively, and/or if the positive responses are sometimes on the right and sometimes on the left, response set can be differentiated from responding to an underlying theoretical dimension. This situation is illustrated causally in Figure 4.2B. In these two situations, the method artifact is undetectable and detectable, respectively. Finally, it should be noted that some respondents are more prone to response set than others are. That is, some respondents react mainly to the content of the items, whereas others are more influenced by the form in which the items are presented.

We now want to create hypothetical data that embodies the foregoing characteristics. Specifically, the data must reflect the notion that concept X is actually two distinguishable but correlated concepts, Xa and Xb. Furthermore, it must reflect the notion that concept Y is a single theoretical dimension but that the measurement of Y is infested with the method artifact, response set. Table 5.1 creates these data.

The columns of Table 5.1 represent manipulations of the variables to create the situation observed in Figure 5.1. Variable Xa, presented in column a, has a mean of 0 and a variance of 1 (that is, it is a standardized variable). A standardized variable, independent of Xa, is labeled W_1 and is presented in column (b) [that is, the value in column (b) is uncorrelated with the value in column (a)]. The value in column (c) is the addition of Xa and W_1. Column (d) presents the standardization of the variable in column (c). This variable is denoted as Xb. We created these variables such that Xa causes half of the variance in Xb. However, in the context of this example, we consider them to be merely correlated with each other. A standardized variable, independent of Xa, Xb, and W_1, is presented in column (e) and is denoted W_2. The value in column (f) is the addition of Xa and W_2.

Table 5.1. *Creation of variables representing the causal diagram in Figure 5.1*

Xa (a) Xa	(b) W₁	(c) (a)+(b)	Xb (d) c_z	(e) W₂	(f) (a)+(d)	Y (g) f_z	(h) W₃	(i) (g)+(h)	Y+ (j) i_z	(k) (g)−(h)	Y− (l) k_z
1	1	2	1.4142	1	2	1.4142	1	2.4142	1.7071	.4142	.2929
1	1	2	1.4142	1	2	1.4142	−1	.4142	.2929	2.4142	1.7071
1	1	2	1.4142	−1	0	0	1	1	.7071	−1	−.7071
1	1	2	1.4142	−1	0	0	−1	−1	−.7071	1	.7071
1	−1	0	0	1	2	1.4142	1	2.4142	1.7071	.4142	.2929
1	−1	0	0	1	2	1.4142	−1	.4142	.2929	2.4142	1.7071
1	−1	0	0	−1	0	0	1	1	.7071	−1	−.7071
1	−1	0	0	−1	0	0	−1	−1	−.7071	1	.7071
−1	1	0	0	1	0	0	1	1	.7071	−1	−.7071
−1	1	0	0	1	0	0	−1	−1	−.7071	1	.7071
−1	1	0	0	−1	−2	−1.4142	1	−.4142	−.2929	−2.4142	−1.7071
−1	1	0	0	−1	−2	−1.4142	−1	−2.4142	−1.7071	−.4142	−.2929
−1	−1	−2	−1.4142	1	0	0	1	1	.7071	−1	−.7071
−1	−1	−2	−1.4142	1	0	0	−1	−1	−.7071	1	.7071
−1	−1	−2	−1.4142	−1	−2	−1.4142	1	−.4142	−.2929	−2.4142	−1.7071
−1	−1	−2	−1.4142	−1	−2	−1.4142	−1	−2.4142	−1.7071	−.4142	−.2929

Column (g) presents the standardization of the variable in column (f). This variable is denoted as Y. Xa causes half of the variance in Y. We have now created Xa, Xb, and Y.

In order to add response set to Y, we will use the standardized variable W_3 that is presented in column (h). W_3 is independent of Xa, Xb, Y, W_1, and W_2. The value in column (i) is the addition of Y and W_3. Column (j) presents the standardization of the variable in column (i). This variable is denoted as $Y+$. The value in column (k) is Y minus W_3. Column (l) presents the standardization of the variable in column (k). This variable is denoted as $Y-$. In the process of creating $Y+$ and $Y-$, we have systematically altered the Y scores in such a fashion that $Y+$ and $Y-$ will correlate similarly with Xa and Xb, but that the correlation between $Y+$ and $Y-$ will be reduced because the $Y+$ values are comparable to positively stated questionnaire items, whereas the $Y-$ values are comparable to negatively stated items.

As we noted above, method artifacts such as response set may affect some individuals but not others. Therefore, to analyze the data, we will create 16 respondents who are affected by response set and 16 respondents who are not. These data are presented in Table 5.2. Those respondents labeled with single letters (A through P) are nonresponse setters, whereas those labeled with double letters (AA through PP) are response setters. We shall refer to these two sets of observations as the trait observations and the response set observations, respectively. For the trait observations (A through P), the value of $Y+$ in column (c) is equal to the value of $Y-$ in column (d). For the response set observations (AA through PP), the value of $Y+$ is not the same as the value of $Y-$. For these observations, the differences in the value of $Y+$ and $Y-$ represent the variance in the scores due to response set. The $Y+$ and $Y-$ values for the trait observations came from column (g) of Table 5.1; the $Y+$ and $Y-$ values for the response set observations came from columns (j) and (l) of Table 5.1, respectively.

Because these variables are in standardized form, the sum of their cross-products divided by N is the correlation. Because the sum of column (e) in Table 5.2 divided by N is .7071, it can be seen that the correlation between Xa and Xb is .7071. That value squared is the proportion of variance that Xa and Xb share (that is, $.7071^2 = .5$). When Xa and Xb were created in Table 5.1, they were constructed so that they would share half of their variance.

To simplify matters, we set the correlations between Xa and Xa_i and between Xb and Xb_i equal to 1.0. It must be recalled, however, that we do not know about the theoretical differentiation between Xa and Xb. Rather, we think that all the Xa_i and Xb_i actually measure the same theoretical construct. To confirm this expectation, we per-

Table 5.2. *Correlations among created variables for 32 observations*

Obs.	(a) Xa	(b) Xb	(c) Y+	(d) Y−	(e) XaXb	(f) XaY+	(g) XaY−	(h) XbY+	(i) XbY−	(j) Y+Y−
A	1	1.4142	1.4142	1.4142	1.4142	1.4142	1.4142	2.0	2.0	2.0
B	1	1.4142	1.4142	1.4142	1.4142	1.4142	1.4142	2.0	2.0	2.0
C	1	1.4142	0	0	1.4142	0	0	0	0	0
D	1	1.4142	0	0	1.4142	0	0	0	0	0
E	1	0	1.4142	1.4142	0	1.4142	1.4142	0	0	2.0
F	1	0	1.4142	1.4142	0	1.4142	1.4142	0	0	2.0
G	1	0	0	0	0	0	0	0	0	0
H	1	0	0	0	0	0	0	0	0	0
I	−1	0	0	0	0	0	0	0	0	0
J	−1	0	0	0	0	0	0	0	0	0
K	−1	0	−1.4142	−1.4142	0	1.4142	1.4142	0	0	2.0
L	−1	0	−1.4142	−1.4142	0	1.4142	1.4142	0	0	2.0
M	−1	−1.4142	0	0	1.4142	0	0	0	0	0
N	−1	−1.4142	0	0	1.4142	0	0	0	0	0
O	−1	−1.4142	−1.4142	−1.4142	1.4142	1.4142	1.4142	2.0	2.0	2.0
P	−1	−1.4142	−1.4142	−1.4142	1.4142	1.4142	1.4142	2.0	2.0	2.0
Σ	0	0	0	0	11.3136	11.3136	11.3136	8	8	16
Σ/N	0	0	0	0	.7071	.7071	.7071	.5	.5	1.0

AA	1	1.4142	1.7071	.2929	1.4142	1.7071	.2929	2.4142	.4142	.5
BB	1	1.4142	.2929	1.7071	1.4142	.2929	1.7071	.4142	2.4142	.5
CC	1	1.4142	.7071	-.7071	1.4142	.7071	-.7071	1.0	-1.0	-.5
DD	1	1.4142	-.7071	.7071	1.4142	-.7071	.7071	-1.0	1.0	-.5
EE	1		1.7071	.2929	0	1.7071	.2929	0	0	.5
FF	1		.2929	1.7071	0	.2929	1.7071	0	0	.5
GG	1		.7071	-.7071	0	.7071	-.7071	0	0	-.5
HH	1		-.7071	.7071	0	-.7071	.7071	0	0	-.5
II	-1		.7071	-.7071	0	-.7071	.7071	0	0	-.5
JJ	-1		-.7071	.7071	0	.7071	-.7071	0	0	-.5
KK	-1		-.2929	-1.7071	0	.2929	1.7071	0	0	.5
LL	-1		-1.7071	-.2929	0	1.7071	.2929	0	0	.5
MM	-1	-1.4142	.7071	-.7071	1.4142	-.7071	.7071	-1.0	1.0	-.5
NN	-1	-1.4142	-.7071	.7071	1.4142	.7071	-.7071	1.0	-1.0	-.5
OO	-1	-1.4142	-.2929	-1.7071	1.4142	.2929	1.7071	.4142	2.4142	.5
PP	-1	-1.4142	-1.7071	-.2929	1.4142	1.7071	.2929	2.4142	.4142	.5
Σ	0	0	0	0	11.3136	8	8	5.6568	5.6568	0
Σ/N	0	0	0	0	.7071	.5	.5	.3535	.3535	0
$\Sigma\Sigma$	0	0	0	0	22.6272	19.3136	19.3136	13.6568	13.6568	16
$\Sigma\Sigma/N$	0	0	0	0	.7071	.6035	.6035	.4268	.4268	.5

Table 5.3. *Factor analysis of Xa$_i$ and Xb$_i$*

Item	Unrotated			Rotated		
	1	11	h^2	1	11	h^2
Xa_1	.924	.383	1.00	.924	.383	1.00
Xa_2	.924	.383	1.00	.924	.383	1.00
Xa_3	.924	.383	1.00	.924	.383	1.00
Xa_4	.924	.383	1.00	.924	.383	1.00
Xb_1	.924	−.383	1.00	.383	.924	1.00
Xb_2	.924	−.383	1.00	.383	.924	1.00
Xb_3	.924	−.383	1.00	.383	.924	1.00
Xb_4	.924	−.383	1.00	.383	.924	1.00
Eigenvalue	6.83	1.17		4.00	4.00	
Variance explained	85.4%	14.6%		50%	50%	

formed a common factor analysis (with SMCs in the main diagonal) on the eight X indicants, which is presented in Table 5.3. The factors as extracted from the correlation matrix are presented on the left and are denoted I and II, the factors as rotated 45° to approximate a varimax solution are presented on the right and are denoted I' and II'. In point of fact, factor I of the unrotated factor matrix accounts for 85% of the variance, and we might be strongly tempted to conclude that those eight indicants of X do, in fact, form a single theoretical dimension. However, since we do not want to make the error of allowing our theory to blind us from alternative interpretations of the data, we seriously consider the approximation to the varimax rotational scheme on the right. An examination of factors I' and II' in Table 5.3 reveals what is actually the case in the causal model: that there are really two theoretical concepts, Xa and Xb. These concepts are correlated but are definitely distinguishable from each other.

At this point, we cannot make a definitive evaluation concerning the dimensional nature of the indicants measuring the concept X, based upon the factor analysis. The Xa_i indicants are definitely distinguishable from the Xb_i indicants. However, based upon the data, we do not know whether this is due to inadequate conceptualization of X or to some method artifact that has artificially altered the structure of the correlation matrix to provide this real but theoretically meaningless second factor. Because we created the causal structure underlying the data, we know that the real problem is the inadequate conceptualization of X. In other words, there is no method artifact influencing the factor structure. Rather, the X indicants represent two separate theoretical concepts.

Table 5.4. *Factor analysis of* Y_i

Item	Unrotated			Rotated		
	1	11	h^2	1	11	h^2
Y_1	.866	.500	1.00	.966	.259	1.00
Y_2	.866	−.500	1.00	.259	.966	1.00
Y_3	.866	.500	1.00	.966	.259	1.00
Y_4	.866	−.500	1.00	.259	.966	1.00
Y_5	.866	.500	1.00	.966	.259	1.00
Y_6	.866	−.500	1.00	.259	.966	1.00
Y_7	.866	.500	1.00	.966	.259	1.00
Y_8	.866	−.500	1.00	.259	.966	1.00
Eigenvalue	6.00	2.00		4.00	4.00	
Variance explained	75%	25%		50%	50%	

Let us now turn our attention to the dimensionality of Y_i. The intercorrelations among $Y_{i\ odd}$ equal 1.0's, as do the intercorrelations among the $Y_{i\ even}$. However, because of M, the intercorrelations between $Y_{i\ odd}$ and $Y_{i\ even}$ are .5 [as shown in column (j), Table 5.2]. A factor analysis of the eight Y_i indicants is presented in Table 5.4. The unrotated factors as extracted from the correlation matrix are presented on the left and are denoted I and II, whereas the factors as rotated to 45° to approximate a varimax solution are presented on the right and are denoted I' and II'. Factor I of the unrotated factor matrix accounts for 75% of the variance, and we might be tempted to assert that those eight indicants of Y do, in fact, form a single theoretical dimension. However, when we considered X, where factor I accounted for 85% of the variance, we thought it necessary and appropriate to consider the approximation to the varimax rotational scheme. Clearly, we should make the same decision here. An examination of factors I' and II' in Table 5.4 reveals that the bifactorial interpretation of the Y indicants is a real possibility.

Based upon the way in which the Y scores were created, we know that the substantive bifactorial interpretation of Y is incorrect. That is, these Y indicants only reflect a single theoretical concept. However, the evidence provided by the factor analysis suggests that the theoretical bifactorial interpretation of the Y_i is more compelling than the theoretical bifactorial interpretation on the X_i. This is because the high factor loadings in the rotated factor matrix in Table 5.4 are *higher* than the corresponding loadings in Table 5.3, and the low factor loadings in the rotated factor matrix in Table 5.4 are *lower* than the corresponding loadings in Table 5.3.

Table 5.5. *Correlation matrix of* X_a, Xb, $Y+$, *and* $Y-$

	Xa	Xb	Y+	Y−
Xa	—	.7071	.6035	.6035
Xb		—	.4268	.4268
Y+			—	.5000
Y−				—

Originally, it was hypothesized that each of the two sets of indicants tapped its respective single theoretical concept. However, the factor analyses reveal two empirical factors for each set of indicants. These factors can be interpreted in two ways. First, the factors can be conceived of as representing distinct theoretically meaningful concepts. Alternatively, the two empirical factors underlying each set of items can represent a single theoretical concept, with the second factor being a method artifact factor. Within a strictly factor-analytic framework, we cannot differentiate between these two interpretations.

At this point, we can turn to evidence concerning external associations to assess the construct validity of these measures. As we pointed out earlier, construct validation implies that multiple indicants providing an empirical approximation of the *same* theoretical concept should correlate similarly with theoretically relevant external variables. On the other hand, if multiple indicants designed to measure the same theoretical concept in fact provide empirical approximations of different theoretical concepts, the indicants should correlate dissimilarly with these same theoretically relevant external variables. In other words, the absence of consistent external associations implies that the indicants are *not* measuring the same concept. X and Y provide theoretically relevant external variables for each other. Therefore, an examination of the intercorrelations of scales made up of Xa, Xb, $Y+$, and $Y-$ should provide evidence of the theoretical bidimensionality of the X_i's and the theoretical unidimensionality of the Y_i's. In an actual research situation, these scales would be constructed by summing the values of the indicants of Xa, Xb, $Y+$, and $Y-$, respectively, or by appropriate use of factor scores. These correlations are computed from Table 5.2 and are placed in matrix form in Table 5.5.

The correlation of Xa with $Y+$ is higher than the correlation of Xb with $Y+$; the correlation of Xa with $Y-$ is higher than the correlation of Xb with $Y-$. This evidence, showing that Xa and Xb relate differentially to $Y+$ and $Y-$, suggests that these empirical factors (Xa and Xb) represent two genuinely distinguishable theoretical concepts. Alternatively stated, we can say that the absence of consistent external associations displayed by these two empirical factors is consistent with the hypothesis that they measure *different* theoretical concepts. On the other hand, since the correlation of $Y+$ and Xa is identical to the correlation of $Y-$ with Xa and since the correlation of $Y+$ with Xb is identical to the correlation of $Y-$ with Xb, it does not appear that $Y+$ and $Y-$ represent different theoretical concepts. On the contrary, this evidence concerning external associations suggests that these two empirical factors ($Y+$ and $Y-$) represent a *single* theoretical concept. Thus, this analysis based on the logic of construct validation indicates that while there are four empirical factors underlying these data, only three of these factors are theoretically meaningful and significant.

With this information, we can make a more definitive decision about which factor structure in Tables 5.3 and 5.4 properly describes the data. In Table 5.3, the rotated factor matrix on the right is the preferred orthogonal structure, because it is consistent with the finding that the X indicants are measuring different theoretical concepts. An oblique rotation would place dimensions directly through the two clusters of items representing Xa and Xb. The angle intersecting these two dimensions is 45°. The cosine of 45° is .7071, which is the correlation between Xa and Xb given in Table 5.2. Given the appropriateness of the theoretical bidimensionality underlying the X_i's, all the variance of both the Xa and Xb indicants is both reliable and valid.

In Table 5.4, the unrotated factor matrix on the left is the preferred orthogonal structure. This structure is consistent with the finding that all of the Y_i indicants are empirical approximations of the same theoretical construct. Although all the variance of the Y_i indicants is reliable, only 75% of it is valid. The angle between the $Y+$ and $Y-$ clusters of indicants is 60°. The cosine of 60° is .5, which is the correlation between $Y+$ and $Y-$ in column j of Table 5.2. Although this is empirically true, it is theoretically irrelevant, because the proper interpretation of the Y_i's is that they all measure the same theoretical concept: Y.

Now that the measures of the theoretically relevant variables have been established, we can solve for the structural parameters and the epistemic correlations (that is, the path coefficients) in Figure 5.2. An examination of Figure 5.2 reveals that the Xb indicants and the Xa indicants perfectly represent their theoretical concepts. This is not the case with the Y indicants. We concluded that the unrotated factor I in Table 5.4 represents the relationships between each indicant of Y with Y. These factor loadings specify the degree to which Y causes each of the respective Y_i. Therefore, these factor loadings are used as empirical estimates of the causal effects of Y on the respective Y_i. We also concluded that the unrotated factor II in Table 5.4 represents the correlation of each indicant of Y with M (the method artifact).

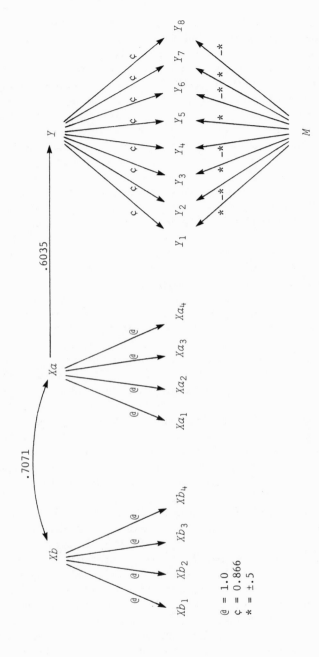

Figure 5.2. Structural measurement model containing empirical estimates.

@ = 1.0
ç = 0.866
* = ±.5

These factor loadings specify the degree to which M causes each respective Y_i. Therefore, these factor loadings are used as empirical estimates of the causal effects between M and the respective Y_i.

The structural parameter linking Xa to Y is slightly underestimated. In actuality, it should equal .7071, as we created it in Table 5.1, instead of its estimated value of .6035. Finally, based upon the data, we cannot specify the causal relationship between Xa and Xb. All we can say is that they are correlated substantially (.7071). In summary, the correspondence between the underlying causal model and the one inferred from the analysis is rather close. Other than slightly underestimating ρ_{X_aY}, the causal model is properly solved. Difficulties in inferring ρ_{x_ay} and solving for the partitioning of the variance into true, systematic error, random error, and covariance components will be more fully discussed in Chapter 6.

Qmatrix factor analysis and method artifacts

Earlier, it was noted that response set may affect some subjects but not others. (It may also affect subjects in varying degrees.) Data were then created such that response set affected only half of the observations. We will now describe a set of procedures by which those respondents who emitted response set bias can be distinguished from those who responded solely to the content of the items by performing a qmatrix factor analysis (Nunnally, 1967; Rummel, 1970). Instead of factoring correlations among the variables (that is, factoring the correlations among the columns in Table 5.2), the correlations among observations are factored (we will factor the correlations among the rows in Table 5.2). The resulting qmatrix factor analysis, rotated to a varimax solution, is presented in Table 5.6.

An examination of Table 5.6 reveals three distinct factors which account for approximately equal proportions of the variance in the matrix. Factor I is defined by observations C, D, E, F, K, L, M, N, CC, DD, EE, FF, KK, LL, MM, and NN; factor II is defined by A, B, G, H, I, J, O, P, GG, HH, II, and JJ; and factor III is defined by all the double-lettered observations. Interpretation of these factors can be aided by making a series of computations. For each factor, the observations can be divided into three categories: (1) those that define the factor positively, (2) those that define the factor negatively, and (3) those that do not define the factor at all. If we choose a factor loading of .5 as the cutoff for defining a factor, then if an observation has a factor loading of between .5 and 1.0, it defines the factor positively; if an observation has a factor loading of between −.5 and −1.0, it defines the factor negatively; and if an observation has a factor loading between .5 and −.5, it does not define the factor.

Table 5.6. *Qmatrix factor analysis of data*

Obs.	1	11	111	h^2
A	−.06	−1.00	.00	1.00
B	−.06	−1.00	.00	1.00
C	.95	.30	.00	1.00
D	.95	.30	.00	1.00
E	−.99	.12	.00	1.00
F	−.99	.12	.00	1.00
G	.07	1.00	.00	1.00
H	.07	1.00	.00	1.00
I	−.07	−1.00	.00	1.00
J	−.07	−1.00	.00	1.00
K	.99	−.12	.00	1.00
L	.99	−.12	.00	1.00
M	−.95	−.30	.00	1.00
N	−.95	−.30	.00	1.00
O	.06	1.00	.00	1.00
P	.06	1.00	.00	1.00
AA	.30	−.14	.94	1.00
BB	.30	−.14	−.94	1.00
CC	.74	.23	.63	1.00
DD	.74	.23	−.63	1.00
EE	−.60	.26	.75	1.00
FF	−.60	.26	−.75	1.00
GG	.05	.65	.76	1.00
HH	.05	.65	−.76	1.00
II	−.05	−.65	.76	1.00
JJ	−.05	−.65	−.76	1.00
KK	.60	−.26	.75	1.00
LL	.60	−.26	−.75	1.00
MM	−.74	−.23	.63	1.00
NN	−.74	−.23	−.63	1.00
OO	−.30	.14	.94	1.00
PP	−.30	.14	−.94	1.00
Eigenvalue	11.7	10.7	9.7	
Variance explained	36.5%	33.3%	30.2%	

For each of these groups of observations, the mean value for each of the four variables Xa, Xb, $Y+$, and $Y-$ was calculated. An examination of Table 5.7 shows that factor I differentiates Xb from Y. A positive loading on factor I indicates a high Xb score and low $Y+$ and $Y-$ scores; a negative loading on factor I indicates a low Xb score and high $Y+$ and $Y-$ scores. Factor II differentiates Xa from the other variables. A positive loading on factor II indicates a high value on Xa and low values on Xb, $Y+$, and $Y-$; a negative loading on factor II indicates a low value on Xa and high values on Xb, $Y+$, and $Y-$. Factor III differentiates $Y+$ from $Y-$. A positive factor loading on

Table 5.7. *Means of observations defined on each factor*

	Xa	Xb	Y+	Y−
Factor I				
Positive	0	.7071	−.6035	−.6035
Negative	0	−.7071	.6035	.6035
Undefined	0	0	0	0
Factor II				
Positive	.3333	−.4714	−.4714	−.4714
Negative	−.3333	.4714	.4714	.4714
Undefined	0	0	0	0
Factor III				
Positive	0	0	.7071	−.7071
Negative	0	0	−.7071	.7071
Undefined	0	0	0	0

factor III indicates a high value on $Y+$ and a low value on $Y-$; a negative loading on factor III indicates a low value on $Y+$ and a high value on $Y-$.

Since $Y+$ and $Y-$ represent one underlying theoretical concept and response set, those subjects that define factor III are the response setters; the observations that are undefined on factor III have responded solely to the underlying theoretical content tapped by the items. In this case, the correlation of $Y+$ and $Y-$ will be low for those who define factor III and high for those who do not define factor III. An examination of Table 5.2 shows that the correlation between $Y+$ and $Y-$ among observations A through P (who are undefined on factor III) is 1.0, whereas the correlation between $Y+$ and $Y-$ among observations AA through PP (who do define factor III) is 0.0.

Given that qmatrix factor analysis has differentiated the response set observations from the trait observations, one can now estimate the structural/measurement model for each of these subpopulations separately. These estimates as shown in the causal diagrams are presented in Figure 5.3A and B, respectively. For the trait observations, Figure 5.3A perfectly corresponds with the construction of the data in Table 5.1. There is no method artifact; all variables are perfectly reliable and valid; and all paths are properly specified. However, the distortion in Figure 5.3B representing the response set observations is substantial. Y only accounts for half of the variance in each of the Y_i, and the path from Xa to Y is significantly underestimated. In other words, identification and elimination of respondents who are not responding to the theoretical content of the items substantially improves the degree to which the underlying theory can be inferred from the data.

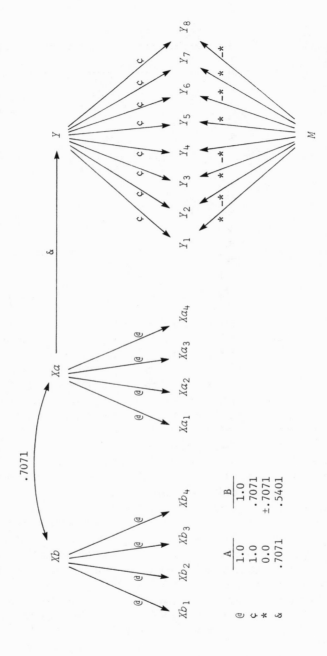

Figure 5.3. Structural measurement model containing empirical estimates for (A) trait observations (observations A through P) and (B) response set observations (observations AA through PP).

Theoretical misspecification

What would the consequences be if the correlation between Xa and $Y+$ were higher than the correlation between Xb and $Y+$ but the opposite were true for $Y-$? In other words, what would the proper inference about the underlying model be if the factor-based scales did not include a method artifact but rather represented four separate theoretical concepts? To answer this question, we return to the original causal relationship between the two theoretical concepts:

$$X \rightarrow Y$$

This time, however, let us suppose that errors have been made in the conceptualization of both X and Y. Although it is assumed that both X and Y are unidimensional concepts, in fact, the measurement of each is made up of two correlated but definitely distinguishable theoretical dimensions. These dimensions can be referred to as Xa, Xb, Ya, and Yb, respectively. Given that the actual theoretical dimensionality of X and Y do not correspond with their conceptualization, the causal relations among them must now be reformulated to coincide with their actual state. In actuality, Xa causes Ya and Xb causes Yb. Although we do not know and cannot infer the causal relationship between Xa and Xb, we do know that they are correlated with each other. Moreover, Ya and Yb share no variance apart from their dependence on Xa and Xb, respectively. A model of the actual causal relationship underlying this analysis is as follows:

$$Yb \leftarrow Xb \longleftrightarrow Xa \rightarrow Ya$$

The appropriate causal model with the paths designating the effects of the concepts on the respective empirical indicants is presented in Figure 5.4.

Table 5.8 creates data that embody these characteristics. Columns (a) through (g) were created in a fashion identical to Table 5.1. We will now refer to the variable in column (g) as Ya. W_3, a standardized variable uncorrelated with Xa, Xb, Ya, W_1, and W_2, is presented in column (h). The value in column (i) is the addition of Xb and W_3. Column (j) standardizes the variable in column (i) and is referred to as Yb. The entire causal model, including Xa, Xb, Ya, and Yb, has now been created. A factor analysis of the X indicants is identical to the factor analysis presented in Table 5.3; a factor analysis of the Y indicants is similar (but not identical) to the factor analysis presented in Table 5.4. Based upon the factor analyses, it is not possible to determine whether X and Y have been inadequately conceptualized or whether a method artifact has artificially altered the structure of the correlation matrix to provide this "real" but theoretically meaningless second factor for each set of indicants. Because we created the

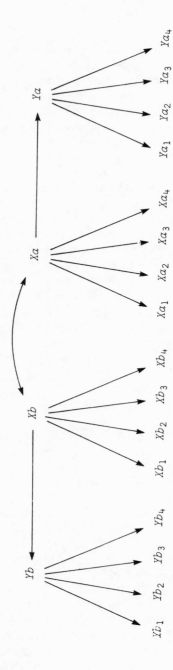

Figure 5.4. Structural measurement model illustrating specification errors.

Table 5.8. *Creation of variables representing the causal diagram in Figure 5.4*

Xa			Xb			Ya			Yb
(a) Xa	(b) W₁	(c) (a)+(b)	(d) c_z	(e) W₂	(f) (a)+(e)	(g) f_z	(h) W₃	(i) (d)+(h)	(j) i_z
1	1	2	1.4142	1	2	1.4142	1	2.4142	1.7071
1	1	2	1.4142	1	2	1.4142	-1	.4142	.2929
1	1	2	1.4142	-1	0	0	1	2.4142	1.7071
1	1	2	1.4142	-1	0	0	-1	.4142	.2929
1	-1	0	0	1	2	1.4142	1	1	.7071
1	-1	0	0	1	2	1.4142	-1	-1	-.7071
1	-1	0	0	-1	0	0	1	1	.7071
1	-1	0	0	-1	0	0	-1	-1	-.7071
-1	1	0	0	1	0	0	1	1	.7071
-1	1	0	0	1	0	0	-1	-1	-.7071
-1	1	0	0	-1	-2	-1.4142	1	1	.7071
-1	1	0	0	-1	-2	-1.4142	-1	-1	-.7071
-1	-1	-2	-1.4142	1	0	0	1	-.4142	-.2929
-1	-1	-2	-1.4142	1	0	0	-1	-2.4142	-1.7071
-1	-1	-2	-1.4142	-1	-2	-1.4142	1	-.4142	-.2929
-1	-1	-2	-1.4142	-1	-2	-1.4142	-1	-2.4142	-1.7071

Table 5.9. *Correlation matrix of Xa, Xb, Ya, and Yb*

	Xa	Xb	Ya	Yb
Xa	—	.7071	.7071	.5000
Xb		—	.5000	.7071
Ya			—	.3536
Yb				—

causal structure underlying the data, we know that the source of the problem is the inadequate conceptualization of each underlying concept, but the evidence provided by the factor analyses does not allow us to make that inference.

At this point, we can turn again to evidence concerning external associations to assess the construct validity of the factor-based scales. An examination of the intercorrelations of scales made up of Xa, Xb, Ya, and Yb should provide evidence of the theoretical bidimensionality of both the X and Y indicants. These correlations are computed from Table 5.8 and placed in matrix form in Table 5.9.

The correlation of Xa with Ya is .7071, whereas the correlation of Xb with Ya is .5. Similarly, the correlation of Xa with Yb is .5, but the correlation of Xb with Yb is .7071. The fact that Xa and Xb relate differentially to these theoretically relevant external variables (Ya and Yb) suggests that these two sets of indicants reflect different concepts. The correlation between Ya and Xa is .7071, whereas the correlation between Yb and Xa is .5. Similarly, the correlation between Yb and Xb is .7071, whereas the correlation between Yb and Xa is .5. This pattern of differential external associations indicates that Ya and Yb represent two genuinely distinguishable concepts. Thus, in this case, the second empirical factors emerging from each factor analysis reflect theoretically meaningful and interpretable concepts. Now that the measures of the theoretically relevant variables have been properly inferred, the researcher can solve for the appropriate effect parameters using the procedures outlined for Figure 5.2.

A substantive example: FIRO-B

The previous sections of this chapter have used hypothetical data to illustrate how systematic sources of error – whether they are due to method artifacts or theoretical misspecification – can be analyzed within the integrated approach to measurement developed in Chapter 4. This section of the chapter applies this measurement strategy to nonhypothetical data – the three-by-two dimensional theory of interpersonal behavior formulated by Schutz (1966).

This theory, the *Fundamental Interpersonal Relations Orientation of Behavior (FIRO-B)*, stipulates that every individual has three interpersonal needs: the need for inclusion, the need for control, and the need for affection (Schutz, 1966:13). The word "interpersonal" refers to relations that occur between people, and thus an interpersonal need is one that can only be satisfied through the successful attainment of satisfactory relationships with others. Failure to achieve this relation in any of the need areas leads to a condition of anxiety for the individual in question. Schutz (1966:13) also states that *inclusion, control, and affection* constitute a sufficient set of areas of interpersonal behavior for the prediction of interpersonal phenomena. This implies that behavior relative to the three interpersonal need areas must be capable of measurement if social interaction is to be predicted.

In addition, the interpersonal behavior relative to each interpersonal need area is specified as being composed of two orthogonal dimensions: behavior that the subject expresses toward others, and how the subject wants others to behave toward him. To accommodate these theoretical notions, FIRO-B requires the development of six scales, to reflect the following concepts:

A   *Expressed* interpersonal need for *inclusion*.
B   *Wanted* interpersonal need for *inclusion*.
C   *Expressed* interpersonal need for *control*.
D   *Wanted* interpersonal need for *control*.
E   *Expressed* interpersonal need for *affection*.
F   *Wanted* interpersonal need for *affection*.

These six concepts are thought to be orthogonal to one another and to independently predict interpersonal behavior. Schutz "validated" his measuring instruments using scalogram analysis. For a discussion of his procedures, see Wallace and Zeller (1974a). The remainder of this section will present evidence relevant to the theoretical notions which Schutz has proposed. Through the use of factor analysis, it is possible to determine those groups of indicants which best represent empirical dimensions within the data. These dimensions can then be compared with the hypothesized concepts using the procedures outlined earlier in this chapter.

The application of factor analysis is not without precedent in the analysis of FIRO-B. Indeed, Schutz himself (1966:54) proposed a factor-analytic solution as empirical evidence of the existence of the three-by two-dimensional (conceptual) structure. Table 5.10 presents the 54 FIRO-B items used by Schutz. Nine items were designed to approximate each concept. Using the 54 items as an appropriate battery of measures of interpersonal behavior, it is possible to test the resulting factor structure against the hypothesized one.

Table 5.10. *FIRO-B scales*

Item	Statement	Response[a]
Expressed inclusion (e^1)		
1	I try to be with people.	a
2	I join social groups.	a
3	I tend to join social organizations when I have an opportunity.	a
4	I try to be included in informal social activities	a
5	I try to include other people in my plans.	a
6	I try to have people around me.	a
7	When people are doing things together I tend to join them.	a
8	I try to avoid being alone.	a
9	I try to participate in group activities.	a
Wanted inclusion (w^1)		
10	I like people to include me in their activities.	a
11	I like people to invite me to things.	a
12	I like people to invite me to join their activities.	a
13	I like people to invite me to participate in their activities	a
14	I like people to invite me to things.	b
15	I like people to invite me to join their activities.	b
16	I like people to include me in their activities.	b
17	I like people to ask me to participate in their discussions.	b
18	I like people to invite me to participate in their activities.	b
Expressed control (e^C)		
19	I try to be the dominant person when I am with people.	a
20	I try to take charge of things when I am with people.	b
21	I try to have other people do things I want done.	a
22	I try to influence strongly other people's actions	a
23	I try to influence strongly other people's actions.	b
24	I try to have other people do things the way I want them done.	a
25	I try to have other people do things the way I want them done.	b
26	I take charge of things when I'm with people.	a
27	I try to take charge of things when I'm with people.	a
Wanted control (w^C)		
28	I let other people decide what to do.	a
29	I let other people decide what to do.	b
30	I let other people take charge of things.	b
31	I let other people strongly influence my actions.	b
32	I let other people strongly influence my actions.	a
33	I let other people control my actions.	a
34	I am easily led by people.	a
35	I let people control my actions.	b
36	I am easily led by people.	b

Expressed affection (e^A)

37	I try to be friendly to people.	b
38	My personal relations with people are cool and distant.	b
39	I act cool and distant with people.	b
40	I try to have close relationships with people.	a
41	I try to have close, personal relationships with people.	a
42	I try to have close relationships with people.	b
43	I try to get close and personal with people.	b
44	I try to have close, personal relationships with people.	b
45	I try to get close and personal with people.	c

Wanted affection (w^A)

46	I like people to act friendly toward me.	b
47	I like people to act cool and distant toward me.	a
48	I like people to act distant toward me.	a
49	I like people to act cool and distant toward me.	b
50	I like people to act distant toward me.	b
51	I like people to act close toward me.	b
52	I like people to act close and personal with me.	a
53	I like people to act close and personal with me.	b
54	I like people to act close toward me.	a

^a Response code: (a) usually   often   sometimes   occasionally   rarely   never; (b) most people   many people   some people   a few people   one or two people   nobody; (c) usually   often   sometimes   a few people   one or two people   nobody.

The data for analysis of the FIRO-B instrument were gathered in three undergraduate sociology classes at SUNY at Buffalo in 1973. The questionnaire presented in Table 5.10 was described as a test designed to elicit the actual behavior of subjects with regard to the questions asked. Students were told to circle the response most nearly true for them for each statement. Items were not presented in the order shown in Table 5.10, but in a random fashion. The total sample was composed of 226 subjects. Using Schutz's own procedures, we establish that the retest data was a good approximation of the original Schutz data. For further information on this problem, see Wallace and Zeller (1974a).

Factor analysis was used to assess the empirical structure of the 54 FIRO-B items. Subject responses were coded according to Likert scoring procedures. For each scale item, response categories were coded from 6, for the most positive category, to 1, for the least positive category. Table 5.11 presents a common factor analysis (using SMCs in the main diagonal) of the FIRO-B items. Five factors were extracted and rotated to a varimax solution. The extraction and rotation of additional factors lacked interpretational import. Through the analysis of the results of Table 5.11, it should be possible to determine if the FIRO-B scales possess the conceptual properties hypothesized by Schutz.

Table 5.11. *Common factor analysis of FIRO-B items rotated to varimax solution*

Concept	Item	I	II	III	IV	V	h^2
Expressed inclusion	1	.52	−.08	.13	.14	−.24	.37
	2	.59	.05	.04	.08	.13	.37
	3	.66	−.02	.00	.10	.20	.49
	4	.69	.12	−.02	.12	.15	.53
	5	.61	−.01	−.01	.15	.38	.55
	6	.62	−.05	.11	.23	.20	.48
	7	.69	.06	−.14	.02	.25	.56
	8	.54	.02	−.01	−.01	.21	.33
	9	.74	.08	−.06	.14	.16	.61
Wanted inclusion	10	.62	.05	.23	.19	.16	.50
	11	.80	.11	.10	.09	.18	.70
	12	.83	.13	.10	.07	.16	.74
	13	.77	.08	.10	.13	.15	.65
	14	.79	.09	.05	.15	.19	.69
	15	.67	.14	.17	.16	.19	.56
	16	.64	.12	.10	.13	.26	.52
	17	.56	.15	−.06	.31	.23	.49
	18	.73	.07	.12	.09	.22	.61
Expressed control	19	.19	.75	−.07	.05	−.01	.60
	20	.17	.78	−.07	−.08	.18	.68
	21	−.01	.67	.14	.00	.00	.47
	22	.12	.75	.06	−.09	.04	.59
	23	.09	.77	.10	−.06	.09	.63
	24	−.15	.65	.08	.10	.03	.46
	25	−.03	.76	.06	−.02	.07	.59
	26	.14	.82	−.08	−.11	.02	.70
	27	.18	.80	.00	−.15	.07	.70
Wanted control	28[a]	−.10	−.24	.40	.06	.10	.24
	29[a]	.02	−.19	.46	−.09	.07	.26
	30[a]	.01	.02	.59	−.22	.09	.40
	31	.17	.22	.78	−.13	.14	.72
	32	.13	.17	.82	−.05	.09	.73
	33	.10	.07	.76	.18	−.02	.63
	34	.04	−.01	.81	.14	.10	.68
	35	.11	.19	.80	−.10	.03	.71
	36	.12	.07	.81	−.03	.12	.69
Expressed affection	37[a]	.20	−.05	−.11	.31	.19	.18
	38	−.30	.14	.15	−.62	−.26	.58
	39	−.26	.06	.13	−.68	−.25	.62
	40	.36	.02	.05	.19	.72	.69
	41	.40	−.11	.00	.18	.65	.63
	42	.28	−.01	.15	.12	.80	.75
	43	.32	.15	.24	.15	.72	.72
	44	.32	.15	.10	.08	.81	.79
	45	.33	.13	.11	.07	.77	.74

Wanted	46[a]	.39	.00	.15	.37	.20	.36
affection	47	−.28	.00	−.03	−.80	−.11	.72
	48	−.20	.08	−.05	−.84	−.15	.78
	49	−.11	.02	.02	−.87	−.14	.78
	50	−.12	.07	.05	−.83	−.07	.71
	51	.26	.09	.16	.14	.72	.65
	52	.39	.04	.15	.15	.67	.65
	53	.31	.12	.08	.17	.75	.70
	54	.35	.08	.06	.23	.69	.66
Eigenvalue		10.1	5.6	5.6	4.7	6.6	32.6
Percent of variance		18.7%	10.4%	10.4%	8.7%	12.2%	60.4%

[a] Scale items that were rejected because they were weak and failed to properly correspond to the proper concept.

The five factors presented account for 59.3% of the total variance in the 54-item matrix. An examination of Table 5.11 reveals that the inclusion items load heavily on factor I, the control items load heavily on factors II and III, and the affection items load heavily on factors IV and V. The inclusion factor, the control factors, and the affection factors account for 18.7%, 20.8%, and 20.9% of the variance, respectively.

Inclusion
The factor analysis fails to distinguish between the wanted inclusion and expressed inclusion sets of items. Rather, factor I in Table 5.11 suggests that the 18 inclusion items measure a single underlying concept: inclusion. A separate factor analysis of the inclusion items clearly indicates that the items cannot be interpreted as representing a two-factor structure. The cluster of items designed to empirically represent expressed inclusion were indistinguishable from the cluster of items designed to empirically represent wanted inclusion (that is, items 1 through 9 were indistinguishable from items 10 through 18). Thus, factor analysis suggests that items 1 through 18 are an empirical representation of a single concept (and/or method artifact). Later in this chapter, we will argue that these items are due to both the concept "inclusion" and an undetectable method artifact.

Table 5.12A presents evidence pertaining to the construct validity of the inclusion scales. In addition to the six FIRO-B scales proposed by Schutz, there exist two empirically constructed scales representing inferred concepts. They are "Cool and Distant" (on factor IV) and "Close and Personal" (on factor V). In spite of the evidence supporting the unidimensional interpretation of inclusion, it is possible to treat expressed inclusion as distinguishable from wanted inclusion, as we have done in Tables 5.10, 5.11, and 5.12A.

Table 5.12. *Correlation among external variables to assess construct validity of FIRO-B*

A. Inclusion items	e^C	w^C	e^A	w^A	Close and Personal	Cool and Distant
e^I	.15	.18	.53	.48	.44	.57
w^I	.21	.21	.49	.49	.34	.57
Difference	−.06	−.03	.04	−.01	.10	.00

B. Control items	e^I	w^I	e^A	w^A	Close and Personal	Cool and Distant
e^C	.15	.21	.10	.09	−.04	.17
w^C	.18	.21	.09	.09	−.01	.27
Difference	−.03	.00	−.01	.00	−.03	−.10

C. Affection items	e^I	w^I	e^C	w^C
e^A	.53	.49	.10	.09
w^A	.48	.49	.09	.09
Difference	.05	.00	.01	.00

Note: External variables are scales constructed as follows: e^I = sum of items 1 through 9; w^I = sum of items 10 through 18; e^C = sum of items 19 through 27; w^C = sum of items 31 through 36; e^A = sum of items 38 through 45; w^A = sum of items 47 through 54. Close and Personal = sum of items 40 through 45 and 51 through 54. Cool and Distant = sum of items 38, 39, 47, 48, 49, and 50.

An examination of Table 5.12A reveals that a correlation between the wanted inclusion scale and the FIRO-B scales e^C, w^C, e^A, and w^A is similar to the correlation between the expressed inclusion items and the same FIRO-B scales. The difference between the correlation of wanted inclusion and expressed inclusion with these external variables is less than .07. Furthermore, expressed inclusion is indistinguishable from wanted inclusion for the created empirical constructs, "Close and Personal" and "Cool and Distant." Thus, both internal and external evidence suggests that items 1 through 18 are an empirical representation of a single theoretical dimension of inclusion.

Control
The evidence from the factor analysis suggests that wanted control is distinguishable from expressed control. Factors II and III in Table 5.11 clearly differentiate between expressed control and wanted con-

Table 5.13. *Common factor analysis of control items* ($N = 226$)

Item	Rotation A			Rotation B		
	I	II	h^2	I	II	h^2
19	.48	.58	.57	.75	−.07	.56
20	.50	.60	.61	.78	−.07	.61
21	.57	.37	.46	.66	.14	.46
22	.57	.49	.56	.75	.06	.56
23	.62	.47	.60	.77	.11	.60
24	.52	.40	.43	.65	.08	.43
25	.58	.49	.58	.76	.06	.58
26	.52	.63	.67	.81	−.08	.67
27	.56	.56	.62	.79	.00	.62
31	.71	−.40	.66	.21	.78	.65
32	.70	−.46	.70	.17	.82	.70
33	.58	−.49	.58	.06	.76	.58
34	.57	−.59	.67	−.01	.82	.67
35	.70	−.43	.67	.19	.80	.68
36	.60	−.52	.63	.06	.79	.62
Eigenvalue	5.19	3.82		5.15	3.84	
Percent of variance	34.6%	25.5%	60.1%	34.3%	25.6%	59.9%

trol. Items 19 through 27, designed as measures of expressed control, strongly define factor II; items 31 through 36, designed as measures of wanted control, define factor III. An investigation of the communalities for each of the control items led us to suspect that items 28, 29, and 30 did not represent wanted control. A factor analysis of the 18 control items, based upon the extraction and rotation of both two and three factors, reveals that these items were defined, in a weak and uninterpretable fashion, on a third factor. Hence, items 28, 29, and 30 were omitted from further consideration.

A factor analysis of the control items is presented in Table 5.13. Sixty percent of the variance was removed on the first two factors. Rotation A reveals two strong factors. Factor I is a general control factor; all items loaded positively on it. The expressed control items load positively on factor II while the wanted control items load negatively on this factor. Rotation B provides a different interpretation, for there is no general factor. Instead, factor I is defined by the expressed control items, and factor II is defined by the wanted control items.

There are two possible interpretations for these factor-analytic results, analogous to the interpretational possibilities presented for self-esteem. In one interpretation, the evidence can be seen to indicate two theoretical concepts: expressed control and wanted control. In the other interpretation, the evidence can be viewed as indicating a single theoretical concept, control, and a method artifact, response set.

Evidence relating to construct validity suggests that wanted control is indistinguishable from expressed control. For Table 5.12B reveals that the correlations between the wanted control scale and the FIRO-B scales e^I, w^I, e^A, and w^A are similar to the correlations between the expressed control scale and the four FIRO-B scales. The difference between the correlation of wanted control and expressed control with these external variables is less than .04. Moreover, an examination of the correlations of these scales with "Close and Personal" and "Cool and Distant" further supports the view that expressed control is indistinguishable from wanted control.

Although factor analysis suggests that wanted control is distinguishable from expressed control, the externally based evidence used to assess their construct validity suggests that the items represent a single dimension of control. This two-factor solution may be a function of a single theoretical concept, control, contaminated by a method artifact, response set.

To evaluate this interpretation further, an additional type of factor analysis was performed on the data. As described in Chapter 2 and illustrated earlier in this chapter, a Qmatrix factor analysis of these data (performed in four separate runs of 56 or 57 subjects each) reveals a first factor accounting for approximately 31% of the variance among subjects. Approximately half of the subjects had a factor loading of greater than .5 or less than −.5 on this factor, while the remaining group had factor loadings between .5 and −.5. These first two groups of observations may be referred to as the high- and low-variance observations, respectively.

A separate factor analysis of the control items for the low- and high-variance observations is presented in Table 5.14. A comparison of these factor solutions shows that 53.7% and 75.5% of the variance was removed on the first two factors of each analysis, respectively. That more variance was extracted from the high-variance subjects comes as no surprise, because the groups were established by examining the factor loadings on the first factor of the Qmatrix factor analysis. The proper theoretical interpretation of the control items can be facilitated by assessing the construct validity of the scales based on membership in groups established by Qmatrix factor analysis.

The factor analysis for the low-variance group indicates a strong factor I and a weak and relatively uninterpretable factor II. Subjects in the low-variance group appear to respond to the control items in a unifactorial space. Thus, for these subjects, both the internal and external evidence is consistent: both converge on a unifactorial in-

Table 5.14. *Common factor analysis of control items for low-and high-variance groups*

	Low-variance group (N = 110)			High-variance group (N = 116)					
				Rotation A			Rotation B		
Item	I	II	h^2	I	II	h^2	I'	II'	h^2
19	.57	.20	.36	.48	−.72	.75	.86	−.13	.75
20	.60	.48	.59	.52	−.72	.79	.88	−.10	.79
21	.67	.13	.47	.56	−.49	.55	.74	.08	.55
22	.62	.48	.61	.60	−.59	.71	.84	.04	.71
23	.64	.40	.57	.66	−.56	.75	.86	.11	.75
24	.58	−.45	.54	.57	−.48	.56	.74	.10	.56
25	.67	−.13	.47	.63	−.54	.69	.82	.10	.69
26	.65	.35	.55	.53	−.74	.83	.90	−.11	.83
27	.73	.35	.66	.55	−.61	.67	.82	−.01	.67
31	.65	.41	.59	.68	.66	.90	−.03	.95	.90
32	.77	−.15	.62	.57	.74	.87	−.16	.92	.87
33	.65	−.31	.52	.49	.73	.77	−.21	.85	.77
34	.62	−.31	.48	.47	.77	.81	−.25	.87	.81
35	.66	.40	.60	.62	.66	.82	−.07	.90	.82
36	.61	.21	.42	.55	.74	.85	−.17	.91	.85
Eigenvalue	6.30	1.75	8.05	4.85	6.47	11.32	6.38	4.94	11.32
Percent of variance	42.0%	11.7%	53.7%	32.3%	43.1%	75.5%	42.5%	32.9%	75.5%

terpretation of control; for these subjects, expressed control is indistinguishable from wanted control.

In contrast, the factor analysis for the high-variance group reveals, in rotation A, two strong factors. Factor I is a general control factor, and appears to correspond to factor I for the low-variance subjects. Factor II differentiates expressed control from wanted control in a fashion similar to their differentiation in Table 5.13, rotation A. Again, rotation B provides no general factor; instead, factor I is defined by the expressed control items and factor II is defined by the wanted control items. Indeed, in rotation B, there is virtual independence between the expressed control and the wanted control dimensions.

Although the data for the low-variance subjects do not support a bidimensional interpretation of control for all subjects, it could be argued that control is bidimensional for the high-variance subjects. If this is the case, one would expect differential correlations between the expressed control scale and the external variables, as compared to the wanted control scale, for the high-variance subjects. The relevant findings, as presented in Table 5.15, indicate that the correlation between the expressed control scale and the theoretically relevant

Table 5.15. *Correlation between external variables and control scale for low- and high-variance groups*

	External variables				
	Incl.	e^A	w^A	Close and Personal	Cool and Distant
A. *Low-variance group*					
Expressed control	.34	.16	.09	.27	−.10
Wanted control	.38	.25	.22	.33	.03
Difference	−.04	−.09	−.13	−.06	−.13
B. *High-variance group*					
Expressed control	.10	.05	.05	.10	−.05
Wanted control	.14	.14	.14	.25	−.03
Difference	−.04	−.09	−.09	−.15	−.02

Note: External variables are scales constructed as follows: Incl. = sum of items 1 through 18, as suggested in the analysis above. e^A = sum of items 38 through 45. w^A = sum of items 47 through 54. Close and Personal = sum of items 40 through 45 and 51 through 54. Cool and Distant = sum of items 38, 39, 47, 48, 49, and 50. Expressed control = sum of items 19 through 27. Wanted control = sum of items 31 through 36.

external variables are almost identical to the correlations between the wanted control scale and these external variables. None of the differences between external variable correlations is statistically significant.

This evidence strongly suggests that rotation A in Table 5.14 is the preferred interpretational scheme for the high-variance group. Factor I of this rotation is based upon these subjects' variation caused by the differential levels of control that they exhibit; we shall refer to the sum of items 19 through 27 and 31 through 36 as the empirical scale "control." Factor II of rotation A is based upon the tendency of subjects to respond in a systematic fashion to items independent of the content of those items. A careful examination of items 19 through 36 and the response categories of those items indicates that if a person simply marks down one side of the questionnaire (or the other), the responses will be systematic yet independent of the content of the items. This method artifact is reponse set. Therefore, one can interpret factor II of rotation A as "response set," where positive factor loadings indicate a tendency to respond positively to the wanted items and negatively to the expressed items, whereas negative factor loadings indicate a tendency to respond positively to the expressed control items and negatively to the wanted items, or vice versa. In sum, both the internal and external evidence suggest that the "expressed" versus "wanted" difference is not supported with respect to control for either the high-variance or low-variance groups.

By recombining the high- and low-variance groups, it is possible to present schematically a causal measurement model of the effects of the underlying substantive concept, control, and the response set on each of the control items. The causal measurement model is presented in Figure 5.5. The causal diagram shows how response set systematically affects the scores on the control items, increasing the correlation among items 19 through 27, increasing the correlations among items 31 through 36, and decreasing the correlations between the two groups of items.

Affection
The factor-analytic evidence suggests that there are two distinguishable dimensions in the affection items, but that these two dimensions do not correspond to the wanted affection and expressed affection dimensions as hypothesized by Schutz. Both factors IV and V in Table 5.11 are defined by the affection items. Additional factor analyses and interpretation suggested that items 37 and 46 represented an uninterpretable third dimension of affection. Hence, items 37 and 46 were omitted from further consideration. However, this factor structure does not correspond to the expressed and wanted affection dimensions. Instead, the items whose content centers on being cool and distant define factor IV, whereas the items whose content centers on being close and personal define factor V. We shall call the sum of items 38, 39, 47, 48, 49, and 50 the "cool and distant" scale, and the sum of items 40 through 45 and 51 through 54 the "close and personal" scale. Evidence relating to construct validation also indicates that wanted affection is indistinguishable from expressed affection because Table 5.12C reveals that the correlations between the wanted affection scale and the FIRO-B scales e^I, w^I, e^C, and w^C are quite similar to the correlations between the expressed affection scale and those same FIRO-B scales.

However, the evidence also suggests that "Cool and Distant" is distinguishable from "Close and Personal." Inclusion correlates .67 with Close and Personal and .44 with Cool and Distant (p difference between correlations $< .001$). Control correlates .22 with Close and Personal and $-.04$ with Cool and Distant (p difference between correlations $< .01$). Thus, both the factor analysis and the assessment of construct validity indicate that the Close and Personal items represent one concept and the Cool and Distant items represent another. A causal measurement model of the effects of the underlying theoretical concepts Close and Personal and Cool and Distant is presented in Figure 5.6. If the amount of response set observed in the control items is any guide, the affection items could be seriously biased by response set. If so, the model as solved in Figure 5.6 must be interpreted with great caution. The reason for this caution focuses upon

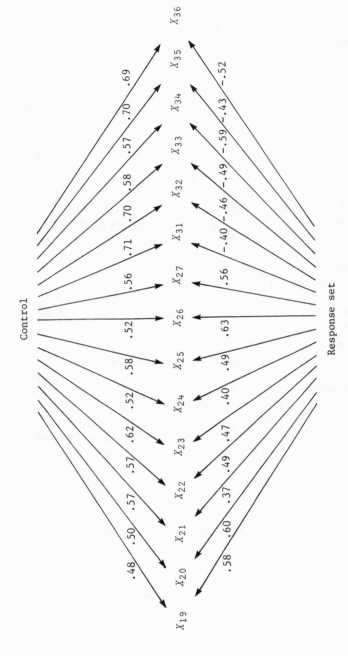

Figure 5.5. Relationship of control and response set to 15 control items. Coefficients correspond to factor loadings for specified items in Table 5.13, rotation A, designed to correspond to the interpretation presented in the text.

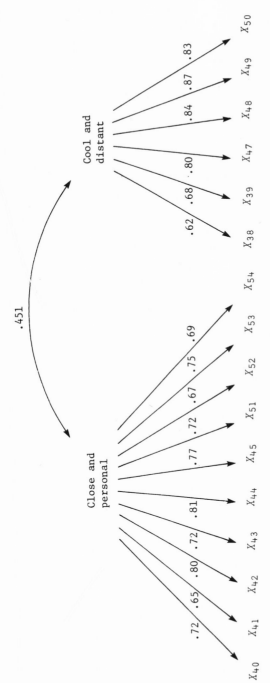

Figure 5.6. Relationship of Close and Personal to Cool and Distant in affection items. Path coefficients correspond to factor loadings for specified items in Table 5.11. The Cool and Distant items report the factor loadings on factor IV; the Close and Personal items report the factor loadings on factor V.

the effects of a method artifact that cannot be detected using empirical means, which, nevertheless, affects the estimation of the parameters of a model. This problem will be discussed in more detail in Chapter 6 (especially, Figure 6.4).

The foregoing analysis has led to a reformulation of the underlying dimensions of FIRO-B. The results of the factor analyses, together with the evidence relating to construct validation, indicate the the 54 FIRO-B items measure four theoretical concepts: inclusion, control, and two aspects of affection, Close and Personal and Cool and Distant. However, this analysis did not support the theoretical differentiation between expressed and wanted behavior. On the other hand, inclusion, control, and the two aspects of affection were clearly distinguishable and provide support for this aspect of Schutz's theoretical formulation.

Conclusion

This chapter has formulated a general strategy for assessing systematic measurement error. This type of measurement error does not yield easily to analysis and estimation. Indeed, it is most usefully detected and estimated through a combination of inferences based on factor analysis and construct validation. Thus, although the approach outlined and illustrated here cannot be applied indiscriminantly or mechanistically, it does have, we would argue, generalized applicability in the social sciences.

6 Integrating reliability and validity

The previous chapters of this volume have considered a variety of specific issues related to measurement in the social sciences. Chapter 1 discusses the role of measurement in social science, emphasizing how it provides a connecting link between theory and research, and introducing the language of measurement. Chapter 2 provides a non-technical treatment of factor analysis, paying particular attention to its uses in measurement. Chapters 3 and 4 focus on various ways of assessing reliability and validity, respectively. Chapter 5 demonstrates how systematic sources of measurement error can contaminate the empirical dimensionality of theoretical concepts, and provides a comprehensive and coherent strategy for detecting and estimating the most prevalent forms of systematic error: method artifacts.

The primary purpose of this chapter is to outline and further explain an approach to measurement that combines and intergrates reliability and validity assessment. More specifically, this chapter has the following purposes: (1) to explain the differences between detectable and undetectable measurement artifacts, (2) to differentiate between the measurement properties of an indicant and the measurement properties of a scale, and (3) to apply this integrated measurement approach to the examples of self-esteem and interpersonal needs.

Detectable and undetectable method artifacts

Figure 4.2A presented a causal measurement model where the d_i represented the epistemic correlations and e represented the structural relationship between the concepts. Specifically, $d_i = .8$ and $e = .5$ in that particular structural/measurement model. We now wish to discuss that model for various values of d_i and e. Specifically, Table 6.1 presents a variety of information about Figure 4.2A when $d_i = .5$, .7, and .9 and $e = .2$, .4, .6, and .8. The first four rows of each combination of d_i and e present the factor loadings on factors 1 and 2 for items 1 through 4 and 5 through 8, respectively; this information is comparable to the rotated factor structure presented in Table 4.3. Next, we present the communality for each item. Notice that the communality of the indicants depends totally on the value of d_i. When

Table 6.1. *Information relevant to Figure 4.2A for varying values of d_i and e*

d_i	Information	e			
		.2	.4	.6	.8
.5	Factor 1: 1–4	.497	.489	.474	.447
	Factor 1: 5–8	.050	.102	.158	.223
	Factor 2: 1–4	.050	.102	.158	.223
	Factor 2: 5–8	.497	.489	.474	.447
	Communality	.249	.250	.250	.250
	α	.571	.571	.571	.571
	Angle between clusters	78°30′	66°30′	53°	37°
	Cosine of angle	.199	.399	.602	.799
	ρ	.114	.229	.343	.457
	ρ corrected	.200	.401	.601	.800
.7	Factor 1: 1–4	.697	.684	.664	.626
	Factor 1: 5–8	.069	.144	.221	.313
	Factor 2: 1–4	.069	.144	.221	.313
	Factor 2: 5–8	.697	.684	.664	.626
	Communality	.491	.489	.490	.490
	α	.793	.793	.793	.793
	Angle between clusters	78°30′	66°30′	53°	37°
	Cosine of angle	.199	.399	.602	.799
	ρ	.159	.317	.476	.635
	ρ corrected	.201	.400	.600	.801
.9	Factor 1: 1–4	.895	.882	.853	.805
	Factor 1: 5–8	.091	.183	.285	.402
	Factor 2: 1–4	.091	.183	.285	.402
	Factor 2: 5–8	.895	.882	.853	.805
	Communality	.809	.811	.809	.811
	α	.945	.945	.945	.945
	Angle between clusters	78°30′	66°30′	53°	37°
	Cosine of angle	.199	.399	.602	.799
	ρ	.189	.378	.567	.756
	ρ corrected	.200	.400	.600	.800

$d_i = .5$, $h^2 = .25$; when $d_i = .7$, $h^2 = .49$; and when $d_i = .9$, $h^2 = .81$. That is, if there is no method artifact present in the data, the square root of the communality is equal to the epistemic correlation. The observed correlation between an indicant of T_1 (say indicant 2) and an indicant of T_2 (say indicant 6) equals the product of the paths as follows:

$$\rho_{i_2 t_1}\rho_{t_1 t_2}\rho_{i_6 t_2} = (.5)\,(.2)\,(.5)\ = .05$$

The observed correlation equals the correlation between the two concepts after correcting for attenuation using Formula 3.11 as follows:

$$\rho_{t_1 t_2} = \frac{\rho_{26}}{\sqrt{\rho_{22'} \rho_{66'}}} = \frac{.05}{\sqrt{(.25)(.25)}} = \frac{.05}{.25} = .2$$

The reliability coefficients are equal to .25 rather than .5 because although we solved for them assuming a single measurement, the correction for attenuation formula assumes that the two "variables" of the reliability correlation are both subject to error. We comply with this requirement using Formula 5.1 as follows:

$$\rho_{66'} = \rho_{t_2 i_6} \rho_{t_2 i'_6} = (.5)(.5) = .25$$

Composite scales can be calculated by unit weighting the standardized indicants and summing them. These sums are then standardized, producing a scale with a variance of 1.00. In Figure 4.2A, the path coefficient from T_1 to a scale made up of indicants 1, 2, 3, and 4 equals $\sqrt{\alpha}$. The alpha reliability coefficient for a scale made up of indicants 1 through 4 with a .25 correlation in each off-diagonal location, using Formula 3.5, is

$$a = 4 \qquad b = 1.5$$

$$\alpha = \frac{a}{a-1}\left(1 - \frac{a}{a+2b}\right) = \frac{4}{3}\left[1 - \frac{4}{4+(2)(1.5)}\right] = .571$$

Thus, the epistemic path coefficient from T_1 to scale 1–4 is equal to $\sqrt{.571} = .756$. In other words, the specific value of Cronbach's alpha depends only on the values of the epistemic correlations. Specifically, when $d_i = .5$, $\alpha = .571$; when $d_i = .7$, $\alpha = .793$; and when $d_i = .9$, $\alpha = .945$.

The relationship between the underlying theoretical concepts can be inferred by observing the angle between the two sets of indicants, as shown in Table 6.1 and Figure 6.1. That is, the smaller the angle between these two sets of clusters, the higher the correlation between the two underlying concepts. This can be seen by observing the factor loadings for each combination of d_i and e in Figure 6.1. Angle .2–0–.2′ corresponds to the factor analysis when $e = .2$, angle .4–0–.4′ when $e = .4$, and so on. When $e = .2$, angle .2–0–.2′ is 78°30′; when $e = .4$, angle .4–0–.4′ is 66°30′; when $e = .6$, angle .6–0–.6′ is 53°; and when $e = .8$, angle .8–0–.8′ is 37°. Thus, the value of the angle intersecting the two clusters of indicants depends upon the correlation between the underlying concepts. Moreover, the cosine of each respective angle is equal to the value of e. Thus, within the limits of rounding error, the cosine of 78°30′ $= .2$; the cosine of 66°30′ is .4; the cosine of 53° is .6; and the cosine of 37° is .8. Hence, the cosine

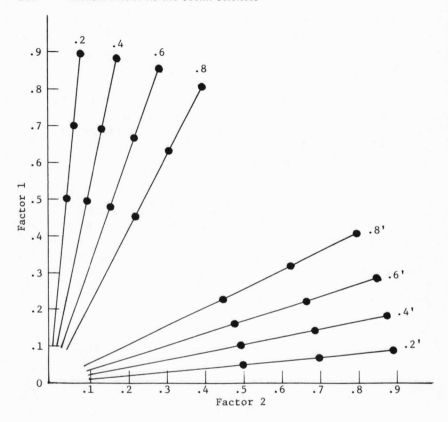

Figure 6.1. Graphic plot of factors 1 and 2 from Table 6.1.

of the angle between the two clusters of indicants is equal to the structural parameter, e, regardless of the values of the epistemic correlations, the d_i. This property of factor analysis was noted by Stinchcomb (1971).

The observed correlation between scale 1–4 and scale 5–8 will equal the product of the paths as follows:

$$\rho_{\text{scale}\,1-4,\,t\,1}\,\rho_{t_1 t_2}\,\rho_{\text{scale}\,5-8,\,t\,2} = (\sqrt{.571})\,(.2)\,(\sqrt{.571}) = .114$$

Using formula 3.11, this correlation can be corrected for attenuation as follows:

$$\rho_{t_1 t_2} = \frac{\rho_{\text{scale}\,1-4,\,\text{scale}\,5-8}}{\sqrt{\rho_{\text{scale}\,1-4\ \text{reliability}}\,\rho_{\text{scale}\,5-8\ \text{reliability}}}} = \frac{.114}{\sqrt{(.571)\,(.571)}} = .200$$

This value corresponds to the value of e. The correlation between scale 1–4 and scale 5–8 depends on both the value of e and d_i, but that correlation corrected for attenuation depends entirely on the value of e. That is, when $e = .2$, the corrected $\rho = .2$; when $e = .4$, the corrected $\rho = .4$; when $e = .6$, the corrected $\rho = .6$; and when $e = .8$, the corrected $\rho = .8$.

The most interesting result from this analysis is that if there is no method artifact in the underlying causal model, the cosine of the angle between a scale made up of items 1–4 (the empirical approximation of T_1) and scale of items 5–8) (the empirical approximation of T_2) equals the value of the structural parameter, e, *regardless of the degree to which the indicants are caused by the underlying concept* (assuming that this is a nonzero value). In other words, one can approximate the proper value of the correlation between the theoretical concepts while tolerating fluctuations in the reliability and validity of the empirical scales.

Differentiating validity from reliability
Recall that we have not shown that there is no method artifact in the model. In the structural/measurement model presented in Figure 6.2, T_1 causes T_2; T_1 causes indicants 1, 2, 3, and 4; and T_2 causes indicants 5, 6, 7, and 8. In this figure,there is an undetectable method artifact, M, which positively affects all eight indicants. Let $k = .4$ and $l_i = .7$. With these values for k and l_i, if $m_i = 0$, the information in the first column of Table 6.2 corresponds to the information in the second row, the second column in Table 6.1 (where $d_i = .7$ and $e = .4$). This is because there is no method artifact in this case. Table 6.2 presents the particular information when $m_i = .0, .2, .4,$ and $.6$, respectively. Given the same theoretical structure (represented by $k = .4$ and $l_i = .7$) but a method artifact of varying strength, a variety of changes occur in the summary coefficients. First, the factor loadings and communalities increase. When $m_i = 0$, each item has a communality of $.49$; when $m_i = .6$, each item has a communality of $.49 + .36 = .85$. As m_i increases, Cronbach's alpha increases. When $m_i = 0$, α for each scale $= .793$; when $m_i = .6$, α of each scale is $.958$. In the latter case, not all of the reliable variance is valid because although some of it is due to the concept, some of it is also due to the method artifact. As m_i increases, the angle between the two clusters becomes smaller. When $m_i = 0$, the angle between the two clusters of indicants is $66°30'$; when $m_i = .6$, the angle between the two clusters is $48°30'$. As m_i increases, the cosine associated with the angle between the clusters of indicants also increases. When $m_i = 0$, the cosine of the angle $= .4$ (the value of k); when $m_i = .6$, the cosine of the angle is $.66$

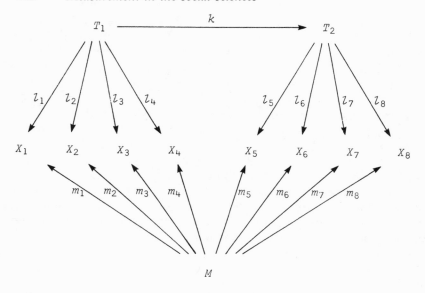

Figure 6.2. Structural measurement model with an undetectable method artifact.

Table 6.2. *Information relevant to Figure 6.2 for varying values of* m_i

Information	m_i			
	.0	.2	.4	.6
Factor 1: 1–4	.684	.709	.771	.864
Factor 1: 5–8	.144	.167	.232	.332
Factor 2: 1–4	.144	.167	.232	.332
Factor 2: 5–8	.684	.709	.771	.864
Communality	.486	.531	.648	.850
α	.793	.818	.881	.958
Angle between clusters	66°30'	63°30'	57°	48°30'
Cosine of angle	.399	.446	.545	.663
ρ	.317	.364	.483	.626
ρ corrected	.400	.446	.548	.664

(substantially higher than the value of k). As m_i increases, the correlation between scales formed from the two clusters of indicants increases. When $m_i = 0$, $\rho = .317$; when $m_i = .6$, $\rho = .626$. As m_i increases, the correlation between scales formed from the two clusters of indicants as corrected for attenuation also increases. When $m_i = 0$, corrected $\rho = .400$ (the value of k); when $m_i = .6$, corrected $\rho = .664$.

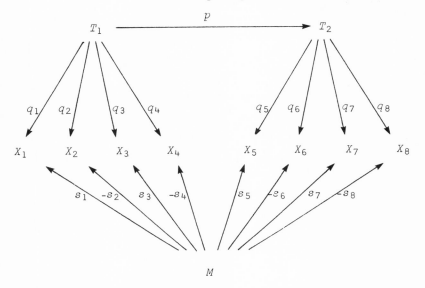

Figure 6.3. Structural measurement model with a detectable method artifact.

In sum, the appropriate inferences about the theoretical structure is seriously distorted by undetectable method artifacts. Moreover, there is no way within the analysis to detect and estimate this distortion. The reason for our inability to detect and estimate this method artifact is that it has the same positive effect on all the indicants.

Fortunately, many of the method artifacts in social science are detectable. For example, a method artifact such as response set would be approximated by Figure 6.2 if all questions were asked positively, but good methodological procedure specifies that one should word half of the questions positively and half of them negatively. Figure 6.3 presents a causal model that includes a detectable method artifact. Again, T_1 causes T_2; T_1 causes indicants 1, 2, 3, and 4; and T_2 causes indicants 5, 6, 7, and 8. In Figure 6.3, however, the method artifact affects indicants 1, 3, 5, and 7 positively but it affects indicants 2, 4, 6, and 8 negatively. If $p = .4$, each $q_i = .7$, and each $s_i = 0$, the correlation matrix associated with Figure 6.3 is presented in Table 6.3. Again, the information relevant to this theoretical structure is identical to that found in the first column of Table 6.2. If $s_i = .1$, the italicized correlations in Table 6.3 will increase in value by .01 and the remaining correlations will decrease by .01. If $s_i = .2$, the encircled correlations will increase by .04 and the remaining correlations will decrease by .04. Because a method artifact systematically alters the correlation matrix of indicants, it will also alter the factor structure of those same

Table 6.3. *Correlation matrix for Figure 6.3*

	1	2	3	4	5	6	7	8
1	—	.49	.49	.49	.196	.196	.196	.196
2		—	.49	.49	.196	.196	.196	.196
3			—	.49	.196	.196	.196	.196
4				—	.196	.196	.196	.196
5					—	.49	.49	.49
6						—	.49	.49
7							—	.49
8								—

indicants. The point is that *a factor analysis will detect the method artifact only if it has differential effects on the indicants that is not confounded with the underlying causal effects*.

If $s_i = .5$, the results of the factor analysis of the model are presented in Table 6.4. The three factors can be interpreted as follows: factor 1 roughly defines the cluster of indicants designed to measure T_1; factor 2 roughly defines the cluster of indicants designed to measure T_2; and factor 3 represents the method artifact. Thus, it is possible to isolate the method artifact and remove it from the analysis if the method artifact has differential effects on the indicants of each concept.

Reliability and validity of indicants and scales

We will now discuss how it is that the observed variance of an indicant or scale can be partitioned into the components specified in Formula 1.15 so that the reliability and validity coefficients described in Formulas 1.16 and 1.17 can be specified, as follows:

$$\sigma_x^2 = \sigma_t^2 + \sigma_s^2 + \sigma_r^2 + 2 \text{ Cov } TS$$

The main difficulty in estimating these components rests on the unobservability of T, S, and Cov TS. Although one cannot observe these components, they can, under certain circumstances, be estimated if the systematic error is detectable. If the systematic error is undetectable (that is, if T is perfectly confounded with S, as shown in Figure 6.2), one cannot estimate these variance components. Thus, the way to make systematic error detectable is to make S unconfounded with T. This can be achieved, for example, with Likert items by reversing the response categories or reversing the direction of the items.

If the systematic error is perfectly unconfounded with T (as it is when half of one's items are stated positively and half negatively for response set, as shown in Figure 6.3), Cov $TS = 0$, and the remaining

Table 6.4. *Factor analysis of correlation matrix in Table 6.3 with each italicized correlation increased by .25 and all other correlations decreased by .25*

	Factor				
	1	2	3	h_{12}	h_{123}
1	.684	.144	.500	.489	.739
2	.684	.144	−.500	.489	.739
3	.684	.144	.500	.489	.739
4	.684	.144	−.500	.489	.739
5	.144	.684	.500	.489	.739
6	.144	.684	−.500	.489	.739
7	.144	.684	.500	.489	.739
8	.144	.684	−.500	.489	.739
Eigenvalue	1.95	1.95	2.00		

problem concerns the estimation of σ_t^2 and σ_s^2. Let us illustrate the estimation of σ_t^2 and σ_s^2 on the analyses performed in Chapters 3 and 4. Since the validity and reliability effect parameters were given, solving for the foregoing values for each indicant is not difficult. For example, in Figure 3.1, σ_s^2 and Cov TS equal zero. As shown in Figure 3.1A, the epistemic correlation of each concept with its respective indicant is .676. The square of this value, .457, is equal to the true variance, namely σ_t^2. Hence, 45.7% of the variance of each item is associated with the factor structure. Because each indicant's relationship to the causal structure is through its respective concept (that is, because $\sigma_s^2 = 0$), the communality is equal to the true variance. The remaining variance, $1 - .457 = .543$, represents random error.

Similarly in Figure 3.1B, the epistemic correlation between each concept and its respective three-indicant scale is .846; $.846^2 = .716$; hence, 71.6% of the variance in each of these three-indicant scales is true variance; the remaining variance, $1 - .716 = .284$, is random error variance. Finally, in Figure 3.1C, the epistemic correlation from each concept to its respective six-indicant scale is .914; $.914^2 = .835$; hence, 83.5% of the variance in each of these six-indicant scales is true variance; the remaining variance, $1 - .835 = .165$, is random error variance. As pointed out earlier, an increase in the number of items results in a decrease in the random error. When there is no systematic error (and no Cov TS), the result is an increase in the true variance.

As implied above, factor loadings and communalities are quite relevant to the estimation of reliable and valid variance. In the present example, we have thus far assumed a known amount of random error, an infinite sample size, and perfect measurement. In actual research situations, however, none of these assumptions is fully met. A more realistic account of estimating the true variance is provided by the Monte Carlo simulation in Chapter 3. Specifically, the first factor loading on the first principal factor extracted from each set of items designed to measure its respective concept may be taken as the estimate of the epistemic correlation. These factor loadings, presented in Table 3.8, hover closely around their theoretical value of .676. The square of these factor loadings estimates the true variance that each item shares with the concept. The remaining variance is random error, because the remaining factors are statistically unimportant and substantively uninterpretable. Hence, the correlation between X_1 and X_t, as estimated by the factor analysis, is .663; hence, 44% of the variance in X_1 is estimated "true" variance for that item. Similar calculations can be performed for all X_i and Y_i in Table 3.10. These values are presented in Figure 3.3.

The value of the epistemic correlation from each concept to its respective six-indicant scale depends upon the particular reliability coefficient that one uses to estimate the internal consistency of the scale. As shown in Chapter 3, there is usually only a small difference among the numerical values of α, θ, and Ω.

The attentive reader will note that we have assumed that all the reliable variance is valid. That is, there is no systematic error variance in the model. This raises the question: What will happen when neither the true variance nor the systematic error variance equal zero? This question was partially answered in Chapters 4 and 5 when, on a per Y-indicant basis, it was assumed that $\sigma_t^2 = .75$, $\sigma_s^2 = .25$, and $\sigma_r^2 = .00$. The epistemic correlation (in Figure 5.2) from Y to each T_i equals .866; the method aritfact effect from M to each Y_i is ±.5, with the sign depending upon the direction of the effect of M on the respective Y_i. Hence, on a per indicant basis, $.866^2 = .75$ of the variance is true, whereas $(\pm.5)^2 = .25$ of the variance is systematic error.

Assessing the true and systematic error variance of a composite scale is more difficult, for one must consider the possible multidimensionality of the scale. Indeed, the scale is made up of not one but two dimensions, as demonstrated in Table 5.4. The Y_{odd} define one factor and the Y_{even} define the other. Moreover, construct validation demonstrates that this bidimensionality of the Y indicants is due to the existence of a single theoretical concept plus a method artifact. Tables 6.5 and 6.6 address the question of the reliability and validity of such multidimensional scales. Table 6.5 presents the reliabilities for various levels of σ_t^2, σ_s^2, and σ_r^2 when the value of σ_t^2 is set at .1, .3, .5, and .7 and the values of σ_s^2 and σ_r^2 are varied by intervals of .1 throughout the remaining possible intervals such that the sum of the three components of the variance equal 1.00.

First, as the systematic error increases while the random error decreases, the reliability of a scale made up of indicants similarly affected by a method artifact increases, approaching unity as the proportion of random error approaches zero. The evidence in support of this assertion concerns the scales made up of odd (or even) items in Table 6.3. As shown in the row labeled $\alpha_{2,2}$ of Table 6.5, if one has two such items where $\sigma_t^2 = .1$, $\sigma_s^2 = .0$, and $\sigma_r^2 = .9$, the alpha reliability coefficient would equal .182; when $\sigma_t^2 = .1$, $\sigma_s^2 = .1$, and $\sigma_r^2 = .8$, the alpha would equal .333, and so on. As one moves from left to right in this row, representing two such items, the alpha coefficient approaches 1.000; this holds true regardless of whether $\sigma_t^2 = .1, .3, .5,$ or .7. Indeed, alpha = .947 when $\sigma_r^2 = .1$ with varying σ_t^2's and σ_s^2's in columns (i), (q), (w), and (aa), respectively. Alpha equals .889 in columns (h), (p), (v), and (z), where $\sigma_r^2 = .2$ with varying σ_t^2's and σ_s^2's. This regularity is mirrored for four, six, and eight items in the remainder of section 1, Table 6.5.

Second, as the systematic error increases while the random error decreases, the α reliability of a scale made up of indicants differentially affected by a method artifact decreases. The evidence in support of this assertion concerns scales made up of positive and negative indicants in Table 6.3. As shown in the row labeled $\alpha_{2,1}$ of Table 6.5, if one had one item positively affected while the other item is negatively affected by the method artifact, and when $\sigma_t^2 = .1$, $\sigma_s^2 = .1$, and $\sigma_r^2 = .8$, the alpha reliability coefficient would equal .000; when $\sigma_t^2 = .1$, $\sigma_s^2 = .2$, and $\sigma_r^2 = .7$, alpha would equal $-.222$, and so on. As one moves from left to right in this row, representing two items oppositely affected by the method artifact, the alpha coefficient decreases in value. This holds true regardless of whether σ_t^2 equals .1, .3, .5, or .7. This regularity is mirrored for four, six, and eight items in the subsequent three rows of section 2, Table 6.5.

We are thus presented with the following paradox: when items are similarly affected by a method artifact, the less random error, the higher the alpha reliability coefficient; when items are differentially affected by a method artifact, the less random error, the lower the alpha reliability coefficient. The way out of this paradox involves the dimensional structure that is assumed to underlie alpha. Alpha assumes, to use Bohrnstedt's (1970:90) words "that the scale is factorially homogeneous (unidimensional)." Although that assumption is plausible (if misleading) when items are similarly affected by a method artifact, it is not plausible when items are differentially affected by the method artifact. The important point is that despite the empirical bidimensionality of items differentially affected by a method artifact,

Table 6.5. *Reliabilities for various levels of* σ_t^2, σ_s^2, *and* σ_r^2

	(a)	(b)	(c)	(d)	(e)	(f)	(g)	(h)	(i)	(j)	(k)	(l)
σ_t^2	.1	.1	.1	.1	.1	.1	.1	.1	.1	.1	.3	.3
σ_s^2	.0	.1	.2	.3	.4	.5	.6	.7	.8	.9	.0	.1
σ_r^2	.9	.8	.7	.6	.5	.4	.3	.2	.1	.0	.7	.6
1 $\alpha_{2,2}$	.182	.333	.462	.571	.667	.750	.824	.889	.947	1	.462	.571
$\alpha_{4,4}$	.308	.500	.632	.727	.800	.857	.903	.941	.973	1	.632	.727
$\alpha_{6,6}$	.400	.600	.720	.800	.857	.900	.933	.960	.982	1	.720	.800
$\alpha_{8,8}$	.471	.667	.774	.842	.889	.923	.949	.970	.986	1	.774	.842
2 $\alpha_{2,1}$	.182	.0	−.222	−.500	−.857	−1.333	−2.000	−3.000	−4.667	−8	.462	.333
$\alpha_{4,2}$	.308	.222	.121	.0	−.148	− .333	− .517	− .889	−1.333	−2	.632	.593
$\alpha_{6,3}$	.400	.343	.277	.200	.109	.0	− .133	− .300	− .514	−.800	.720	.700
$\alpha_{8,4}$	.471	.429	.381	.327	.264	.190	.104	.0	− .127	−.286	.774	.762
3 $\Omega_{2,1}$	.182	.200	.222	.250	.286	.333	.400	.500	.667	1	.462	.500
$\Omega_{4,2}$	.308	.333	.364	.400	.444	.500	.571	.667	.800	1	.632	.667
$\Omega_{6,3}$	.400	.429	.462	.500	.545	.600	.667	.750	.857	1	.720	.750
$\Omega_{8,4}$	.471	.500	.533	.571	.615	.667	.727	.800	.889	1	.774	.800

these items represent a single theoretical dimension, as they all measure a single concept.

Third, as the systematic error increases while the random error decreases, the behavior of the Ω reliability of a scale made up of indicants differentially affected by a method artifact depends upon the number of factors contributing to the coefficient. If one considers only the first extracted factor from a causal structure such as presented in Figure 4.2B, the omega reliability is equal to the alpha reliability as described above. As demonstrated in Chapter 3, $\alpha \leq \Omega$. The difference between these two parameters concerns a weighting of items according to their factor loadings. For this discussion, however, we are not concerned with this difference. Usually, the difference between alpha and omega is trivial. However, as we will show in this discussion, the difference between these two parameters is of crucial importance in the presence of detectable systematic error. In order that this difference be most clearly made, we will for the purposes of this discussion operate as if all items contribute equally to σ_t^2 and σ_s^2. Under these conditions, when systematic error is undetectable or nonexistent, $\alpha = \Omega$.

On the other hand, if one considers both factors from that model as contributing to the systematic variance, then as the systematic error increases, the omega reliability of a scale made up of such indicants will also increase. This is shown in section 3 of Table 6.5, in the row

(m)	(n)	(o)	(p)	(q)	(r)	(s)	(t)	(u)	(v)	(w)	(x)	(y)	(z)	(aa)	(bb)
.3	.3	.3	.3	.3	.3	.5	.5	.5	.5	.5	.5	.7	.7	.7	.7
.2	.3	.4	.5	.6	.7	.0	.1	.2	.3	.4	.5	.0	.1	.2	.3
.5	.4	.3	.2	.1	.0	.5	.4	.3	.2	.1	.0	.3	.2	.1	.0
.667	.750	.824	.889	.947	1	.667	.750	.824	.889	.947	1	.824	.889	.947	1
.800	.857	.903	.941	.973	1	.800	.857	.903	.941	.973	1	.903	.941	.973	1
.857	.900	.933	.960	.982	1	.857	.900	.933	.960	.982	1	.933	.960	.982	1
.889	.923	.949	.970	.986	1	.889	.923	.949	.970	.986	1	.949	.970	.986	1
.182	.0	−.222	−.500	−.857	−1.333	.667	.571	.462	.333	.182	.0	.824	.750	.667	.571
.549	.500	.444	.381	.308	.222	.800	.778	.754	.727	.698	.667	.903	.889	.874	.857
.678	.655	.629	.600	.568	.533	.857	.847	.836	.825	.813	.800	.933	.927	.921	.914
.749	.735	.720	.703	.686	.667	.889	.883	.877	.871	.864	.857	.949	.946	.942	.939
.545	.600	.667	.750	.857	1	.667	.714	.769	.833	.909	1	.824	.875	.933	1
.706	.750	.800	.857	.923	1	.800	.833	.870	.909	.952	1	.903	.933	.966	1
.783	.818	.857	.900	.947	1	.857	.882	.909	.938	.968	1	.933	.955	.977	1
.828	.857	.889	.923	.960	1	.889	.909	.930	.952	.976	1	.949	.966	.982	1

labeled $\Omega_{2,1}$. If one had two such items where $\sigma_t^2 = .1$, $\sigma_s^2 = .0$, and $\sigma_r^2 = .9$, the omega reliability coefficient would equal .182; when $\sigma_t^2 = .1$, $\sigma_s^2 = .1$, and $\sigma_r^2 = .8$, omega would equal .200, and so on. As one moves from left to right in this row, representing two such items, the omega coefficient approaches 1.000; this holds true regardless of whether $\sigma_t^2 = .1$, .3, .5, or .7.

An examination of this table reveals the effect of a detectable method artifact upon the reliability estimates. For example, let us consider six such items. If $\sigma_t^2 = .1$ and $\sigma_s^2 = .0$, then 40% of the variance is systematic. However, if $\sigma_t^2 = .1$ and $\sigma_s^2 = .1$, the reliability of the scale depends upon whether the items are phrased in a similar or opposite way. That is, if the items are phrased in a similar way, $\alpha_{6,6}$ (and $\Omega_{6,6}$) increase dramatically to .600, as demonstrated in Table 6.5, section 1, column b. On the other hand, if three items are phrased positively and the other three items are phrased negatively, $\Omega_{6,3}$ based on two factors increases modestly to .429, as demonstrated in Table 6.5, section 3, column b. The corresponding alpha ($\alpha_{6,3}$), based only on the first factor extracted, decreases in value to .343, as shown in Table 6.5, section 2, column b.

The omega coefficient comes closest to our understanding of what is actually occurring in this situation. With three positive items and three negative ones, the systematic error variance is being "offset." That is, if a respondent is answering the questions in response set

Table 6.6. *Epistemic correlations for various levels of* σ_t^2, σ_s^2, *and* σ_r^2

	(a)	(b)	(c)	(d)	(e)	(f)	(g)	(h)	(i)	(j)	(k)	(l)	(m)
σ_t^2	.1	.1	.1	.1	.1	.1	.1	.1	.1	.1	.3	.3	.3
σ_s^2	.0	.1	.2	.3	.4	.5	.6	.7	.8	.9	.0	.1	.2
σ_r^2	.9	.8	.7	.6	.5	.4	.3	.2	.1	.0	.7	.6	.5
1 $\rho_{y_t y_1}$	.316	.316	.316	.316	.316	.316	.316	.316	.316	.316	.548	.548	.548
2 $\rho_{y_t y_{2,2}}$	.426	.408	.392	.378	.365	.354	.343	.333	.324	.316	.680	.655	.633
$\rho_{y_t y_{4,4}}$	.555	.500	.459	.426	.400	.378	.359	.343	.329	.316	.795	.739	.693
$\rho_{y_t y_{6,6}}$	.632	.548	.490	.447	.414	.387	.365	.346	.330	.316	.849	.775	.718
$\rho_{y_t y_{8,8}}$	.686	.577	.508	.459	.422	.392	.368	.348	.331	.316	.880	.795	.731
3 $\rho_{y_t y_{2,1}}$	.426	.447	.471	.500	.535	.577	.632	.707	.816	1	.680	.707	.739
$\rho_{y_t y_{4,2}}$	.555	.577	.603	.632	.667	.707	.756	.816	.894	1	.795	.817	.841
$\rho_{y_t y_{6,3}}$	.632	.654	.679	.707	.739	.775	.816	.866	.926	1	.849	.866	.885
$\rho_{y_t y_{8,4}}$	.686	.707	.730	.756	.784	.816	.853	.894	.943	1	.880	.895	.910
4 $\rho_{y_s y_1}$	.000	.316	.447	.548	.632	.707	.775	.837	.894	.949	.000	.316	.447
5 $\rho_{y_s y_{2,2}}$	.000	.408	.555	.655	.730	.791	.840	.882	.918	.949	.000	.378	.516
$\rho_{y_s y_{4,4}}$	.000	.500	.649	.739	.800	.845	.880	.907	.930	.949	.000	.426	.566
$\rho_{y_s y_{6,6}}$	.000	.547	.693	.775	.828	.866	.894	.917	.934	.949	.000	.447	.586
$\rho_{y_s y_{8,8}}$	.000	.577	.718	.795	.843	.877	.902	.921	.936	.949	.000	.459	.596

format, such responses will be higher than they should be for the positive (or negative) items and lower than they should be for the remaining items.

Table 6.6 presents the epistemic correlations for various levels of σ_t^2, σ_s^2, and σ_r^2 when the value of σ_t^2 is set at .1, .3, .5, and .7 while the values of σ_s^2 and σ_r^2 are varied by intervals of .1 throughout the remaining possible intervals such that the sum of the three components of the variance equal 1.0.

In Table 6.6, the correlation between any single indicant on a concept and the concept is equal to the square root of the true variance regardless of the proportions of systematic error and random error. In Table 6.6 in the row labeled $\rho_{y_t y_1}$, when $\sigma_t^2 = .1, \rho_{y_t y_1} = .316$ regardless of σ_s^2 and σ_r^2; when $\sigma_t^2 = .3$, $\rho_{y_t y_1} = .548$ regardless of σ_s^2 and σ_r^2, and so on.

Second, as the systematic error increases while the random error decreases, the correlation between a scale made up of indicants similarly affected by a method artifact and the concept decreases approaching the square root of the true variance as the random error variance approaches zero. This assertion is supported in Table 6.6 in the rows labeled $\rho_{y_t y_{n,n}}$. In the row labeled $\rho_{y_t y_{2,2}}$, the epistemic correlation between the concept and a scale made up of two indicants

(n)	(o)	(p)	(q)	(r)	(s)	(t)	(u)	(v)	(w)	(x)	(y)	(z)	(aa)	(bb)
.3	.3	.3	.3	.3	.5	.5	.5	.5	.5	.5	.7	.7	.7	.7
.3	.4	.5	.6	.7	.0	.1	.2	.3	.4	.5	.0	.1	.2	.3
.4	.3	.2	.1	.0	.5	.4	.3	.2	.1	.0	.3	.2	.1	.0
.548	.548	.548	.548	.548	.707	.707	.707	.707	.707	.707	.837	.837	.837	.837
.613	.594	.578	.562	.548	.816	.791	.767	.745	.725	.707	.907	.882	.858	.837
.655	.622	.594	.569	.548	.894	.845	.803	.769	.735	.707	.950	.907	.870	.837
.671	.633	.600	.572	.548	.926	.866	.816	.775	.739	.707	.966	.917	.874	.837
.680	.638	.603	.574	.548	.943	.877	.823	.778	.740	.707	.974	.921	.876	.837
.775	.817	.866	.923	1	.816	.845	.877	.913	.953	1	.907	.935	.966	1
.866	.895	.926	.961	1	.894	.913	.932	.953	.976	1	.950	.966	.983	1
.905	.926	.949	.974	1	.926	.939	.953	.968	.983	1	.966	.977	.988	1
.927	.943	.961	.980	1	.943	.953	.964	.976	.988	1	.974	.983	.991	1
.548	.632	.707	.775	.837	.000	.316	.447	.548	.632	.707	.000	.316	.447	.548
.612	.686	.745	.795	.837	.000	.354	.485	.577	.649	.707	.000	.333	.459	.548
.655	.718	.767	.805	.837	.000	.378	.508	.594	.658	.707	.000	.343	.465	.548
.671	.730	.775	.809	.837	.000	.387	.516	.600	.661	.707	.000	.346	.467	.548
.679	.736	.778	.811	.837	.000	.392	.521	.603	.662	.707	.000	.348	.468	.548

that are similarly affected by the method artifact is .426, the square root of the alpha reliability (that is, $\sqrt{.182} = .426$). However, as the systematic error variance increases while the random error decreases (that is, as you move from left to right in this row of Table 6.6), the epistemic correlation between the concept and the scale decreases, approaching $\sqrt{\sigma_t^2}$.

Third, as the systematic error increases while the random error decreases, the correlation between a scale made up of indicants differentially affected by a method artifact and the concept increases approaching unity as the random error variance approaches zero. This assertion is supported in Table 6.6, in the rows labeled $\rho_{y_t y_{o,m/2}}$. In the row labeled $\rho_{y_t y_{2,1}}$, the epistemic correlation between the concept and a scale made up of two indicants that are differentially affected by the method artifact is .426. However, as the systematic error variance increases while the random error decreases, the epistemic correlation between the concept and the scale increases, approaching unity.

One is thus presented with a more perplexing paradox: *When items are similarly affected by a method artifact, the less random error, the higher the alpha reliability but the lower the epistemic correlation; on the other hand, when items are differentially affected by a method artifact, the less the random error, the lower the alpha reliability but the higher the epistemic correlation.*

The way out of this paradox has to do with the nature of epistemic correlations. When a scale correlates with something other than the concept (that is, with a method artifact), that correlation places a limit on the strength of the epistemic correlation. Indeed, as the systematic error variance increases, the correlation of the $Y_{n,n}$ scale with the concept decreases. On the other hand, when the systematic error variance is offsetting, as it is in the $Y_{n,n/2}$ scale, there is no correlation of that scale with the method artifact; hence, when the random error approaches zero, the epistemic correlation approaches unity. This leads to our next conclusion.

Fourth, the correlation between any single indicant of a concept and the method artifact is equal to the square root of the systematic error variance regardless of the true and random error variance. In Table 6.6 in the row labeled $\rho_{y_s y_1}$, when $\sigma_s^2 = .1, \rho_{y_s y_1} = .316$ regardless of σ_t^2 and σ_r^2; when $\sigma_s^2 = .2$, $\rho_{y_s y_1} = .447$ regardless of σ_t^2 and σ_r^2; and so on.

Fifth, as systematic error increases while the random error decreases, the correlation between a scale made up of indicants similarly affected by a method artifact and the method artifact increases approaching the square root of the systematic error variance as the random error variance approaches zero. This assertion is supported in Table 6.6 in the rows labeled $\rho_{y_s y_{n,n}}$. In the row labeled $\rho_{y_s y_{2,2}}$, the correlation between the method artifact and a scale made up of two indicants that are similarly affected by the method artifact is zero when there is no systematic error variance. However, as the systematic error variance increases, this correlation approaches $\sqrt{\sigma_s^2}$.

Finally, a scale made up of across-method artifact indicants is uncorrelated with the method artifact regardless of the true, systematic error, or random error variances. This assertion is not presented in Table 6.6 because all appropriate entries into the table would have values of .000.

The problem associated with detectable method artifacts concerns the estimation of the reliability and validity of scales. As shown in Table 6.5, one can estimate the valid variance and the reliable variance of any specific indicant. However, as shown in section 2 of Table 6.5, the greater the systematic error variance, the lower the α reliability coefficient. The reason for this, of course, is the lack of unidimensionality of the indicants. But, as we have seen, this empirical bidimensionality is not indicative of a theoretical bidimensionality; instead, it is indicative of a theoretical unidimensionality. However, since the empirical bidimensionality has the effect of reducing (and possibly making negative) the alpha, a unidimensional assessment of reliability, the question then becomes: How can the correlation between the concepts be estimated when the correction for attenuation along with the alpha reliability becomes substantively meaningless.

For the answer to this question, we note that $\Omega_{n,n/2}$ coefficient, in Table 6.5, section 3, is the square of the epistemic correlation in Table 6.6, section 3. Hence, if we have worked through a measurement problem in such a fashion that we decide that there is a single underlying concept and a method artifact in a two-factor structure, we can estimate the epistemic correlation between the scale made up by a sum of those items and the concept. This value is, quite simply, the square root of the omega coefficient based upon the two-factor structure. Moreover, it is important to recall that the cosine of the angle intersecting the valid factors, as presented in Table 6.1 and Figure 6.1, was equal to e, the correlation between the concepts. As such, the cosine of the angle between the clusters of items represented in factors 1 and 2 of Table 6.4 will equal the correlation between the concepts. In this case, the method artifact has been detected in factor 3, and has been removed (or, more accurately, set aside for the purposes of estimating the correlation between the concepts). Hence, we can solve for p in Figure 6.3 even though the italicized correlations in Table 6.3 are increased by .25 and the remaining correlations are decreased by .25.

The Appendix to this chapter provides the derivation of the functions that allow us to generalize the results of Tables 6.5 and 6.6 to any number of items with any value for σ_t^2 and σ_s^2. Consistent with our discussion, the sum of σ_t^2 and σ_s^2 cannot exceed unity.

This analysis has important implications. Proper inference of the epistemic correlation between an item and its corresponding concept depends upon the detection and removal of systematic error variance. The detection of systematic error variance depends upon making it unconfounded with the concept. When this occurs, the method artifact will have differential effects on different indicants designed to measure the concept. In this situation, the best measurement strategy appears to be choosing items that have equal and opposite distortion from the method artifact. Such a strategy will increase one's ability to properly infer the correlation between the concepts (which is, after all, our major substantive purpose). At the same time, such a measurement strategy will decrease the observed reliability of the scale and its factor structure will be contrary to the usual pattern of factor loadings required of such analysis. Indeed, the analysis gives credibility to the assertion by Curtis and Jackson (1962:199) that "two equally valid indicators of the same concept may . . . be strongly related to one another, or they may be totally unrelated [or negatively related]."

Self-esteem

Using the Appendix to this chapter, we can estimate the relevant parameters for the 10-item self-esteem scale. That is, we can estimate the correlation between this scale, the underlying concept of self-esteem, and the method artifact, response set. In addition, we can estimate the alpha and omega values. As shown in Table 4.5, $\sigma_t^2 = .341$ while $\sigma_s^2 = .067$. The alpha, as derived in the Appendix to this chapter, is applied to the 10-item self-esteem scale as follows:

$$\alpha_{10,5} = \frac{10}{9}\left\{1 - \frac{10}{10 + 2[(20)(.408) + (20)(.274)]}\right\} = .813$$

Applying Formula 3.5 to the correlations in Table 4.4, we get

$$\alpha_{10,5} = \frac{10}{9}\left[1 - \frac{10}{10 + (2)(14.487)}\right] = .826$$

Within the limits of rounding error and the approximations built into each of these formulas, these values equal one another.

The omega, as derived in the Appendix to this chapter, is applied to the 10-item self-esteem scale as follows:

$$\Omega_{10,5} = 1 - \frac{(10)(.592)}{10 + (2)[(20)(.408) + (20)(.274)]} = .841$$

Applying Formula 3.10 to the correlations in Table 4.4, we get

$$\Omega_{10,5} = 1 - \frac{10 - .408}{10 + (2)(14.487)} = .848$$

Within the limits of rounding error and the approximations built into each of these formulas, these values equal one another.

The epistemic correlation of the self-esteem scale with the concept of self-esteem is calculated using the formula derived in the appendix as follows:

$$\rho_{y_t y_{10,5}} = \frac{10\sqrt{.341}}{\sqrt{10 + (2)[(20)(.408) + (20)(.274)]}} = .954$$

We cannot, of course, compare this value to the "true" correlation between the self-esteem scale and concept. The reason for our inability to do this is because the concept of self-esteem, like all concepts, is by definition not empirical.

The correlation between the self-esteem scale and the method artifact is zero, because there is an equal number of equally weighted positive and negative items in the scale.

Given this information, we can solve for the parameters of Formula 1.15 as follows:

$$\sigma_x^2 = \sigma_t^2 + \sigma_s^2 + \sigma_r^2 + 2 \text{ Cov } TS$$

where $\sigma_t^2 = \rho_{y_t y_{\text{scale}}}^2$ $\qquad\qquad\qquad\qquad = .910$

$\qquad\sigma_s^2 = \rho\ _{y_s y_{\text{scale}}}^2$ $\qquad\qquad\qquad\qquad = .000$

$\qquad\sigma_r^2 = 1 - \Omega$ $\qquad\qquad\qquad\qquad = .159$

$2\text{ Cov } TS = 1 - (\sigma_t^2 + \sigma_s^2 + \sigma_r^2)$

$\qquad\qquad = \Omega - \rho_t^2 - \rho_s^2 = .841 - .910 = -.069$

Substituting this information into the reliability and validity Formulas 1.14 and 1.15, we get

$$\text{Reliability} = \frac{\sigma_x^2 - \sigma_r^2}{\sigma_x^2} = \frac{1 - .159}{1} = .841 = \Omega$$

$$\text{Validity} = \sigma_t^2 / \sigma_x^2 = .910/1 = .910$$

FIRO-B

Similarly, we can estimate the relevant parameters for the 15-item control scale. As shown in Table 5.13, the estimated true variance is .346 and the estimated systematic error variance is .255 for the total sample. As shown in Table 5.14, for the low-variance subjects, $\sigma_t^2 = .420$ and there is no σ_s^2; for the high-variance subjects $\sigma_t^2 = .323$ and $\sigma_s^2 = .431$. These values, together with the corresponding parameters and scale properties, are presented in Table 6.7. An examination of Table 6.7 reveals that the low-variance group had a higher validity but a lower reliability than did the high-variance group. This analysis is consistent with the assertions that we made about these groups in Chapter 5. Moreover, in spite of a substantial amount of systematic variance in each item, there was only a small amount of systematic error in the scale. This systematic error was not dominant in the scale because nine of the items were phrased positively and six were phrased negatively. In this circumstances, the systematic error was almost, but not quite, offset in the high-variance group; there was no systematic error in the low-variance group.

We have already warned against the hazards of interpreting a scale that is contaminated with undetectable method artifact variance. Hence, while the inclusion and affection scales have attractive factor analytic properties, the confidence that a researcher would have in assuming that they are good approximations of their respective concepts is tempered by the reasoned judgment that they are contaminated by a substantial amount of undetectable method artifact.

Let us speculate on the effect of this undetectable method artifact upon the dimensions of affection as seen in Figure 5.6. Suppose, for example, that we have the same proportions of true and systematic error variance in the affection measures as we observed in the control measures. (We see this assumption about our measures as being reasonable.) Hence, $.346/.601 = .576$ of the nonrandom variance is associated with the respective concept, whereas $.255/.601 = .424$ of the

Table 6.7. *Analysis for FIRO-B control dimension*

Factors in analysis	Total	Low variance	High variance
	2	1	2
Parameters			
α	.885	.916	.871
Ω	.931	.916	.954
$\rho_{u_t u}$scale	.951	.957	.952
$\rho_{u_s u}$scale	.163	.000	.222
Item properties			
σ_t^2	.346	.420	.323
σ_x^2	.255	.000	.431
Scale properties			
σ_t^2	.904	.916	.906
σ_x^2	.027	.000	.049
σ_r^2	.069	.084	.046
2 Cov TS	.000	.000	$-.001$
Reliability	.931	.916	.954
Validity	.904	.916	.906

nonrandom variance is due to response set. Using these proportions, the estimated model in Figure 5.6 must be reformulated to include response set. This reformulated model is presented in Figure 6.4. To approximate the parameters of this model, the following formulas were used:

$$f_j = \sqrt{(.576)f_i^2}$$
$$f_k = \sqrt{(.424)f_i^2}$$

where f_i = factor loading for the ith item from Table 5.11
        f_j = effect of the respective concept on the measure
        f_k = effect of response set on the measure
        .576 = proportion of nonrandom variance that is true variance
        .424 = proportion of nonrandom variance that is systematic error variance

The correlation between Close and Personal and Cool and Distant in Figure 6.4 is the difference between the correlation between the two scales minus the correlation that occurs due to the effect of response set corrected for attenuation.

A comparison of Figures 5.6 and 6.4 reveals some striking differences. First, the effects of the respective concepts upon their measures are noticeably weaker in Figure 6.4 than in Figure 5.6. In substantive terms, we are reporting weaker epistemic correlations in the model that acknowledged response set. Second, the effects of response set on the measures are unacknowledged in Figure 5.6; these effects are

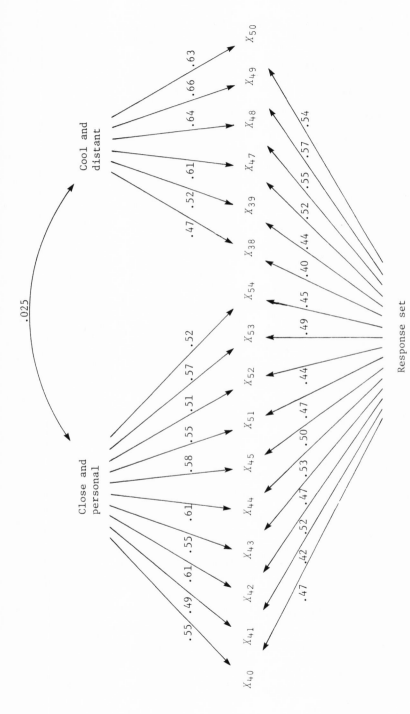

Figure 6.4. Reestimated relationship between Close and Personal and Cool and Distant.

of substantial size in Figure 6.4. Third, the reported correlation between the two concepts is a substantial .451 in Figure 5.6; in Figure 6.4, it vanishes to a trivial .025. In substantive terms, if we do not acknowledge response set, we report a substantial correlation between the two dimensions of affection; if we do acknowledge response set, we report a trivial correlation between these dimensions.

The models in both Figure 5.6 and 6.4 are speculative. Each depends for its veracity upon the proper characterization of the proportions of true and systematic error variance. The vexing question is: Are the affection measures beset with response set or not? We cannot, within the context of our data, answer this question. Response set, if it is affecting our measures, is undetectable. However, as we have shown, an undetectable method artifact has even more serious substantive ramifications than a detectable one does.

Conclusion

It is perhaps fitting to conclude this final chapter with a brief restatement of the book's principal arguments together with their implications for social science measurement. Measurement can be most usefully conceived of, we argued, as the process of linking abstract concepts to empirical indicants. Abstract concepts, such as prestige, social trust, and political participation, are the most important terms used in social theory. Their principal purpose is to identify, describe, and explain socially, psychologically, economically, and politically relevant beliefs and behaviors. But although abstract concepts play an indispensable role in the social sciences, they have the crucial limitation of not being directly observable nor measurable. This means that the systematic testing and evaluation of theories in the social sciences requires the use of empirical indicants, designed to represent given abstract concepts. In other words, empirical indicants are intended to approximate empirically specific theoretical concepts.

Thus, the social sciences require the use of both abstract concepts and empirical indicants. Indeed, they are both indispensable, for as Greer (1969:160) has aptly observed, "Our creations in the world of possibility must be fitted in the world of probability; in Kant's epigram, 'Concepts without percepts are empty.' It is also the process of relating our observation to theory; to finish the epigram, 'Percepts without concepts are blind.'" And it is measurement that provides the connecting link between these formulations.

But how does one know if a particular set of empirical indicants does provide an adequate empirical approximation of a given theoretical concept? In other words, according to what criteria are empirical measures evaluated? The two basic criteria of "good" measurements are that they be reliable and valid. Reliability implies both repeatability and consistency; it can be assessed within the context of classical test theory. For example, if an identical measure of political participation is used to determine the level of political activity among a group of individuals, the measure is considered reliable if the same or highly similar ratings are obtained on two or more separate occasions. On the other hand, if divergent results are obtained, it is concluded that the measure is unreliable – assuming that there has been no real change in political participation between the test intervals. Similar reasoning is applicable when assessing the consistency of different measures of the same concept. Thus, if two or more indicants of the same theoretical concept provide roughly similar ratings, the indicants are considered reliable. Conversely, if multiple indicants provide very different ratings, indicants are considered unreliable.

As is clear from this discussion, the focus of attention in reliability assessment is random error. Specifically, the greater the random error, the lower the reliability; the lower the random error, the higher the reliability. If the correlations among multiple indicants of the same theoretical concept are perfect (1.00), reliability will equal 1.00, indicating that there is no random error in the measurement process. Precise estimations of the reliability of empirical measurements can be obtained through the use of factor analysis models, as described earlier in this book.

Nevertheless, perfect reliability does not guarantee that the empirical indicants are actually measuring the theoretical concept of interest. That is, a reliable measure is not necessarily a valid one. Indeed, it is possible that a perfectly reliable measure can be totally invalid if the indicants are completely affected by systematic error. This systematic error can be due to other theoretical concepts, to method artifacts, or to a combination of the two. Unfortunately, assessing validity is thus far more difficult than estimating reliability, precisely because of the possible presence of systematic error. Indeed, the difference between the estimated values of validity and reliability is a function of the amount of systematic error in the measurement process. Of course, if there is no systematic error in the measurement process, validity will equal reliability and both will be reduced by the amount of random error. However, both systematic and random error is probably contained in the measurement of most theoretical concepts used in the social sciences.

By necessity, assessing systematic error and hence, indirectly, validity is more a theoretical problem than a purely statistical one. Indeed, there is no mechanical procedure by which systematic error can be estimated. The strategy developed here for assessing validity focuses on the theoretical implications of empirical measurements.

Thus, it is argued that validity presumes that an empirical measure of a given theoretical concept will behave toward theoretically relevant external variables in a manner that is consistent with theoretical expectations. It is also the case that one's confidence in the validity of any empirical measurements is increased substantially when the measure has successfully met multiple tests of its construct validation.

Finally, we have argued that while reliability assessment and validity assessment are separate concerns, they must be considered simultaneously to ensure adequate measurement of the theoretical concepts. For empirical measures must possess the statistical characteristics relating to reliability and the theoretical content implied by validity to approximate the complex abstract concepts used in the social sciences.

Appendix: Functions for tables 6.5 and 6.6*

1    $$\alpha_{n,m} = \frac{n}{n-1}\left(1 - \frac{n}{n+2b}\right)$$

where n = number of indicants
b = sum of the nonredundant off-diagonal correlations
m = number of positive indicants
$n - m$ = number of negative indicants
$\sigma_t^2 + \sigma_s^2$ = correlation between each pair of similar indicants
$\sigma_t^2 - \sigma_s^2$ = correlation between each pair of opposite indicants

Under these conditions,

$$b = \left[\frac{m(m-1)}{2} + \frac{(n-m)(n-m-1)}{2}\right](\sigma_t^2 + \sigma_s^2) +$$
$$(m)(n-m)(\sigma_t^2 - \sigma_s^2)$$

When $n = m$ or when $m = 0$, b reduces to

$$b = \frac{n(n-1)}{2}(\sigma_t^2 + \sigma_s^2)$$

2    $$\Omega_{n,m} = 1 - \frac{n - \Sigma h^2}{n + 2b}$$

where Σh^2 = sum of the communalities of the n indicants = $n(\sigma_t^2 + \sigma_s^2)$. Thus,

* The authors appreciate the assistance of L. David Sabbagh in the derivation of these functions.

$$\Omega_{n,m} = 1 - \frac{n(1 - \sigma_t^2 - \sigma_s^2)}{n + 2b}$$

3    $\rho_{y_t y_{n,m}} = e/\sqrt{n + 2b}$

where $e = n\sqrt{\sigma_t^2}$

4    $\rho_{y_s y_{n,m}} = e/\sqrt{n + 2b}$

where $\left| m - (n - m) \right|$ = absolute difference between m and

$$n - m$$
$$e = \left| m - (n - m) \right| \sqrt{\sigma_s^2}$$

Appendix: Multiple indicators

JOHN P. McIVER, EDWARD G. CARMINES, AND RICHARD A. ZELLER

Two principal approaches have been used to select and identify indicants of theoretical concepts. Empirical variables are chosen on the basis of theoretical appropriateness or empirical consistency (as determined through a factor analysis of a set of indicants). Both criteria are important. Yet, there is disagreement over the appropriate application of these criteria. Theory may correctly specify the dependence of a set of variables on a common trait, but traditional tests of validity may fail if error systematically biases the relationships between sets of variables. Alternatively, empirical evidence may support an incorrect theory due to various types of random and nonrandom error. Scale construction requires evaluation of the hypothesis that some of the systematic variance in a set of items is contributed by other concepts or methods rather than the hypothesized concept. This alternative hypothesis may take many forms. Response set may affect each of a set of variables. Two subsets of variables may be spuriously related because of the effects of either another method or another concept. Independent sets of variables may not be independent; indicants of one concept may share a common source of variance with indicants of another concept.

Identification of systematic error, as we have seen, requires some a priori knowledge of possible sources of such biases. Without such information, the search for such errors can be tedious for simple models and boundless for complex models. We do not have the capabilities to engage in a general search for nonrandom error. Only specific types can be identified. Indeed, the major focus of this volume has been to guide the search for systematic error. The purpose of this work has been to sensitize the researcher to the types of systematic error that are likely to occur in data and to propose ways of eliminating the distortions in the inference process that occur because of systematic error. Our approach is not the only approach designed to discover and

The empirical data presented in this appendix were provided by the Workshop in Political Theory and Policy Analysis at Indiana University. Data collection was funded by NSF Grant GI-43949. The opinions expressed herein are those of the authors and do not necessarily reflect the views of the funding agency.

describe such errors. We now turn to a discussion of two alternative strategies for the discovery and description of systematic errors.

Two methods have been proposed to formalize the identification of specific types of systematic error. The first, a path-analytic model with multiple indicators (Costner, 1969), provides two criteria for evaluating the consistency of path estimates. These criteria permit evaluation of four specific types of systematic biases in overidentified models. Problems do arise, however, in application of these rules to sample data. Furthermore, efficient estimation of path coefficients is not possible.

The second method is more general in its ability to deal with the various types of systematic errors and permits efficient parameter estimation. A model for the analysis of covariance structures (Jöreskog, 1967, 1969, 1970, 1971) may be used to identify errors and test for their statistical significance. Below, we will analyze six survey items using both Costner's path-analytic and Jöreskog's confirmatory factor-analytic methods. Inferences drawn from these techniques will be compared with conclusions based on the methods discussed in the first six chapters.

An empirical example

During the summer of 1977, the staff of the workshop in Political Theory and Policy Analysis at Indiana University, in conjunction with researchers from the Center for Urban and Regional Studies at the University of North Carolina, undertook a large-scale study to evaluate police services in metropolitan areas. Data were collected on many aspects of policing in 60 neighborhoods in the St. Louis, Rochester, and Tampa–St. Petersburg metropolitan areas. In the course of this research, the citizen's perspective on the quality of police services received was obtained through the use of a structured interview schedule. An attitude victimization survey was completed by three local survey research firms operating as subcontractees. Over 11,000 telephone interviews, approximately 200 per neighborhood, were completed.

Six questions were designed to elicit evaluations of the quality of police services. These items are:

1   How would you rate the overall quality of police services in your neighborhood? Remember, we mean the two or three blocks right around your home. Are they outstanding, good, adequate, inadequate, or very poor?

2   Do you think that your police department tries to provide the kind of services that people in your neighborhood want? (Responses: Yes/No)

Table A.1. *Interitem correlation matrix*

	X_1	X_2	X_3	X_4	X_5	X_6	X_7	X_8	X_9
X_1 Police service	—	.498	.411	.334	.284	.296	−.240	−.231	−.205
X_2 Responsiveness		—	.349	.289	.259	.274	−.189	−.192	−.181
X_3 Response time			—	.305	.270	.286	−.171	−.165	−.140
X_4 Honesty				—	.521	.476	−.131	−.109	−.150
X_5 Courtesy					—	.438	−.106	−.089	−.105
X_6 Equality of treatment						—	−.147	−.129	−.134
X_7 Probability of burglary							—	.580	.474
X_8 Probability of vandalism								—	.420
X_9 Probability of robbery									—

3 When the police are called to your neighborhood, in your opinion, do they arrive very rapidly, quickly enough, slowly, or very slowly? (Also coded: Not at all)

4 Policemen in your neighborhood are basically honest. Do you agree or disagree? Do you feel strongly about this?

5 The police in your neighborhood are generally courteous. Do you agree or disagree? Do you feel strongly about this?

6 The police in your neighborhood treat all citizens equally according to the law. Do you agree or disagree? Do you feel strongly about this?

Each of these questions was asked at the beginning of the telephone interview, which lasted 25 to 50 minutes depending on the respondent's victimization history. At the end of the interview, the first question was repeated as a test for attitude consistency over the course of the interview.

Using data from a similar 1972 study, McIver and Ostrom (1976) constructed a unidimensional evaluation scale composed of eight items on citizen experiences with the police ($\alpha = .85$). On the basis of this prior research, we hypothesized a unidimensional evaluation scale of the six items included in the current study. Preliminary data analysis, however, suggested a second possibility—evaluation of police as measured by the six foregoing survey questions is multidimensional. We will now explore the basis of this possibility. Table A.1 presents the interitem correlation matrix of these six items, together with three victimization items that will be used later in the analysis. Using Formula 3.5, the alpha for this six item set equals .766. Although this reliability coefficient is lower than that observed by McIver and Ostrom (1976), both meet the usual standards by which attitude measures are evaluated. Moreover, a visual examination of the matrix reveals that the six items are positively and significantly intercorrelated.

However, further visual examination of this matrix reveals that X_1, X_2, and X_3 form one cluster of items and X_4, X_5, and X_6 form another. Specifically, whereas the intercorrelations among X_1, X_2, and X_3 av-

Table A.2. *Factor analysis of measures of the perceived quality of police services*

	Extracted		Rotated		
	I	II	I'	II'	h^2
X_1	.653	.398	.737	.207	.585
X_2	.568	.317	.619	.200	.423
X_3	.524	.169	.481	.268	.304
X_4	.686	−.302	.246	.708	.562
X_5	.622	−.307	.199	.664	.481
X_6	.599	−.219	.248	.587	.406

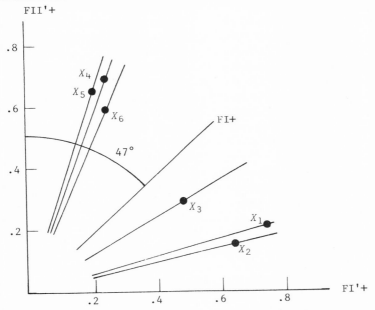

Figure A.1. Graphic plot of factor loadings from Table A.2.

erage .419 and the intercorrelations among X_4, X_5, and X_6 average .478, the intercorrelations between these two sets of items average only .288. This result is mirrored in the common factor analysis of these items (using SMCs in the main diagonal) as presented in Table A.2. This factor structure, presented in both the extracted form and rotated to a varimax solution, bears a striking resemblance to the factor structure in Table 4.3. As noted above, the appropriate interpretation for this factor structure could be described graphically in Figure 4.2 A or B. Figure A.1 presents a graphic plot of the factor loadings. Factors II' and I', as rotated, are presented on the vertical and horizontal axes, respectively. The Varimax rotation resulted in a clockwise rotation of 47°. This figure bears a strong resemblance to Figure 4.3.

Table A.3. *Correlation of scales with crime probabilities*

		Crime Fighting	Police Style	p^a
X_7	Probability of burglary	$-.255$	$-.158$	.01
X_8	Probability of vandalism	$-.250$	$-.135$	.01
X_9	Probability of robbery	$-.243$	$-.161$	.01

$^a p$ describes the probability that these two correlations equal one another.

Moreover, this analysis has placed the data analyst in the same interpretational difficulty as was faced in Tables 5.3 and 5.4. The question is: How many substantive dimensions underlie the items, one or two? There is a reasonable substantive interpretation for either answer to this question. On the one hand, the scale was originally conceived of as unidimensional. From this perspective, the higher the scale score, the higher the respondent perceives the quality of police services received to be. On the other hand, an examination of the questionnaire items leads to a possible interpretation of this factor structure as rotated to the Varimax solution. Factor I' evaluates the performance of police in crime-related duties; factor II' evaluates the interaction style of the police. For convenience, we will label these the "Crime Fighting" and the "Police Style" factors.

As described in Chapter 5, the procedure for handling such an interpretational difficulty lies in an examination of the relationship between scales generated on the basis of this factor analysis and external variables. A first approximation to this activity involves a scale constructed by summing items X_1, X_2, and X_3 into a "Crime Fighting" scale and summing X_4, X_5, and X_6 into a "Police Style" scale. The relevant external variables for this analysis, as presented in Table A.1, are the probabilities of the various crimes: burglary, vandalism, and robbery (X_7, X_8, and X_9, respectively).

Table A.3 presents the intercorrelations of these three measures with the Crime Fighting and Police Style scales computed form Table A.1 using Formula 3.1. An examination of Table A.3 reveals that the probability of these crimes varies inversely with both the Crime Fighting and the Police Style scales. More important for our purposes, however, is the fact that the Crime Fighting scale correlates more strongly with each of these probabilities than does the Police Style scale. Hence, we have met the criteria for establishing the substantive differentiation of two dimensions from what was originally considered to be a single concept.

Now that we have established that Crime Fighting and Police Style are important dimensions separate and distinguishable from one another, we are faced with the task of solving for the measurement model that accounts for the relationship between these two concepts. To do this, we must establish the measurement properties of each indicant as a measure of its respective concept and we must estimate the correlation between the two concepts. We now turn to these tasks.

Epistemic correlations
Our first estimation task concerns the degree to which each indicant is caused by its respective concept. Within this process, we must be on the lookout for indicants whose empirical properties lead us to suspect that they are less than optimal measures of their respective concepts. This process involves a variety of bits of information which, taken together, constitute compelling evidence for the strength of some indicants and the weakness of others.

One indication of the strength of the indicant involves its communality with other indicants within a factor analysis. As noted in Figure 6.1 and Table 6.1, when an indicant is not distorted by systematic error, the communality is the square of the epistemic correlation. Hence, one indication of a weak indicant is a low communality. An examination of the communalities in Table A.2 reveals that X_1 and X_4, with communalities of .585 and .562, respectively, are the strongest indicants; X_3, with a communality of .304, is the weakest indicant of the six. From this evidence, we are alerted to the fact that the measurement properties of X_3 are suspect.

A second indication of the degree to which an indicant reflects its respective concept concerns the clustering of the set of indicants which measure that concept. An examination of Figure A.1 reveals a well-defined cluster of indicants X_4, X_5, and X_6. These indicants occur within a close proximity of one another. Moreover, the angles intersecting them with the origin are small, with the angle between X_5 and X_6 being only 6°30'. On the other hand, X_1, X_2, and X_3 do not have such a well-defined cluster. While items X_1 and X_2 are in relatively close proximity to one another, X_3 is some distance away. Moreover, while the angle between X_1 and X_2 is a mere 2°, the angles between these two variables and X_3 are 14° and 16°, respectively. This constitutes additional evidence which suggests that X_3 has suboptimal measurement properties. In addition, however, this points to the specific form of the measurement ambiguity associated with X_3. Specifically, X_3 has suboptimal properties because it is defined statistically on both the Crime Fighting and the Police Style dimensions. An examination of the content is consistent with this interpretation. Although responsiveness to citizen demands for service is primarily a matter of Crime Fighting, it is apparent that, to some slight degree, respondents also saw this characteristic as a matter of police style.

Now that we have established the measurement characteristics of the indicants, we turn to the task of estimating the correlation between the inferred concepts.

Estimate of the correlation between concepts

In order to estimate the correlation between the concepts of Crime Fighting and Police Style, recall that the angle of intersection between the clusters is equal to the correlation between the two concepts, as shown in Table 6.1 and Figure 6.1. The estimate that we derive from this correlation depends upon whether we include X_3 in the analysis. If we include X_3, then the angle between the Crime Fighting cluster (X_1, X_2, and X_3) and the Police Style cluster (X_4, X_5, and X_6) is 51°10'. The cosine of this angle is .628; hence, when X_3 is included as a measure of Crime Fighting, .628 is the estimated correlation between the concepts of Crime Fighting and Police Style.

On the other hand, because we have two reasons to suspect the measurement properties of X_3 as a measure of Crime Fighting, we may wish to exclude it from consideration. In this case, the angle between the Crime Fighting cluster (X_1 and X_2) and the Police Style cluster (X_4, X_5, and X_6) is 56°10'. The cosine of this angle is .557. Thus, when X_3 is excluded from consideration, the estimated correlation between Crime Fighting and Police Style is .557.

An important point emerges from this discussion: namely, the measurement decisions that a researcher makes will affect the inferences that are ultimately drawn from the research. Since the evidence presented above suggests that X_3 is affected by both concepts and since we are attempting to assess the correlation between those two concepts, the .557 estimate of the correlation between the concepts is to be preferred.

Using Formula 3.1 and Table A.1, the correlation between these two scales is estimated as follows:

$$r_{1-2,4-6} = \frac{e}{\sqrt{a + 2b} \sqrt{c + 2d}} = \frac{1.736}{\sqrt{2.996} \sqrt{5.870}} = .414$$

$$r_{1-3,4-6} = \frac{2.597}{\sqrt{5.516} \sqrt{5.870}} = .456$$

These correlations can be corrected for attenuation using Formula 3.11 as follows:

$$r_{1-2,4-6 \text{ cor}} = \frac{r}{\sqrt{\Omega_{1\times2}} \sqrt{\Omega_{4\times6}}} = \frac{.414}{\sqrt{.669} \sqrt{.736}} = .590$$

$$r_{1-3,4-6 \text{ cor}} = \frac{.456}{\sqrt{.694} \sqrt{.736}} = .638$$

Thus, with some tolerance for rounding error and approximations, the correlation between the appropriate unit-weighted scales is equal to the angle between the clusters. Hence, proper use of widely available tools (graph paper, a protractor, a table of cosines, and a desk calculator) and the material in this book will allow a researcher to make evidence-based inferences about the measurement properties of sets of indicants and about the correlations among the concepts that underlie those indicants.

A similar approach can be used to estimate the correlations between Probability of Victimization and each of these concepts. The correlation between Crime Fighting and the Probability of Victimization can be estimated by obtaining a common factor analysis of X_1 through X_9 in Table A.1, calculating the angle between the two clusters of items, and solving for the cosine of that angle. Such a procedure yields an angle of 113°30'; the cosine of this angle is .399. Moreover, the correlation between these two scales, using Formula 3.1, is . −.299. This correlation, corrected for attenuation, is equal to −.414. Omitting X_3 from the analysis, the angle separating the clusters is 113°; the cosine of this angle is −.391; the correlation between these scales is −.293; and this correlation corrected for attenuation is −.413.

Finally, using these procedures, the correlation between Police Style and Probability of Victimization is similarly estimated. The angle between these two clusters of variables is 102°; the cosine of 102° is −.208; the correlation between these two scales is −.186; and this correlation corrected for attenuation is −.250. This value was not altered by the inclusion of exclusion of X_3 as a measure.

The conclusions from this analysis are as follows. First, the probability of Victimization is negatively correlated with both Crime Fighting and Police Style. More important, the Probability of Victimization is correlated more strongly with Crime Fighting than it is with Police Style. Second, Crime Fighting is positively correlated with Police Style. Third, X_3 is an indicant with inferior measurement properties, as it is affected by both Crime Fighting and Police Style; hence, it does not define either concept unambiguously.

Having completed an analysis of these data using the procedures described in this volume, we will now describe two alternative sets of procedures that have been proposed for this purpose. These procedures are Costner's path-analytic approach and Jöreskog's analysis-of-covariance-structures approach to measurement.

Costner's path-analytic approach

Costner (1969) provided the first systematic schema for the identification of certain types of nonrandom errors through the use of multiple

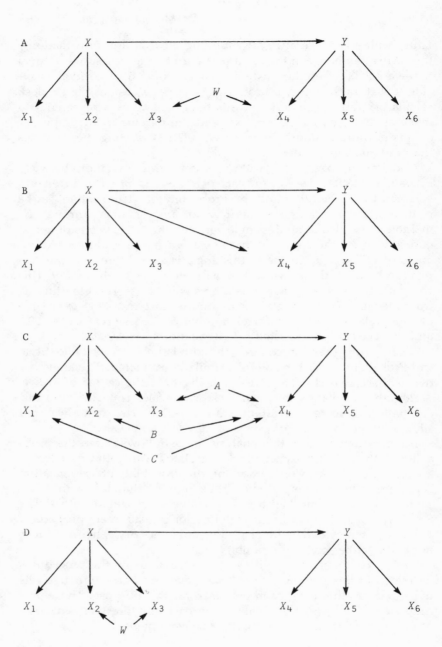

Figure A.2. Types of error identifiable using Costner's consistency criterion.

indicators. Costner reasoned, using path diagrams, that estimates of parameters would be equal in the presence of certain types of "differential bias" and inconsistent in the presence of other types. The patterns of variation of parameter estimates for overidentified models point to the particular types of nonrandom error affecting the sample data. With two indicator models, he argued, error type A may be identified, as shown in Figure A.2A. That is, the presence of W is detectable as an additional source of common variance even if there were only two measures of X and two measures of Y. None of the other types of nonrandom error illustrated in Figure A.2 are detectable with less than three indicators of each concept.

Assuming that the six survey items measure two distinct components of evaluation, Costner's path analytic approach was applied to the two concept/three indicator model. The results are presented in Table A.4. (Estimates of the correlation between the two concepts are the focus of the analysis although estimates of any parameter might be used.)

Examination of Table A.4A suggests that there is no type A error in our data. Differences in estimates of the correlation between the two constructs occur whenever indicants X_1 and X_6 are included in the two-indicator estimates. None of these differences are large enough to be considered substantively interesting. There is an appropriate test of statistical significance for such differences; it is Spearman's "tetrad-difference" criterion (Spearman and Holzinger, 1924). However, since our sample size is 11,000, such a test would have an excessive amount of statistical power to detect what Spreitzer and Chase (1972) refer to as a "substantively meaningless but statistically significant" result.

The results presented in Table A.4B permit distinction between error types A, B, and C. The following rule distinguishes among these errors:

1   If one estimate of nine is deviant, type A error is present.
2   If three estimates of nine are deviant and the model passes the two-indicator test (that is, no difference in estimates occur), type B error is present.
3   If three estimates of nine are deviant and the model fails the two-indicator test, type C error is present.

All three estimates of the correlation between Crime Fighting and Police Style that are based on indicator X_3 are higher than these estimates for any other indicator of either concept. Hence, a type B error appears to be present.

Costner is able to identify one other type of nonrandom error. This systematic error is a source of common variance between indicators

Table A.4. *Costner's consistency criteria test results*

A. Two-indicator test[a]

Indicators of perceived Crime Fighting	Indicators of perceived Police Style		
	4,5	4,6	5,6
1,2	.014	.021	.005
1,3	.012	.019	.006
2,3	.005	.004	.000

B. Three-indicator test[b]

Indicators of perceived Crime Fighting	Indicators of perceived Police Style		
	4	5	6
1	.336	.287	.372
2	.349	.332	.443
3	.572	.529	.708

C. Test for extraneous source of common variance – error type D[c]

Pairs of indicators	Underestimates	Overestimates	Not affected
$X_1 X_2$	.352	.603	.458
$X_1 X_3$	.456	.375	.411
$X_2 X_3$	.480	.331	.398
$X_4 X_5$	.437	.419	.419
$X_4 X_6$	.456	.383	.409
$X_5 X_6$	.395	.507	.439

[a]Cell entries are differences in the 9 pairs of squared estimates of the structural parameter computed according to Costner (1969), equation 20.
[b] Cell entries are 9 squared estimates of the structural parameter, computed according to Costner (1969), equation 42.
[c] Cell entries are the mean of the squared estimates of the structural parameter computed according to Costner (1969), equations 20 and 42.

of the same concept other than their common dependence on that concept (error type D). Table A.4C contains a summary of the evidence marshaled to ascertain the presence of this type of error. If error type D is present between any two indicators, those estimates of the structural correlation that include these indicators in the computation of their numerator will be overestimates, and all estimates that include these indicators in their denominator will be underestimates. Otherwise, the estimates should be unaffected. Examination of Table A.4C suggests that the most serious incident of error type D involves X_1 and X_2.

Figure A.3 is offered as a reconceptualization of the relationship among the six indicators. As we shall see, this model is similar to that produced by the confirmatory factor-analytic techniques. Efficient estimation of parameters, however, is not possible using Costner's approach (Hauser and Goldberger, 1971). Twenty-seven estimates of

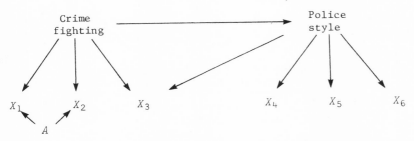

Figure A.3. Reconstruction of the relationship between indicators based on Costner's consistency criteria.

the structural correlation are produced by the two concept/three indicator model. No criteria are provided to access the "best" estimate. In addition, the number of estimates for the model increases geometrically as the number of indicants increases arithmetically.

Jöreskog's analysis-of-covariance-structures approach

Jöreskog's analysis-of-covariance-structures model is a special case of his more general solution of a system of linear structural equations. The general model permits estimation of identified structural equation models containing errors in variables or measurement error and errors in equations (the overlap between the psychometric and econometric approaches to this problem is noted by Goldberger, 1971). The models assume that the "true" dependent variable (η) and the "true" independent variables (ξ) are related by a series of linear structural equations:

$$\beta\eta = \Gamma\xi + \zeta \tag{A.1}$$

where β and Γ represent coefficient matrices and ζ is a residual vector that represents errors in the equations. The term "true" is used as a modifier to describe η and ξ as measured without error or, alternatively, as unobserved variables.

The observed variables, here equivalent to our survey items, are denoted by the vectors Y and X. These observed variables are related to the "true" variables by a series of measurement equations. Assuming that these observed variables are standardized to simplify presentation, these equations are

$$Y = \Lambda_y\eta + \epsilon \tag{A.2}$$
$$X = \Lambda_x\xi + \delta \tag{A.3}$$

where Λ_y and Λ_x are coefficient matrices and ϵ and δ are vectors representing measurement errors.

Either of the two measurement equations is structurally equivalent to the factor-analytic model. The factor model may be written as

$$X = \Lambda f + \epsilon \tag{A.4}$$

where

X = vector of observed scores ($p \times 1$)
Λ = matrix of factor loadings ($p \times k$)
f = vector of common factors ($k \times 1$)
ϵ = vector of unique scores ($p \times 1$)

Four assumptions are necessary to estimate this model.

1    $E(f) = E(\epsilon) = 0$.
2    $E(f\epsilon) = 0$.
3    $E(\epsilon\epsilon^{\tau}) = \psi^2$, a diagonal matrix; that is, cov ($\epsilon_i\epsilon_j$) = 0, $i \neq j$.
4    $E(ff^{\tau}) = \Phi$, the correlation matrix among the factors. This matrix is constrained to be equal to 1 (the identity matrix) in estimating factor loadings. On the basis of these assumptions, the model predicts the expected value of the variance–covariance matrix of the observed variables.

$$
\begin{aligned}
E(xx^{\tau}) &= E(\Lambda f + \epsilon)(\Lambda f + \epsilon)^{\tau} \\
&= E(\Lambda ff^{\tau}\Lambda^{\tau} + \Lambda f\epsilon^{\tau} + \epsilon f^{\tau}\Lambda^{\tau} + \epsilon\epsilon^{\tau}) \\
&= E(\Lambda ff^{\tau}\Lambda^{\tau}) + E(\epsilon\epsilon^{\tau}) \\
&= \Lambda E(ff^{\tau})\Lambda^{\tau} + \Psi^2 \\
&= \Lambda\Phi\Lambda^{\tau} + \Psi^2 = \Sigma
\end{aligned}
\tag{A.5}
$$

If we further assume the observed variables have been standardized, that is, $E(X) = 0$ and Var $(X) = 1.0$, Σ is equal to the predicted correlation matrix between observed variables.

In applying the factor model to a set of data, we hypothesize that the common factors extracted should account for all correlations among the X's. In other words, if the effect of the factors were to be partialed out, no correlation should remain between the items. The ability to replicate observed correlations from factor loadings constitutes one test of the adequacy of this model.

Jöreskog's technique for analysis of covariance structures enables the researcher to generalize the traditional factor model by (1) incorporating restrictions on the factor structure underlying the data in order to test alternative hypotheses, and (2) allowing relaxation of the assumption of no correlation between errors, between factors, or between errors and factors (Jöreskog, 1969).

The parameters of the model are estimated using a maximum likelihood estimation technique originally described in Jöreskog (1967). A test of the overall goodness of fit between the proposed factor model and the original correlation matrix is provided by a chi-square or "likelihood ratio" test.

For very large samples, it is unlikely that any nontrivial model will fit the matrix of correlations between observed variables. As a result, relative fit provides a critical perspective on the value of any particular statistical model. A model may, in fact, fit "too well"; that is, one can relax so many parameters in estimating a model using one data set that it will not fit other sample data. Further discussion of this problem is provided by Jöreskog (1969:201).

If model M_0 can be obtained by constraining one or more parameters of model M_1, it is considered to be "nested" within M_1 for models bearing this relationship to one another, the likelihood ratio test can be used to evaluate the incremental improvement of the fit of the overall model:

$$\chi_d^2 = \chi_{m_1}^2 - \chi_{m_0}^2 \quad \text{with} \quad df_d = df_{m_1} - df_{m_0} \tag{A.6}$$

Significant chi-square values indicate a better fit by model M_0 than M_1. This test provides an additional means to evaluate the ability of the model to replicate the sample covariance matrix. Tucker and Lewis (1973) provide an alternative to the likelihood test. Their coefficient, ρ_q, is not without weaknesses: its sampling distribution is not known. Tucker and Lewis suggest, however, that values above .9 represent "adequate" structures. Thus, ρ_q becomes another descriptive measure for evaluating alternative models based on large samples.

Applying both the likelihood ratio test and the Tucker–Lewis statistic ρ_q to a model, the researcher may determine the fit is a poor one. What can be done? Neither test indicates what part of the proposed model does not accurately represent the structure underlying the data. Several suggestions have been offered. No one approach is unambiguous in its application:

1   Nested models may be evaluated one coefficient at a time using the likelihood ratio text described above.

2   Confidence intervals may be constructed for each parameter estimate of a specific model in order to examine its significance. Standard errors of each estimate are computed using Jöreskog's technique.

3   A first-order derivative test has been proposed by Sörbom (1975) that identifies the parameter constraint that may be relaxed to produce the greatest likelihood ratio test improvement.

4   Identification of which sample covariances the model is unable to predict is possible through examination of the residual variance–covariance matrix. Both Costner and Schoenberg (1973) and Sörbom (1975) have argued that clues provided by this approach may be misleading. However, use of Sörbom's first derivative test without examination of this residual matrix may lead to faulty inferences about the underlying structure.

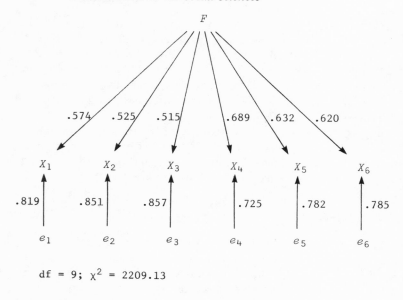

df = 9; χ^2 = 2209.13

Figure A.4. Originally proposed unidimensional model of citizen evaluations.

Two points need to be stressed. These tests are most useful when used in combination. Second, specification of hypothesized deviations from the proposed model will greatly facilitate testing and evaluation and will assist interpretation of a final solution. It is not difficult to apply Jöreskog's models to a set of data without any preconceived expectations of underlying structure and generate complex statistical models. Substantive interpretation of such models may be considerably more difficult. In essence, all of the many critiques applied to the "factor analysis machine" and its proponents in the 1960s can be used with greater force to caution against misuse of the analysis-of-covariance models.

The unidimensional (one-factor) model of citizen evaluations that we originally hypothesized is presented graphically in Figure A.4. The chi-square goodness-of-fit test indicates that the model does not adequately represent the data; that is, statistically significant differences exist between the sample correlation matrix (S) and the correlation matrix predicted by the factor structure (Σ). As noted above, however, given the size of our sample ($N = 11,000$), it is unlikely that any model that does not exhaust the available degrees of freedom will adequately (in the statistical sense implied by the likelihood ratio test) fit the sample data. The test statistic offered by Tucker and Lewis does suggest that the model is not appropriate.

Two alternative hypotheses were posed earlier – (1) two factors, rather than one are operating to produce the sample correlation matrix, and (2) correlated errors are affecting the relationships between the last three indicators. Because correlated errors, if they exist, will affect the factor structure whether one or two factors are present, we will examine the two-factor model first.

The two-factor model is presented in Figure A.5A. The correlation between factors is constrained to equal .0; that is, the factors are orthogonal. This factor model is presented as a baseline against which a two-correlated-factors model can be correctly compared, as the difference in chi-square values between the one-factor and two-correlated-factors model is not a likelihood ratio test (the models are not nested), although chi-square differences may be considered as suggesting evidence.

The orthogonal solution, presented in Figure A.5A, provides a poor fit to the model (χ^2 = 16,567.3). In contrast, the oblique solution, presented in Figure A. 5B, fits considerably better (χ^2 = 128.9). Moreover, the Tucker–Lewis ρ_q also indicates a good fit between sample and predicted covariances (see Table A.6). Examination of the first derivative test shows little evidence of correlated errors among the latter three indicators (see Table A.5).

The likelihood ratio test for the oblique solution indicates that the model may still be improved; that is, a closer fit to the data is possible. The first derivative tests provide indicators of where the model might be improved. Examination of Table A.5 shows that relaxation of the constraint on the correlation between X_1 and X_2 would yield the greatest single improvement in the model. This is, in fact, equivalent to one of the prescriptions offered by the Costner criteria. Yet examination of the residual matrix indicates that the model is deficient primarily in its ability to predict the correlations between X_3 and X_4, X_5, and X_6. The first derivative tests for the variance–covariance matrix of error components shows that releasing any of these coefficients will improve the fit of the model. Given the underestimate between all the indicators of factor 2 and X_3, one plausible interpretation of the pattern of first derivative tests is that the model presented in Figure A.5 misrepresents the relationship between Police Style and X_3. A revised model is offered as Figure A.6. This model fits the data significantly better than the model presented in Figure A.5. The weakness of X_3 as an indicator of Police Style is sustained in this analysis. Evaluation criteria for all factor models are summarized in Table A.6.

The preceding analysis suggests that a two-factor structure underlies the sample correlation matrix. Yet one more rival hypothesis needs to be examined: all six indicators measure citizen evaluations of police, but each cluster is affected by another factor, which results in cor-

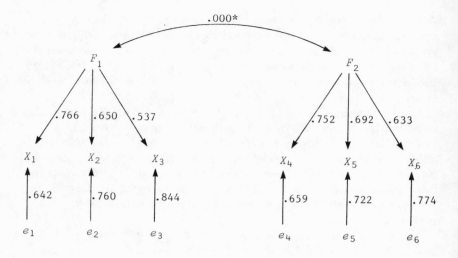

df = 9; χ^2 = 16567.33

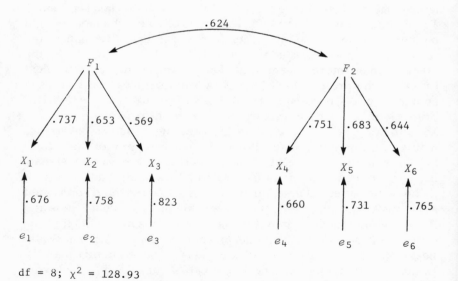

df = 8; χ^2 = 128.93

Figure A.5. Bidimensional model of citizen evaluations. (* This value constrained to equal .000.)

Table A.5. *First-order derivative tests and residual covariance matrix for the model presented in Figure A.5B.*

First-order derivatives
Lambda Y (matrix for structural coefficients)

	1	2
X_1	.000	.028
X_2	−.000	.016
X_3	.000	−.054
X_4	.003	.000
X_5	.021	−.000
X_6	−.026	−.000

Theta EPS (matrix for correlated errors)

	X_1	X_2	X_3	X_4	X_5	X_6
X_1	.000					
X_2	−.066	.000				
X_3	.025	.057	−.000			
X_4	.004	.038	−.041	.000		
X_5	.051	.018	−.026	−.033	−.000	
X_6	.012	−.023	−.064	.030	.005	−.000

Residuals: Σ S
Σ(YY), S(YY)

	X_1	X_2	X_3	X_4	X_5	X_6
X_1	.000					
X_2	−.017	.000				
X_3	.008	.022	.000			
X_4	.012	.017	−.039	.000		
X_5	.030	.019	−.028	−.008	.000	
X_6	.001	−.012	−.057	.008	.002	.000

related errors within each cluster. This hypothesis cannot be dismissed on the basis of evidence supplied by the interitem correlation matrix of the indicators of citizen evaluations. Other variables must be included to identify a model that hypothesizes the differential impact of a third factor on the indicators of Crime Fighting and Police Style. The addition of relevant variables also permits evaluation of the validity of the two-factor model: do the two factors relate differentially to third variables, and do they do so in a predictable fashion?

If a distinction between the two sets of indicators is warranted and if each measures the concept ascribed to it (that is, if Crime Fighting is conceptually distinct from Police Style), then scales of these sets of items should relate differently to certain other variables. In particular, we would expect perceptions of neighborhood crime to be related to evaluations of police services: the higher the perceived crime rate in the neighborhood, the lower the citizen will evaluate the police agency

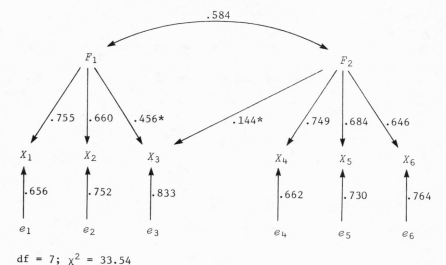

df = 7; χ^2 = 33.54

Figure A.6. Revised bidimensional model of citizen evaluations. (* Major alterations in revision of bidimensional model.)

Table A.6. *Goodness-of-fit tests for confirmatory factor-analytic models*

Model	χ^2	df	Sign	ρ_q
Figure A.4	2,209.13	9	.000	.764
Figure A.5A	16,567.33	9	.000	−.774
Figure A.5B	128.93	8	.000	.985
Figure A.6	33.54	7	.000	.996

serving that area. Perceived crime rate may only be indirectly related to style evaluations offered by citizens.

Three indicators are used to measure perceived probability of crime:

X_7 How likely do you think it is that your home will be burglarized in the next year? Do you think it is very likely, somewhat likely, or not at all likely?

X_8 How about vandalism; how likely do you think it that your home will be vandalized in the next year? Do you think it is very likely, somewhat likely, or not at all likely?

X_9 How likely do you think it is that you will be robbed by someone with a weapon in your neighborhood in the next year? Do you think it is very likely, somewhat likely, or not at all likely?

Assuming these three items to be measures of the concept, perceived crime rate, all nine indicators may be analyzed using the confirmatory factor model. Three correlated factors are hypothesized: two identify the components of evaluation; the third is the citizen's estimate of probability of being victimized in the neighborhood. The correlation between the style and perceived crime factors is initially constrained to equal zero–reflecting the hypothesis that crime rate will only affect the evaluation of Police Style through its effect on evaluation of Crime Fighting (a "halo" effect). All errors are initially assumed to be uncorrelated.

Figure A.7 presents graphically the three concept nine indicator model. Model 1, as we have just described it, sets c_{23}, a'_3, d_{27}, and d_{49} to zero; these parameters will be introduced shortly. The parameters for model 1 are presented in the first column of Table A.7. According to these maximum likelihood estimates, Perceptions of the Crime Rate do affect evaluations of Crime Fighting ability, as hypothesized. The fit of the model is not, however, a good one. Examination of the first-order derivative tests indicate that our second hypothesis is untenable. That is, the constraint on the correlation between Perceived Crime and Police Style should be relaxed.

Model 2 provides the appropriate estimation with this constraint relaxed. Specifically, in model 2, c_{23} is estimated, but a'_3, d_{27}, and d_{49} are set to zero. The fit of the model has improved substantially (chi square = 225.1). Comparison of the relationship of the two evaluation factors with Perceived Crime Rate still supports our interpretation of the first three indicators as Crime Fighting, whereas X_4, X_5, and X_6 are Police Style.

While the Tucker–Lewis statistic would suggest that we have a satisfactory fit with this model, further improvements are possible. The first derivative tests again suggest that Λ_{32} (that is, a'_3) should not be fixed at .000. Model 3 presents such a situation, in which c_{23} and a'_3 are estimated and d_{27} and d_{49} are set to zero. Other coefficients may be released and the model reestimated. Using Sörbom's derivative test, maximum improvements were next made by introducing two correlations between errors. Specifically, d_{49} was estimated in model 4 and both d_{49} and d_{27} were estimated in model 5. The likelihood ratio test results, df, significance level, likelihood test between nested models, and the Tucker–Lewis ρ_q are presented for each of these models.

The introduction of correlated errors has a minimal effect on the fit of the model according to the criterion offered by Tucker and Lewis. This suggestive evidence, the small absolute magnitude of these effects, and the realization that sample size also affects the likelihood ratio difference test point to the conclusion that we have "overfit" the model. Incorporation of the ability of Police Style to directly affect the X_3 does improve the fit of the model. It may not be substantively

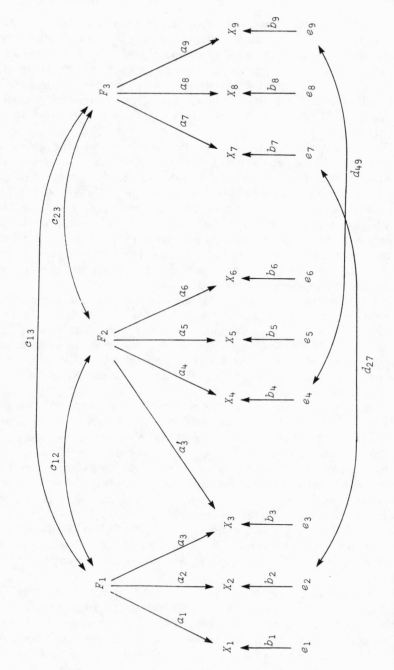

Figure A.7. Tridimensional model.

Table A.7. *Estimators for three-dimensional model*

Model	1	2	3	4	5
a_1	.742	.742	.761	.761	.757
a_2	.650	.650	.654	.654	.657
a_3	.566	.566	.452	.452	.452
a_4	.752	.751	.751	.749	.749
a_5	.685	.682	.682	.682	.682
a_6	.641	.645	.646	.646	.646
a_7	.800	.798	.798	.798	.801
a_8	.724	.723	.723	.723	.721
a_9	.589	.593	.593	.593	.593
b_1	.670	.671	.649	.649	.653
b_2	.760	.760	.756	.756	.753
b_3	.824	.824	.834	.834	.834
b_4	.659	.660	.660	.662	.662
b_5	.729	.731	.731	.731	.731
b_6	.767	.764	.764	.764	.764
b_7	.601	.602	.602	.602	.599
b_8	.689	.691	.691	.691	.693
b_9	.808	.805	.805	.806	.806
$a_3'{}^a$	$.000^b$	$.000^b$	.148	.148	.147
c_{12}	.580	.623	.586	.586	.587
c_{13}	−.316	−.409	−.406	−.407	−.414
c_{23}	$.000^b$	−.237	−.238	−.233	−.233
d_{27}	$.000^b$	$.000^b$	$.000^b$	$.000^b$	.053
d_{49}	$.000^b$	$.000^b$	$.000^b$	−.060	−.060
χ^2	584.99	225.10	128.00	104.17	90.23
df	25	24	23	22	21
Sign	.000	.000	.000	.000	.000
$\Delta\chi^2$	—	359.89	97.10	23.83	13.94
ρ_q	.971	.989	.995	.995	.996

$^a a_3'$ represents the causal effect of F_2 on X_3.
^{b} Constrained to equal .000.

significant, however, as Crime Fighting explains approximately 10 times more of the amount of variance of this indicator than does Police Style. That is, a_3^2 is roughly 10 times larger than $a_3'^2$, as shown in models 3, 4, and 5.

The previous analyses based on Costner's consistency criteria and Jöreskog's analysis-of-covariance-structures model support our initial hypothesis that the six items designed to measure citizen rating of neighborhood police services do, in fact, measure individual evaluations of these services. Two distinct types of ratings were apparent in the responses to the six questions. Police services were evaluated in terms of performance and in terms of style or manner of handling police–citizen contacts. The two three-item clusters that measured these two aspects of citizen evaluations were internally consistent as demonstrated by a factor-analytic model. In addition to having substantial face validity, differences between the two types of ratings was shown in the estimation of a structural model relating perceptions of crime to evaluations of police services. The probability of crime within the neighborhood had a strong effect on the rating of police performance but was only slightly related to ratings of Police Style.

Summary

The preceding example has been used to demonstrate the process of examining empirical data for systematic errors. Costner's criteria are of considerable heuristic value for identifying empirical anomolies in *simple measurement models*. Jöreskog's method, however, permits much greater flexibility, both in terms of the number of indicants it can handle and in the variety of systematic errors that can be modeled and subjected to test. Furthermore, precise structural estimates are produced for identified models. We would, therefore, recommend the Jöreskog approach to those researchers who suspect a particular type of nonrandom error in their data.

Note also that we have examined only several possible sources of systematic bias. Numerous third variables might account for variations in the indicants of Crime Fighting and Police Style. Adequate examination of this possible source of bias will require considerably greater efforts in reestimating the model for each possible source of systematic error. The analysis-of-covariance-structures model also permits examination of external validity in conjunction with the examination of systematic and random errors.

In a wider framework, we have in this appendix compared these two approaches to the approach developed in this volume. We now wish to inquire what substantive differences there were between the inferences made using our procedures and using the procedures discussed in this appendix. In fact, the differences between the results of our approach and these approaches are virtually nil. All approaches inferred two dimensions of the evaluation of police services; all approaches inferred the weakness of X_3 as a measure of Crime Fighting; all approaches sensitized the researcher to possible sources of systematic error; and Jöreskog's approach and ours produced highly similar estimates of the various parameters under the same models.

If Jöreskog's approach and ours produce virtually identical results, on what basis is a researcher to choose between them? We believe that this choice should be based upon three criteria, listed in order of their importance: (1) theoretical clarity, (2) statistical elegance, and

(3) ease of use. Let us evaluate these approaches against these criteria in reverse order.

Our approach is easier to use than Jöreskog's. From our perspective, the researcher can conduct the analysis activities with widely available statistical computer packages and some work on a desk calculator. The Jöreskog approach requires most complex and less widely available computer facilities and training. Both require multiple computer runs.

Jöreskog's approach is far more elegant statistically than is ours. The parameters estimates are maximum likelihood. Statistical tests evaluate the degree to which the nonrandom error has been recomed from the residual matrix. The mathematical basis for the analysis rests upon matrix algebra rather than upon linear algebra.

By far the most important criterion for evaluating these approaches focuses upon the theoretical clarity resulting from their use. On this criterion, the proof will occur substantively, for it is the judgments that are to be made about substance that will determine which approach is most fruitful. From one perspective, Jöreskog's approach to analyzing measurement error can be viewed as a statistical formalization of the conceptual integration we have proposed between factor analysis and construct validation. At the same time, each approach is designed to sensitize the researcher to some kinds of research problems but not others. For example, Jöreskog's approach is well suited to the discovery and description of correlated errors between specific items, such as d_{27} and d_{49} in Figure A.7.

On the other hand, our focus upon the difference between detectable and undetectable method artifacts sensitizes the researcher to discover and describe detectable method artifacts. These models describe the differing measurement structures that underlie the researcher's assumptions about the nature of the method artifact variance that underlies the measurement situation. In our judgment, this is not trivial, for the strength of the epistemic correlations and the strength of the correlation between two concepts depends upon the degree to which undetectable method artifacts distort the estimated model (for example, see Figure 5.6 and 6.4).

Beyond this, we cannot provide extended guidelines under which the procedures offered in this appendix are to be preferred to one another. Extensive Monte Carlo tests of the power of the approaches are not available at this time. Although each approach brings to the study of measurement error a number of advantages, each approach also demands certain restrictive assumptions. In the final analysis, the most useful approach is the approach that provides the firmest basis for social measurement. This basis does not depend upon the desire for social knowledge; it does not depend upon data management ease; it does not depend upon statistical gyrations or ritualistic exercises. Proper social measurement depends upon the creative imagination and persistent persual of important theoretical concerns. With Duncan (1975:150-1) and Borgatta (1969:xiv), we caution against the uncritical use of methodological panaceas to critical problem facing social research. Such fads come and go. Instead, we urge patience, persistence, and soundness in social measurement, for social measurement is the most crucial problem facing modern social science.

BIBLIOGRAPHY

Achen, C. H. 1975. Mass Political Attitudes and the Survey Response. *American Political Science Review, 69,* 1218–31.
Allen, M. P. 1974. Construction of Composite Measures by the Canonical-Factor Regression Method. In H. L. Costner (ed.). *Sociological Methodology 1973–1974,* pp. 51–78. San Francisco: Jossey-Bass.
Althauser, R. P. 1974. Inferring Validity from the Multitrait–Multimethod Matrix: Another Assessment. In H. L. Costner (ed.). *Sociological Methodology 1973–1974,* pp. 106–27. San Francisco: Jossey-Bass.
Althauser, R. P. and Heberlein, T. A. 1970. Validity and the Multitrait–Multimethod Matrix. In E. F. Borgatta and G. W. Bohrnstedt (eds.). *Sociological Methodology 1970,* pp. 151–69. San Francisco: Jossey-Bass.
Althauser, R. P., Heberlein, T. A., and Scott, R. A. 1971. A Causal Assessment of Validity: The Augmented Multitrait–Multimethod Matrix. In H. M. Blalock (ed.). *Causal Models in the Social Sciences.* Chicago: Aldine-Atherton.
Alwin, D. F. 1973. The Use of Factor Analysis in the Construction of Linear Composites in Social Research. *Sociological Methods and Research, 2,* 191–214.
　1974. Approaches to the Interpretation of Relationships in the Multitrait–Multimethod Matrix. In H. L. Costner (ed.). *Sociological Methodology 1973–1974,* pp. 79–105. San Francisco: Jossey-Bass.
American Psychological Association, 1966. *Standards for Educational and Psychological Tests and Manuals.* Washington, D.C.: American Psychological Association.
Armor, D. J. 1974. Theta Reliability and Factor Scaling. In H. L. Costner (ed.). *Sociological Methodology 1973–1974,* pp. 17–50. San Francisco: Jossey-Bass.
Asher, H. B. 1974. Some Consequences of Measurement Error in Survey Data. *American Journal of Political Science, 18,* 469–85.
　1976. *Causal Modeling.* Sage University Paper Series on Quantitative Applications in the Social Sciences, 07–003. Beverly Hills, Calif.: Sage Publications.
Balch, G. I. 1974. Multiple Indicators in Survey Research: The Concept "Sense of Political Efficacy." *Political Methodology, 1,* 1–44.

Bechtolt, H. P. 1959. Construct Validity: A Critique. *American Psychologist, 14*, 619–29.

Beck, P. 1975. Models for Analyzing Panel Data: A Comparative Review. *Political Methodology, 2*, 357–80.

Bierstedt, R. 1959. Nominal and Real Definitions in Sociological Theory. In L. Gross (ed.). *Symposium on Sociological Theory*, pp. 121–44. New York: Harper & Row.

Blalock, H. M. 1963. Making Causal Inferences for Unmeasured Variables from Correlations Among Indicators. *American Journal of Sociology, 69*, 53–62.

1964. *Causal Inferences in Nonexperimental Research*. Chapel Hill, N.C.: University of North Carolina Press.

1968. The Measurement Problem. In H. M. Blalock and A. Blalock (eds.). *Methodology in Social Research*, pp. 5–27. New York: McGraw-Hill.

1969. Multiple Indicators and the Causal Approach to Measurement Error. *American Journal of Sociology, 75*, 264–72.

1970. Estimating Measurement Error Using Multiple Indicators and Several Points in Time. *American Sociological Review, 35*, 101–11.

1974. (Ed.) *Measurement in the Social Sciences: Theories and Strategies*. Chicago: Aldine-Atherton.

Bohrnstedt, G. W. 1969a. A Quick Method for Determining the Reliability and Validity of Multiple-Item Scales. *American Sociological Review, 34*, 542–8.

1969b. Observations on the Measurement of Change. In E. F. Borgatta (ed.). *Sociological Methodology 1969*, pp. 113–33. San Francisco: Jossey-Bass.

1970. Reliability and Validity Assessment in Attitude Measurement. In G. F. Summers (ed.). *Attitude Measurement*, pp. 80–99. Chicago: Rand McNally.

Borgatta, E. F. 1969. The Current Status of Methodology in Sociology. Prologue to E. F. Borgatta (ed). *Sociological Methodology 1969*, pp. ix–xiv. San Francisco: Jossey-Bass.

Brown, W. 1910. Some Experimental Results in the Correlation of Mental Abilities. *British Journal of Psychology, 3*, 269–322.

Burt, R. S. 1973. Confirmatory Factor Analytic Structures and the Theory Construction Process. *Sociological Methods and Research, 2*, 131–90.

1976. Interpretational Confounding of Unobserved Variables in Structural Equation Models. *Sociological Methods and Research, 5*, 3–52.

Campbell, D. T. 1960. Recommendations for APA Test Standards Regarding Construct, Trait, or Discriminant Validity. *American Psychologist, 15*, 546–55.

Campbell, D. T., and Fiske, D. W. 1959. Convergent and Discriminant Validation by the Multitrait–Multimethod Matrix. *Psychological Bulletin, 56*, 81–105.

Carmines, E. G. 1978. Psychological Origins of Adolescent Political Attitudes: Self-Esteem, Political Salience, and Political Involvement. *American Politics Quarterly, 6*, 167–86.

Carmines, E. G., and Zeller, R. A. 1974. On Establishing the Empirical Dimensionality of Theoretical Terms: An Analytical Example. *Political Methodology, 1*, 75–96.

Carmines, E. G. and Zeller, R. A. In preparation. *Reliability and Validity Assessment*, Sage University Paper Series on Quantitative Applications in the Social Sciences. Beverly Hills, Calif.: Sage Publications.

Cattell, R. B. 1964. The Three Basic Factor Analytic Research Designs–The Interrelations and Derivatives. *Personality and Social Psychology*, pp. 667–79. San Diego, Calif.: Knapp.

Costner, H. L. 1969. Theory Deduction, and Rules of Correspondence. *American Journal of Sociology*, 75, 245–63.

Costner, H. L., and Schoenberg, R. 1973. Diagnosing Indicator Ills in Multiple Indicator Models. In A. S. Goldberger, O. D. Duncan, (eds.). *Structural Equation Models in the Social Sciences*, pp. 167–99. New York: Seminar Press.

Cronbach, L. J. 1951. Coefficient Alpha and the Internal Structure of Tests. *Psychometrika*, 16, 297–334.

Cronbach, L. J., and Meehl, P. E. 1955. Construct Validity in Psychological Tests. *Psychological Bulletin*, 52, 281–302.

Crowne, D. P., and Marlowe, D. 1964 *The Approval Motive*. New York: Wiley.

Curtis, R. F., and Jackson, E. F. 1962. Multiple Indicators in Survey Research. *American Journal of Sociology*, 68, 195–204.

Duncan, O. D. 1969. Some Linear Models for Two-Wave, Two-Variable Panel Analysis. *Psychological Bulletin*, 72, 177–82.

  1970. Partials, Partitions, and Paths. In E. F. Borgatta and G. W. Bohrnstedt (ed.). *Sociological Methodology 1970*, pp. 38–47. San Francisco: Jossey-Bass.

  1972. Unmeasured Variables in Linear Models for Path Analysis. In H. L. Costner (ed.). *Sociological Methodology 1972*, pp. 36–82. San Francisco: Jossey-Bass.

  1975. *Introduction to Structural Equation Models*. New York: Academic Press.

Erikson, R. S. 1978. Analyzing One Variable–Three Wave Panel Data: A Comparison of Two Models. *Political Methodology*, 5, 151–66.

Finsterbusch, K. 1976. Demonstrating the Value of Mini Surveys in Social Research. *Sociological Methods and Research*, 5, 117–36.

Gamson, W. A. 1966. Game Theory and Administrative Decision-Making. In C. Press and A. Arian (eds.). *Empathy and Ideology*, pp. 146–61. Chicago: Rand McNally.

  1968. Interaction Processes, Mimeo.

Goldberger, A. G. 1971. Econometrics and Psychometrics: A Survey of Commonalities. *Psychometrika*, 36, 83–107.

Greene, V. 1978. Simultaneous Optimization of Factor Assessibility and Representativeness: An Old Solution to a New Problem. *Psychometrika*, 43, 12–13.

Greene, V., and Carmines, E. G. 1979. Assessing the Reliability of Linear Composites. In K. Schuessler (ed.). *Sociological Methodology, 1980*. San Francisco: Jossey-Bass.

Greer, S. 1969. *The Logic of Social Inquiry*, Chicago: Aldine.

Groat, H. T., and Neal, A. G. 1967. Social Psychological Correlates of Urban Fertility. *American Sociological Review*, 32, 945–59.

1973. Social Class and Alienation Correlates of Protestant Fertility. *Journal of Marriage and the Family*, 35, 83–8.

1975a. Alienation Antecedents of Unwanted Fertility: A Longitudinal Study. *Social Biology*, 22, 60–74.

1975b. A Social Psychological Approach to Family Formation. In K. C. W. Kammeyer (ed.). *Population Studies: Selected Essays and Research*, 2nd ed. pp. 46–59. Chicago: Rand McNally.

Groat, H. T., Neal, A. G., and Knisely, E. C. 1975. Contraceptive Nonconformity Among Catholics. *Journal for the Scientific Study of Religion*, 14, 367–77.

Groat, H. T., Neal, A. G., and Mathews, L. 1976. Social Isolation and Premarital Pregnancy. *Sociology and Social Research*, 60, 188–98.

Groat, H. T., Workman, R. L., and Neal, A. G. 1976. Labor Force Participation and Family Formation: A Study of Working Mothers. *Demography*, 13, 115–25.

Gulliksen, H. 1950. *Theory of Mental Tests*. New York: Wiley.

Guttman, L. 1940. Multiple Rectilinear Prediction and the Resolution into Components. *Psychometrika*, 5, 75–99.

Hannan, M., Rubinson, R., and Wanen, J. T. 1974. The Causal Approach to Measurement Error in Panel Analysis: Some Further Contingencies. In H. M. Blalock (ed.). *Measurement in the Social Sciences: Theories and Strategies*, pp. 293–323. Chicago: Aldine.

Hannan, M. T., and Young, A. A. 1977. Estimation in Panel Models: Results on Pooling Cross-Sections and Time-Series. In D. R. Heise (ed.). *Sociological Methodology 1977*, pp. 52–83. San Francisco: Jossey-Bass.

Harman, H. H. 1967. *Modern Factor Analysis*, 2nd ed. Chicago: University of Chicago.

1976. *Modern Factor Analysis*, 3rd ed. Chicago: University of Chicago.

Hauser, P. 1969. Comments on Coleman's Paper. In R. Bierstedt (ed.). *A Design for Sociology: Scope, Objectives, and Methods*, pp. 122–36. Philadelphia: American Academy of Political and Social Science.

Hauser, R. M., and Golberger, A. S. 1971. The Treatment of Unobservable Variables in Path Analysis. In H. L. Costner (ed.). *Sociological Methodology 1971*, pp. 81–117. San Francisco: Jossey-Bass.

Heise, D. R. 1969. Separating Reliability and Stability in Test–Retest Correlations. *American Sociological Review*, 34, 93–101.

1970. Causal Inference from Panel Data. In E. F. Borgatta and G. W. Bohrnstedt (eds.). *Sociological Methodology 1970*, pp. 3–27. San Francisco: Jossey-Bass.

1974. Some Issues in Sociological Measurement. In H. L. Costner (ed.). *Sociological Methodology 1973–1974*, pp. 1–16. San Francisco: Jossey-Bass.

1975. *Causal Analysis*. New York: Wiley.

Heise, D. R., and Bohrnstedt, G. W. 1970. Validity, Invalidity, and Reliability. In E. F. Borgatta and G. W. Bohrnstedt (eds.) *Sociological Methodology 1970*, pp. 104–29. San Francisco: Jossey-Bass.

Hodgman, C. D. 1959. *Standard Mathematical Tables*, 12th ed. Cleveland: Chemical Rubber Publishing Co.

Hofstetter, C. R. 1971. The Amateur Politician: A Problem in Construct Validation. *Midwest Journal of Political Science, 15,* 31–56.

Hoult, T. F. 1969. *Dictionary of Sociology.* Totowa, N.J.: Littlefield Adams.

Hoyt, C. 1941. Test Reliability Estimated by Analysis of Variance. *Psychometrika, 6,* 153–60.

Jacobson, A. L., and Lula, N. M. 1974. An Empirical and Algebraic Analysis of Alternative Techniques for Measuring Unobserved Variables. In H. M. Blalock (ed.). *Measurement in the Social Sciences: Theories and Strategies,* pp. 215–42. Chicago: Aldine.

Jöreskog, K. G. 1967. Some Contributions to Maximum Likelihood Factor Analysis. *Psychometrika, 32,* 83–107.

   1969. A General Approach to Confirmatory Maximum Likelihood Factor Analysis. *Psychometrika, 34,* 183–202.

   1970. A General Method for the Analysis of Covariance Structures. *Biometrika, 57,* 239–51.

   1971. Statistical Analysis of Sets of Congeneric Tests. *Psychometrika, 36,* 109–33.

Kaplan, A. 1964. *The Conduct of Inquiry.* Scranton, Pa.: Chandler.

Kenny, D. A. 1973. Cross-Lagged and Synchronous Common Factors in Panel Data. In A. S. Goldberger and O. D. Duncan (eds.). *Structural Equation Models in the Social Sciences,* pp. 153–65. New York: Seminar Press.

Kimberly, J. R. 1976. Issues in the Design of Longitudinal Organizational Research. *Sociological Methods and Research, 4,* 321–47.

Krause, M. S. 1972. The Implications of Convergent and Discriminant Validity Data for Instrument Validation. *Psychometrika, 37,* 179–86.

Kuder, G. F., and Richardson, M. W. 1937. The Theory of the Estimation of Test Reliability. *Psychometrika, 2,* 151–60.

Labovitz, S., and Hagedorn, R. 1971. *Introduction to Social Research.* New York: McGraw-Hill.

Lazarsfeld, P. F. 1958. Evidence and Inference in Social Research. *Daedalus, 87,* 99–130.

   1959. Problems in Methodology. In R. K. Merton, L. Broom, and L. S. Cottrell (eds.). *Sociology Today,* pp. 39–78. New York: Harper & Row.

Linehan, W. J. 1967. Models for the Measurement of Political Instability. *Political Methodology, 3,* 441–86.

Long, J. S. 1976. Estimation and Hypothesis Testing in Linear Models Containing Measurement Error: A Review of Jöreskog's Model for the Analysis of Covariance Structures. *Sociological Methods and Research, 5,* 157–206.

Lord, F. M., and Novick, M. R. 1968. *Statistical Theories of Mental Test Scores.* Reading, Mass. Addison-Wesley.

McGaw, D., and Watson, G. 1976. *Political and Social Inquiry.* New York: Wiley.

McIver, J. P., and Ostrom, E. 1976. Using Budget Pies to Reveal Preferences: Validation of a Survey Instrument. In T. N. Clark (ed.). *Citizen Preferences and Urban Public Policy: Models, Measures, Uses.* Sage Contemporary Social Science Issues Vol. 34. Beverly Hills, Calif.: Sage Publications. 87–110.

McPherson, J. M., Welch, S., and Clark, C. 1977. The Stability and Reliability of Political Efficacy: Using Path Analysis to Test Alternative Models. *American Political Science Review, 71,* 509–21.

Magnusson, D. 1967. *Test Theory*. Reading, Mass.: Addison-Wesley.

Merton, R. K. 1957. The Bearing of Empirical Research on Sociological Theory. In R. K. Merton, (ed.). *Social Theory and Social Structure*. New York: Free Press.

Muir, D. E. 1976. Disentangling Instrument Reliability, Validity, and Accuracy in the Social and Behavioral Sciences. Paper read at the Annual Meetings of the American Sociological Association, New York, August.

Namboodiri, N. K., Krishman, N., Carter, L. F., and Blalock, H. M. 1975. *Applied Multivariate Analysis and Experimental Designs*. New York: Mc-Graw-Hill.

Neal, A. G., and Groat, H. T. 1974. Social Class Correlates of Stability and Change in Levels of Alienation: A Longitudinal Study. *Sociological Quarterly, 15*, 548–58.

1975. Alienation Predictors of Differential Fertility: A Longitudinal Study. *American Journal of Sociology, 80*, 1220–6.

Neal, A. G., and Rettig, S. 1963. Dimensions of Alienation Among Manual and Non-Manual Workers. *American Sociological Review, 26*, 599–608.

Novick, M. 1966. The Axioms and Principal Results of Classical Test Theory. *Journal of Mathematical Psychology, 3*, 1–18.

Novick, M., and Lewis, C. 1967. Coefficient Alpha and the Reliability of Composite Measurements. *Psychometrika, 32*, 1–13.

Nunnally, J. C. 1967. *Psychometric Theory*. New York: McGraw-Hill.

1970. *Introduction to Psychological Measurement*. New York: McGraw-Hill.

Payne, J. L. 1975. *Principles of Social Science Measurement*. College Station, Tex.: Lytton.

Pelz, D., and Andrews, F. 1964. Detecting Causal Priorities in Panel Data. *American Sociological Review, 29*, 836–48.

Riley, M. W. 1963. *Sociological Research: A Case Approach*. New York: Harcourt, Brace, and World.

Rock, D. A., Werts, C. E., Linn, R. L., and Jöreskog, K. G. 1977. A Maximum Likelihood Solution to the Errors in Variables and Errors in Equations Model. *Multivariate Behavioral Research, 12*, 187–97.

Rosenberg, M. 1965. *Society and the Adolescent Self-Image*. Princeton, N.J.: Princeton University Press.

Rozeboom. W. W. 1966. *Foundations of the Theory of Prediction*. Homewood, Ill.: Dorsey Press.

Rozelle, R. M., and Campbell, D. T. 1969. More Plausible Rival Hypotheses in the Cross-Lagged Panel Correlation Technique. *Psychological Bulletin, 71*, 74–80.

Rudner, R. S., 1966. *Philosophy of Social Science*, Englewood Cliffs, N.J.: Prentice-Hall.

Rummel, R. J. 1970. *Applied Factor Analysis*. Evanston, Ill.: Northwestern University Press.

Schmitt, N., Coyle, B. W., and Saari, B. B. 1977. A Review and Critique of Analyses of Multitrait–Multimethod Matrices. *Multivariate Behavioral Research, 12*, 447–78.

Schutz, W. C., 1966. *The Interpersonal Underworld*. Palo Alto, Calif.: Science and Behavior Books.

Seeman, M. 1959. On the Meaning of Alienation. *American Sociological Review,* 24, 783–91.

Selltiz, C., Jahoda, M., Deutsch, M., and Cook, S. W. 1959. *Research Methods in Social Relations,* rev. ed. New York: Holt, Rinehart and Winston.

Selltiz, C., Wrightsman, L. S., and Cook, S. W. 1976. *Research Methods in Social Relations,* 3rd ed. New York: Holt, Rinehart and Winston.

Sewell, W. H. 1941. The Development of a Sociometric Scale. *Sociometry, 5,* 279–97.

Siegel, R. W., and Hodge, R. W. 1968. A Causal Approach to the Study of Measurement Error. In H. M. Blalock and A. B. Blalock (eds.). *Methodology in Social Research,* pp. 28–59. New York: McGraw-Hill.

Smith, K. W. 1974a. On Estimating the Reliability of Composite Indexes Through Factor Analysis. *Sociological Methods and Research, 4,* 485–510.
    1974b. Forming Composite Scales and Estimating their Validity Through Factor Analysis. *Social Forces, 53,* 168–80.

Sörbom, D. 1975. Detection of Correlated Errors in Longitudinal Data. *British Journal of Mathematical and Statistical Psychology, 28,* 138–51.

Spearman, C. 1910. Correlation Calculated from Faulty Data. *British Journal of Psychology, 3,* 271–95.

Spearman, C., and Holzinger, K. 1924. The Sampling Error in the Theory of Two Factors, *British Journal of Psychology, 15,* 17–9.

Spreitzer, E., and Chase, L. 1972. A Power Analysis of Published Sociological Literature. Mimeo.

Stanley, J. C. 1971. Reliability. In R. L. Thorndike (ed.). *Educational Measurement.* Washington, D.C.: American Council on Education.

Star, S. A., and Hughes, H. M. 1949–50. Report on an Educational Campaign: The Cincinnati Plan for the United Nations. *American Journal of Sociology, 55,* 389.

Stevens, S. S. 1951. Mathematics, Measurement and Psychophysics. In S. S. Stevens (ed.). *Handbook of Experimental Psychology.* New York: Wiley.
    1968. Measurement, Statistics and the Schemapiric View. *Science, 161,* 849–56.

Stinchcomb, A. L. 1971. A Heuristic Procedure for Interpreting Factor Analysis. *American Sociological Review, 36,* 1080–4.

Sudman, S., and Bradburn, N. 1974. *Response Effects in Surveys.* Chicago: Aldine.

Sullivan, J. A. 1971. Multiple Indicators in Complex Causal Models. In H. M. Blalock (ed.). *Causal Models in the Social Sciences,* pp. 327–34. New York: Aldine-Atherton.
    1974. Multiple Indicators: Some Criteria of Selection. In H. M. Blalock (ed.). *Measurement in Social Sciences: Theories and Strategies,* pp. 243–69. Chicago: Aldine.

Summers, G. F. (ed.) 1970. *Attitude Measurement.* Chicago: Rand McNally.

Thurstone, L. L. 1947. *Multiple-Factor Analysis: A Development and Expansion of the Vectors of Mind.* Chicago: University of Chicago Press.

Torgerson, W. S. 1958. *Theory and Methods of Scaling.* New York: Wiley.

Tucker, L. R., and Lewis, C. 1973. A Reliability Coefficient for Maximum Likelihood Factor Analysis. *Psychometrika, 38,* 1–10.

Upshaw, H. S. 1968. Attitude Measurement. In H. M. Blalock and A. B. Blalock (eds.). *Methodology in Social Research.* New York: McGraw-Hill.

Van Valey, T. L. 1971. On the Evaluation of Simple Models Containing Multiple Indicators of Unmeasured Variables. In H. M. Blalock (ed.). *Causal Models in the Social Sciences,* pp. 320–6. Chicago: Aldine.

Wallace, R. B., and Zeller, R. A. 1974a. FIRO-B: A Reformulation, Mimeo.

1974. Guttman Scaling: Theoretical and Empirical Implications. Mimeo.

Werts, C. E., and Linn, R. N. 1970. Cautions in Applying Various Procedures for Determining the Reliability and Validity of Multiple-Item Scales. *American Sociological Review, 35,* 757–9.

Werts, C. E., Linn, R. L., and Jöreskog, K. G. 1971. Estimating the Parameters of Path Models Involving Unmeasured Variables. In H. M. Blalock (ed.). *Causal Models in the Social Sciences,* pp. 400–9. Chicago: Aldine.

1974. Quantifying Unmeasured Variables. In H. M. Blalock (ed.). *Measurement in the Social Sciences: Theories and Strategies,* pp. 270–92. Chicago: Aldine.

Wheaton, B., Muthen, B., Alwin, D. F., and Summers, G. F. 1977. Assessing Reliability and Stability in Panel Models. In D. R. Heise (ed.). *Sociological Methodology 1977,* pp. 84–136. San Francisco: Jossey-Bass.

Wiley, D. E. 1973. The Identification Problem for Structural Equation Models with Unmeasured Variables. In A. S. Goldberger and O. D. Duncan (eds.). *Structural Equation Models in the Social Sciences,* pp. 69–93. New York: Seminar Press.

Wiley, D. E., and Wiley, J. A. 1970. The Estimation of Measurement Error in Panel Data. *American Sociological Review, 35,* 112–17.

Wilson, W. A., and Tracy, J. I. 1937. *Analytic Geometry.* Boston: Heath.

Yee, D., and Gage, H. L. 1968. Techniques for Estimating the Source and Direction of Causal Influence in Panel Data. *Psychological Bulletin, 70,* 115–25.

Zeller, R. A. 1978. Unmeasured Variables in Panel Analysis: An Analytic Example. Mimeo.

Zeller, R. A., and Carmines, E. G. 1976. Factor Scaling, External Consistency, and the Measurement of Theoretical Constructs. *Political Methodology, 3,* 215–52.

1978. *Statistical Analysis of Social Data.* Chicago: Rand McNally.

Index

A Primary Source History of the Lost Colony of
ROANOKE

BRIAN BELVAL

rosen central
Primary Source™

The Rosen Publishing Group, Inc., New York

To Natalie

Published in 2006 by The Rosen Publishing Group, Inc.
29 East 21st Street, New York, NY 10010

Library of Congress Cataloging-in-Publication Data

Belval, Brian.
A primary source history of the Lost Colony of Roanoke / Brian Belval.—1st ed.
    p. cm.—(Primary sources of the thirteen colonies and the Lost Colony)
Includes bibliographical references and index.
ISBN 1-4042-0435-0 (lib. bdg.)
ISBN 1-4042-0669-8 (pbk. bdg.)
1. Roanoke Colony—Juvenile literature. 2. Roanoke Island (N.C.)—History—16th century—Juvenile literature. 3. Roanoke Colony—Sources—Juvenile literature. 4. Roanoke Island (N.C.)—History—16th century—Sources—Juvenile literature.
I. Title. II. Series.
F229.B45 2006
975.6'175–dc22

2005001389

Manufactured in the United States of America

On the front cover: John White is seen with his group in this nineteenth-century illustration pointing to the inscription of the word CROATOAN, a clue presumably left by residents of his Roanoke colony. At the request of Roanoke's colonists, White had left the settlement to return to England for supplies but was unable to immediately return due to England's war with Spain.

CONTENTS

INTRODUCTION

The Mystery of Roanoke

In 1587, English colonists arrived at Roanoke, an island off the coast of present-day North Carolina. Shortly after their arrival, they worried about their ability to survive. They asked their governor, John White, to go back to England for supplies. White reached England safely, but his return trip to America was delayed after war broke out between England and Spain.

Three years later, White finally returned to Roanoke. When he reached the settlement, he discovered that all of the colonists had disappeared. Their homes were also gone—not a single board remained. The only clue that White found was the word "*CROATOAN*" carved into a fence post. He believed this meant that the colonists had moved to a nearby island. Unfortunately, White never made it there. A violent storm blew his ship off course, and the ship's captain refused to continue the search. White sailed back to England unsure of the fate of the 116 colonists. In the following decades, search parties sought them out, but never found them. To this day, their fate remains a mystery.

Many theories exist concerning the missing colonists. Some people believe that they were killed by Native Americans. Still others believe they attempted to sail back to England but were lost at sea. The most promising of these theories are supported, at least in part, by primary sources such as books, letters, drawings, and paintings that were written or made by people who had witnessed the events they described. These sources tend to be more accurate than sources gathered years later. Because of

A drawing by John White, one of the original colonists in the ill-fated Roanoke expedition of 1585, was the foundation for this sixteenth-century engraving by Theodor de Bry called *The Arrival of the Englishmen in Virginia*. Published in England in 1590, de Bry's engraving showed the sinking of several British ships off the coast of what is now North Carolina, as well as the presence of a mythical sea creature in the Atlantic Ocean. The Roanoke colony (seen here as "Roanoac") is pictured, as are the names of several established Native American villages including Secotan, Weapemeoc, Pasquenoke, and Dasamonquepeuc.

this, historians rely highly on information drawn from primary sources in order to more accurately understand history.

A number of primary sources concerning Roanoke remain. Some of these items are featured throughout this book, giving you the chance to examine them just as a historian would.

CHAPTER 1

In 1492, the Italian explorer Christopher Columbus sailed across the Atlantic Ocean hoping to reach Asia. Instead, he discovered America and claimed it for the king of Spain. Over the next fifty years, Spanish men seeking wealth descended upon America. These men were known as conquistadors, or conquerors. The gold and silver they seized from native populations would make Spain the wealthiest, most powerful kingdom in the world.

While Spain gained wealth from its exploration of the New World, England watched from the outside. At the time, England was a kingdom in turmoil. Its king, Henry VIII, had broken relations with the Roman Catholic Church and declared himself the leader

England Challenges Spain

of a new church he named the Church of England. This caused great turmoil in English society. Many English citizens with ties to the Catholic Church lost their land and homes. These changes led to rebellion, especially in northern England. To make matters worse, England was at war with France and Scotland throughout

Henry's reign. These conflicts depleted England's resources, so instead of funding expeditions to America, England was forced to solve its problems at home.

The situation in England worsened after Henry VIII died. Edward, Henry's only son, became king at age ten. Edward was sickly and died after only six years on the throne. Because of his youth and poor health, he was unable to provide the leadership England needed. Then, Henry's daughter Mary became queen. Mary was a Catholic and felt it was her duty to reestablish

Social and religious reform took shape in England under King Henry VIII (1491–1547), who reigned from 1509 until his death. Pictured (*left*) in an oil portrait by Hans Holbein the Younger, the court painter, King Henry provided solid leadership for England and helped bolster its defense, especially its naval fleet. Despite the king's hopes that his young son would rule after his death, Edward was too sickly and died of tuberculosis in 1553. Taking over for Edward was Henry's daughter, Mary Tudor, though her reign would end with her death in 1558. After, the throne was passed to Mary's half sister Elizabeth (1558–1603, *right*). Despite inheriting a dwindling treasury and a society disunited by religious differences, Queen Elizabeth's forty-four–year legacy was regarded as successful, especially considering her decisions to send expeditions to the New World.

England as a Catholic country. One of her methods to accomplish this goal was to execute people who opposed Catholicism. By the end of her reign, she was known as "Bloody Mary."

To undo the fear and distrust created during Mary's reign, England needed a strong, intelligent, and persuasive leader. Such a person was Queen Elizabeth I, the daughter of Henry VIII and

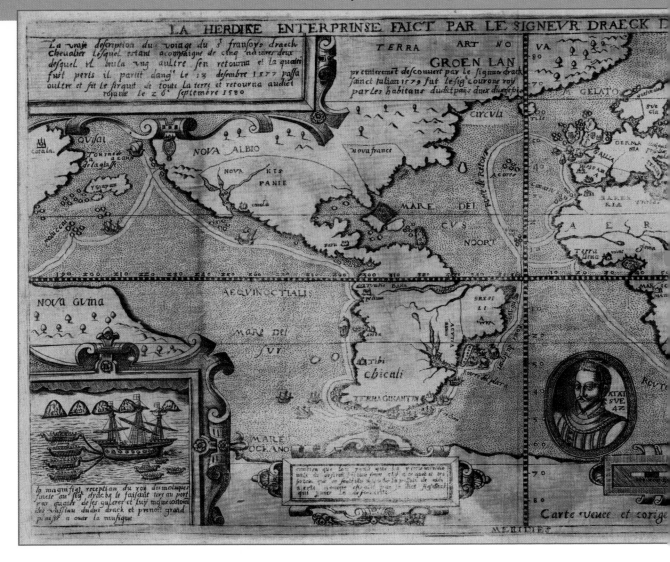

half sister of Mary. Elizabeth was crowned in 1558. One of Elizabeth's first acts was to restore the Church of England. The country rallied around the church, taking pride in the Protestant faith. Then Elizabeth went about improving relations with Scotland and France, two longtime enemies of England. She also passed laws to help improve England's economy. Before long, England prospered and set its sights on America.

During Elizabeth's reign, great mariners of England emerged from a coastal area called Devonshire. Here, generations of

This world map shows the route taken by the English navigator Sir Francis Drake who was knighted by Queen Elizabeth shortly after he returned from his voyage around the world in 1580. Drake returned to England with a tremendous quantity of gold, silver, jewels, and other precious items, which he bestowed upon the queen while recalling tales of his excursions to far-flung places. Because of Drake's success, England's wealth was restored and the country held claims to lands in the New World. When Drake was knighted he was given a coat of arms that read, *Sic Parvis Magna,* Latin for "Greatness from Small Beginnings." Later, in 1588 with England at war with Spain, Drake helped to successfully defend his homeland from Spain's mighty armada.

shipbuilders, merchants, and sailors had established a profitable trade with northern Europe. By the 1560s, they were actively seeking opportunities to expand their trade elsewhere. They were fascinated by the New World, but it was off-limits to them. The king of Spain, Philip II, did not allow his colonies in the Americas to trade with any country except Spain.

John Hawkins was the first of the men from Devonshire to challenge King Philip II. In 1562, Hawkins sailed to the New World with hundreds of African slaves he intended to sell to colonists. He knew his actions were illegal, but the colonists were willing to ignore the law because they desperately needed slaves to work their plantations. In 1567, after two successful slave-trading voyages, Hawkins returned for a third. This time the king was waiting for him. Philip had learned of the illegal trading and sent his warships to attack Hawkins. The warships intercepted Hawkins's fleet near Veracruz, Mexico. Hawkins lost four ships in the ensuing battle, and barely escaped with his life.

An English sailor named Francis Drake fought alongside Hawkins on that fateful day. Enraged by the aggression of the king of Spain, he sought revenge. By 1572, Drake was attacking Spanish ports in Central America and stuffing his vessels full of stolen treasure. Over the next decade, Drake would become the first Englishman to circumnavigate the globe. He returned to England a national hero and was knighted by Queen Elizabeth aboard his ship the *Golden Hind*.

Soon, English sailors had learned the easiest way to get rich was to steal from the Spanish. The Englishmen who challenged Spain in this way became known as "sea dogs," named after a type of shark common in English waters. Often these men received approval and even funds from the queen to rob Spanish ships. This activity was called privateering, and the men who took part in it were known as privateers.

In 1577, a sea dog named Sir Humphrey Gilbert submitted a proposal to the queen entitled *How Her Majesty May Annoy the King of Spain*. Part of Gilbert's plan was to seize Spanish fishing fleets in Newfoundland, a large island on the east coast of Canada. Although the queen disagreed with Gilbert's plan, she did give him permission to start a colony there. She felt, as did Gilbert and others, that the time had come for England to establish itself overseas.

Unfortunately, Gilbert failed. His first attempt to reach the New World in 1578 was disastrous and his ships returned to England. In 1583, Gilbert tried again. He made it to Newfoundland, but problems mounted after his arrival. Some of his men fled, hoping to hitch a ride back home on one of the ships in the harbor. Others decided to hijack a fishing vessel. Then, on a scouting mission off the coast, one of Gilbert's boats sank and their supplies were ruined. After less than a month in Newfoundland, Gilbert abandoned hope of starting a colony. The final disaster occurred on his return voyage when his ship capsized in a storm and he was drowned.

Luckily for England, its desire to settle the New World did not end with Gilbert. The spirit of exploration was passed on to Gilbert's half brother, Sir Walter Raleigh.

CHAPTER 2

Scouting the New World

Sir Walter Raleigh would eventually become the driving force behind the Roanoke colony. Born in 1554 in Devonshire, England, his family was influential in business and politics. At fifteen years of age, Raleigh went to France to make his name as a soldier. He fought beside the Huguenots, Protestant allies of England who were battling Catholic forces for control of the country. When Raleigh returned from France, he attended law school but didn't take his studies seriously. Instead, he spent his time writing poetry and drinking in local taverns. In 1578, he captained a ship in his half brother's unsuccessful attempt to colonize America. Then, in 1580, Raleigh returned to military service. He went to Ireland, where the Irish were rebelling against their English landlords. Raleigh helped put down the rebellion, overseeing the execution of all 600 residents of the town of Smerwick.

Raleigh's service in Ireland attracted the attention of Queen Elizabeth, who was searching for courageous leaders. Soon he became a member of the queen's court. In this position as a courtier, his responsibility was to entertain and flatter the queen. Raleigh excelled as a courtier. His charm, wit, and skill as a poet delighted Queen Elizabeth. She rewarded him with permission to collect taxes from area merchants. By the time of Sir Humphrey Gilbert's death in 1583, Raleigh was wealthy, ambitious, and hungry for fame. It was no surprise, then, that Elizabeth chose to transfer the right of colonization in North America to Raleigh, whom she affectionately referred to as her "Water."

POTENTISSIMAE ELIZABETHAE ANGLIAE REGINAE ad Nobilissimum D.m D.m HENRICUM CAREY, Baron.de HUNSDON, Consobrinum suum in Villa de Hunsdon PROCESSIO REGALIS.

The Royal PROCESSION of QUEEN ELIZABETH to Visit the Right Hon.ble HENRY CAREY Lord HUNSDON, Governor of Berwick upon Tweed, Captain of the Band of Gentlemen Pensioners K.t of the most Noble Order of the Garter, Privy Counsellor and Cousin German to her Majesty by the Lady MARY, Sister to QUEEN ANNA BOLEN.

About 1,000 people made up the court of Queen Elizabeth I at any given time during her reign. Her every need was tended to and she was well guarded from potential adversaries. Even in Elizabeth's private moments, more than six maids could be found in her presence. Of her courtiers, among them Sir Walter Raleigh, the queen expected great intelligence and wit. In this eighteenth-century engraving, Raleigh is pictured among the court procession. Like other monarchs, Elizabeth moved from castle to castle throughout England (at the time of her accession she inherited sixty residences), and in this image she is being carried by armed guard to London.

Raleigh wasted no time putting together his expedition. A month after receiving permission from the queen, he had two ships outfitted to sail to the New World. His mission was to hire a crew to scout suitable locations in America for a colony. Ideally, his crew would locate an area with a harbor close to Spain's colonies, but also

John White (about 1557–1593), sixteenth-century English artist and governor of the 1587 colony, was responsible for some of our most exquisite and valuable paintings of Native American life in Virginia. This watercolor, *The Manner of Their Fishing*, was an invented scene, a combination of several studies of Native Americans and their fishing practices that were observed by White in the New World. According to his notes, the Algonquin used a dip net and spear for day fishing and a fire in a canoe to attract fish at night.

hidden from them. Twenty years earlier, the French had established Fort Caroline in Florida, but the Spanish had destroyed it.

Raleigh wanted the colony to serve as a base for privateering. In the past, privateers would sail across the Atlantic, meet Spanish ships, and then travel back to England. A colony closer to the Spanish treasure fleet would be much more convenient and profitable.

On April 27, 1584, Raleigh's two ships left England. Raleigh chose Philip Amadas to lead the expedition, while Arthur Barlowe captained the smaller vessel. On July 4, after more than two months at sea, they spotted land and claimed it for England.

Initially the men thought they had landed on the North American mainland. However, they soon realized they were on an island about 20 miles (32 kilometers) long and 6 miles (10 km) wide. (Today we know this island as one in the chain off the coast of North Carolina called the Outer Banks. The exact island where they landed is still debated, but it was likely Hatarask Island.) As they explored, the Englishmen found woods full of deer, rabbits, and birds. In the words of Barlowe, the island was teeming with animals "in incredible abundance."

On the third day, a lone Native American appeared on the beach directly across from the Englishmen's ships. A group of Englishmen, including Amadas and Barlowe, rode out to meet him. The Indian delivered a speech to the men, not a word of which they understood. The Englishmen brought the Native American to their ship, where he was given a shirt and a hat. They also offered him wine and meat.

After he was given a tour of both ships, the Native American returned to the shore. He immediately sought out his boat and began fishing. Within thirty minutes he had packed his boat full of fish. On the shore, he neatly divided his catch into two piles. The

Native American pointed at each pile and then to each anchored ship. The fish were gifts in return for the Englishmen's gifts.

In the days that followed, the English traded extensively with the Native Americans, exchanging some of their less valuable items for animal skins, leather, dyes, and coral. The Native Americans also expressed great interest in the Englishmen's metal swords, which were superior to their own wooden ones. But the English refused to trade their swords, fearing they might be used against them.

Throughout this period, the Native Americans were generous. Every day Granganimeo, the brother of the Indian king Wingina, brought the explorers food—deer, rabbit, fish, fruit, melons, walnuts, and an assortment of vegetables including corn. During this time they were also introduced to Granganimeo's wife, whom Barlowe described as being "bashful."

Although the Englishmen and the Native Americans spoke different languages, they were still able to communicate using gestures and sign language. The explorers learned that the king of the tribe was named Wingina and that he had been injured while fighting rival Native Americans. Because he was recuperating in a distant village, Amadas and Barlowe were unable to meet him.

Of course, occasional misunderstandings occurred between the two groups. For example, when the explorers asked one of the Native Americans the name of his country, he misunderstood them, and replied, "Wingandacoa," which meant, "You wear nice clothes." From then on, the explorers mistakenly referred to the country as Wingandacoa.

After establishing good relations with the Native Americans, Barlowe and seven other men decided it was safe to go scouting. Twenty miles (32 km) into their journey, they reached a Native American settlement on the north end of Roanoke Island. As they

This lithograph, a map of the North American coastline and Chesapeake Bay, is a copy of a painting by John White. It was created sometime between 1570 and 1593. Just off the coast of what is now North Carolina, in the mid-left section of the drawing (and in the detail, *inset*), sits Roanoke Island. It was then known as "Roanoac," a name attributed to the Indian king Roanoac, who may have lived there prior to the arrival of the Europeans. To the Algonquin, *Roanoac* may also have meant "northern people" or may have been a reference to shell beads.

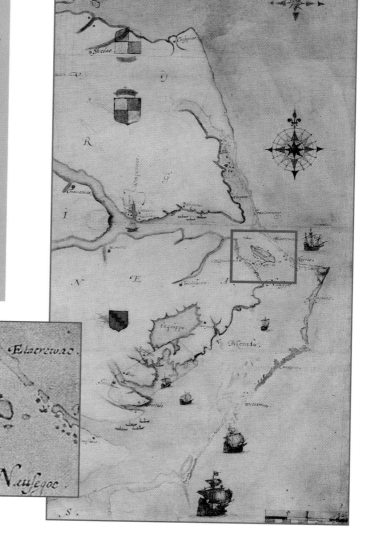

approached, Granganimeo's wife rushed out to meet them, delighted by their surprise visit.

Granganimeo's wife treated the men well. She had them carried back to her village, which consisted of nine homes made out of cedar wood. The explorers were brought inside her home and seated in front of the fire. According to Barlowe, "She took off our clothes and washed them and dried them." Then, her attendants washed the explorers' feet.

The landing of the Englishmen at Roanoke Island is depicted in this nineteenth-century print. Although historians speculate as to when Englishmen first set foot in the New World (some claim as early as 1475), it is well documented that England's finest achievements in exploration came under the leadership of Queen Elizabeth beginning in 1558. Although colonization didn't occur until the late 1580s, many earlier English fishermen wintered in the New World during long expeditions.

After they were refreshed, Granganimeo's wife led the explorers into a room where a feast had been prepared. The men ate happily, enjoying the bounty.

Suddenly, the festive tone of the dinner was interrupted when Barlowe and his men caught sight of a group of Native Americans carrying bows and arrows. Even though they meant no harm, the sight of their weapons alarmed the group. Granganimeo's wife noticed that the Englishmen were uncomfortable. She asked her servants to confiscate the bows. Then, the

Sir Walter Raleigh (1554–1618) is pictured on the engraved title page of *The Historie of the World*, a chronicle of world events first published in 1614. Raleigh began writing his *Historie* while imprisoned in the Tower of London. He was first sent there by Queen Elizabeth after she discovered that he was secretly married to one of her maids, Elizabeth Throckmorton. Though he was soon released, he was again imprisoned in 1603 after James I read *Historie* and found him guilty of treason. Although he was released in 1616, he was executed two years later. See page 54 for an excerpt from *The Historie of the World*.

servants broke the bows to prove that they would not harm their guests.

Still, the Englishmen were worried. When they announced they had to leave, Granganimeo's wife begged them to stay. It did not matter that they'd witnessed the bows destroyed. They knew there were others, and they weren't willing to take any risks. Instead of sleeping in the village, they slept on their boat. When daylight arrived, they returned to the main ships.

By mid-August, the scout group left America for England. Two Native Americans named Manteo and Wanchese joined them. The

Englishmen hoped to teach English to the Native Americans so they could act as interpreters on future voyages.

Back in England, Barlowe prepared a report for Raleigh that said that Roanoke Island appeared to be ideal for a colony. Barlowe noted how it was situated at a safe distance from the Spanish colonies. Roanoke was also hidden from view of passing ships and would be difficult to find if one didn't know exactly where to look. Additionally, Roanoke and the surrounding islands had enough deer and fish to support a colony and its soil was believed to be good for farming. Perhaps most important, the Native Americans were friendly. As Barlowe put it, "We found the people most gentle, loving, and faithful."

CHAPTER 3

The Military Colony

Even before Philip Amadas and Arthur Barlowe returned, Sir Walter Raleigh was busy preparing for the next voyage. The optimistic report he received from Barlowe accelerated his plans. He worked feverishly to find influential people to support his colony. To advertise the project, Manteo and Wanchese were introduced to potential investors, including Queen Elizabeth. Most of the people who met the Indians were impressed by them.

By April of 1585, Raleigh had a fleet ready to sail to Roanoke. His colony was to be named Virginia after Elizabeth, the "Virgin Queen." Elizabeth provided the flagship, the *Tiger*. She also provided an accomplished military leader, Ralph Lane, to act as governor of the colony. Raleigh, however, would not be joining the colonists in America. Elizabeth insisted that he was too valuable in England.

Instead of Raleigh, Sir Richard Grenville was put in charge of the fleet. Grenville, Raleigh's cousin, had distinguished himself as a soldier in Ireland and as a sheriff in England. The lead pilot of the expedition was Simon Fernandez, who was also the pilot on the first voyage to Roanoke. He would be responsible for making sure they reached their destination safely.

On April 9, 1585, with Fernandez at the helm of the *Tiger*, the seven ships left England with 600 men. Their goal was to establish a base for raids against Spanish ships.

On June 22, the fleet arrived at the area now known as the Outer Banks. They sailed to Wococon Island, about 80 miles (129 km) south of Roanoke Island. Grenville and Lane had quarreled for much

Most historians believe this is a portrait of Thomas Harriot (1560–1621, *left*, also spelled Hariot), a friend and colleague of Sir Walter Raleigh's. At various periods, he served as Raleigh's accountant, ship designer, cartographer, and navigational instructor for his crews. In 1585, Harriot accompanied Raleigh's second expedition to Virginia under Sir Richard Grenville and acted as the group's historian. Harriot detailed his observations about the New World in *A Briefe and True Report of the New Found Land of Virginia*, which was first published in 1590. The title page is pictured on the right. See page 54 for a transcription.

of the journey. Each sent letters back to England claiming the other had failed to do his job. According to Lane, Grenville had become so furious that he threatened to execute him.

Then, tragedy nearly struck as Fernandez led the ships too close to land as the fleet approached Wococon. Ocean waves slammed the flagship into a shoal. Fernandez managed to save the ship, but many of their supplies got spoiled. Without these supplies, the colonists would have to find other ways to feed themselves.

While the *Tiger* was being repaired, fifty men in four separate boats traveled to the mainland. Over a week, they visited three Native American villages.

Joining Grenville on this expedition were two men who would become forever associated with the Roanoke colony— Thomas Harriot and John White. Harriot was a scientist, writer, and explorer. Raleigh asked him to join the expedition in order to provide a detailed study of the land and its people. Harriot, three years later, published his findings in *A Briefe and True Report of the New Found Land of Virginia*. In it, Harriot detailed all the American resources that might be of interest to English people. These included sassafras, tobacco, cedar wood, otter furs, iron and copper, pearls, turpentine, corn, oysters, and animal skins. Harriot wrote enthusiastically about both the abundance and the quality of these items. He referred to them as commodities, indicating that he believed they could be sold to English people or people in other countries.

In addition to describing New World resources, Harriot wrote about Native American culture and religion in his book. In one passage, he described how when the Englishmen kneeled to pray, the Indians kneeled and pretended to pray beside them. To the Englishmen, this suggested that the Native Americans were eager to convert to Christianity. In Harriot's words, the Native Americans were "poor souls" who were "very desirous to know the truth." That truth was "the knowledge of the gospel."

White was the colony's artist. His job was to draw the Native Americans, plants, and animals of Virginia. One of White's best drawings is of the village of Secota, which the Grenville party reached on July 15, 1585. Historians have gained an understanding

John White produced this famous drawing of the Indian village of Secota while in the company of Raleigh's 1585 expedition to Roanoke. Researching Native Americans around the Carolina coast, White observed this scene of everyday life. Later, around 1590, Theodor de Bry made engravings based on White's observational drawings, including this one. The de Bry engravings were then printed in Harriot's *A Briefe and True Report of the New Found Land of Virginia.*

of what a sixteenth-century Native American village looked like from his rendering.

The day after visiting Secota, the Englishmen discovered that a silver cup was missing. They determined that it was stolen during their visit to the village of Aquascogoc a few days earlier. Grenville instructed a group to return to the village and ask for the cup back. When the colonists didn't receive it, they burned down the village and its cornfields. The action was meant to discourage Indians from unlawful behavior. This harsh discipline was familiar to Lane, Grenville, and the other soldiers. England's military had been using similar tactics for years in Ireland and France.

After the colonists burned Aquascogoc, they returned to their ships. The *Tiger* had been repaired and they were ready to move north to Roanoke Island. They arrived at the harbor near Roanoke on July 29. Fernandez didn't risk running the boat ashore again. He anchored miles away from the island. By now it was becoming clear to Grenville and Lane that Roanoke and the adjacent islands may not be the best place for their colony. Because of the shallow water surrounding the islands, large ships like the *Tiger* had to stay miles offshore in deeper water. This meant that supplies had to be transferred to the island in small boats. In effect, Roanoke would be acceptable as a temporary colony, but eventually Amadas and Barlowe would need a location where larger ships could more easily make their approach.

Shortly after the ships reached the Roanoke harbor, Granganimeo rowed out to welcome them. The good relations established by Amadas and Barlowe had held, and Granganimeo gave the Englishmen permission to build their fort on Roanoke. Immediately, Grenville dispatched a ship back to England to report the good news.

Once they arrived on the island, the colonists set about building homes and a central fort for protection. By August, the fort was completed. Grenville left Roanoke for England, while 107 men, including Governor Lane, stayed behind. The plan was for Grenville to return with supplies the following spring. In the meantime, Lane's colony was supposed to explore the surrounding area for a more suitable site.

On September 3, Lane wrote a letter to Richard Hakluyt, an important promoter of English colonization. In the letter, Lane wrote about Virginia, "it is the goodliest and most pleasing territory of the world."

Still, one of the most important issues for the colonists was the depletion of food. Since most of their food had spoiled, they would need to find more. Growing crops was not an option because they had arrived too late in the season. Instead the colonists looked to the Native Americans for food. Initially this wasn't a problem. The Native Americans had a surplus of corn and were willing to share it.

By March of the next year, however, the relations between the Indians and the colonists had soured. Part of the problem was that Granganimeo, King Wingina's brother, had passed away. He was a good friend to the colonists and encouraged his people to cooperate with the Englishmen. King Wingina wasn't as friendly. He believed the colonists were a burden to his tribe. They were 107 extra men to feed, but did little to contribute to the health and safety of the community. In fact, as their attack on the village of Aquascogoc illustrated, they were capable of sudden acts of violence.

In March, Lane and a group of Englishmen left Roanoke Island to explore an area to the northwest known today as Albemarle Sound in search of a better location. But Lane was also interested

English writer Richard Hakluyt (1552–1616) was among England's strongest supporters of colonization in the New World. Besides important works including *The Principal Navigations*, in which he wrote about contemporary voyages to the New World, Hakluyt also wrote *Discourse of Western Planting* in 1584, a page of which is pictured here. The overwhelming arguments presented in *Discourse* suggest a variety of economic and political advantages that could be gained by England if the country would fund colonies in America. See the transcription on pages 55-56.

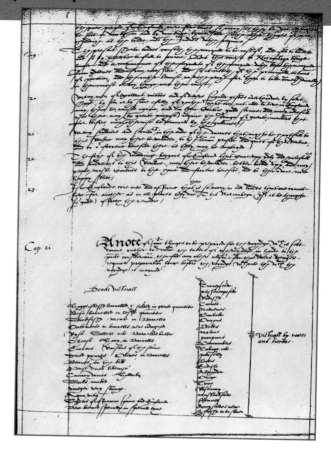

in finding treasure. He had heard of lands that produced copper and pearls in great amounts, and possibly even gold.

The men traveled 130 miles (209 km) to the village of Choanoke. There they met with Menatonon, the Choanoke king. Lane described him as "a man impotent [crippled] in his limbs, but otherwise for a Savage, a very grave and wise man." In order to learn where he could find pearls or gold, Lane and his men took Menatonon prisoner. He confirmed that there were two separate nations, one famous for its pearls, the other for "wassador," which was what the Indians called metal. This area known for its metal (probably copper) was called Chaunis Temoatan. Here, the precious metal was rumored to be so abundant that local tribes built their homes out of it.

While Lane held Menatonon captive, Menatonon confessed that Wingina was conspiring against the Englishmen by spreading rumors that the Englishmen were coming to wage war on Menatonon's tribe. Lane assured Menatonon that this was untrue. He accused Wingina of trying to strike fear into the Choanokes so that they would kill Lane and his men.

Before Lane left Choanoke, he wanted to make sure Menatonon was on his side. So he released Menatonon—and took his son prisoner instead. The son, Skiko, was sent off to Roanoke as a hostage.

The remaining group of thirty men took two boats up the Roanoke River in search of Chaunis Temoaton. They had packed very little food for the journey and hoped to get additional supplies from local Native Americans. However, all of the Native American villages had been deserted. Lane suspected that Wingina had warned the villagers of the Englishmen's approach. Without Indian corn, the Englishmen soon ran out of food. They were forced to turn back. On their return voyage, the situation became so desperate they had to make a stew out of their two guard dogs.

Back at Roanoke, the Englishmen eagerly waited for Sir Richard Grenville to arrive from England with fresh supplies. In the meantime, Lane continued to ask Wingina for food, but every time he was denied. The previous year's surplus of corn was depleted, and the Indians had nothing left to spare. Instead, Wingina planted a field of corn for the Englishmen. However, it would be two months before the corn was ready to harvest.

Lane's men foraged the neighboring islands for food. They survived by eating clams and wild game. These were hard times for the Englishmen. As they faced starvation, they probably blamed their woes on the Native Americans. Now the English and the Indians were enemies.

Richard Grenville (1542–1591) was an English naval officer who commanded the fleet of vessels carrying the first colonists to Virginia in 1585. Not long after his arrival, Grenville burned an Indian village, claiming that local tribes had stolen a silver cup. The burning of the village is re-created in this hand-colored woodcut.

Soon, a rumor reached Lane. Wingina was planning a surprise attack. The plan was to burn the fort and the surrounding homes and drive the Englishmen off the island. After weighing his options, Lane decided to act first. On the night of June 1, 1586, Lane and twenty-five men crossed Roanoke Sound to Wingina's village, Dasemunkepeuc. Pretending to want to meet with the king on friendly terms, the men were allowed to enter the village. Once inside, Lane shouted the signal to attack, "Christ Our Victory!" The Englishmen opened fire. A number of Indians were hit, including Wingina, who fell to the ground. Miraculously, Wingina got up and sprinted toward the woods. A number of English soldiers gave chase. A few minutes later, an English soldier emerged from the woods carrying Wingina's head.

While Lane attacked Wingina at Dasemunkepeuc, a fleet of thirty ships approached Roanoke. On June 8, one of Lane's soldiers spotted the English fleet. It was Sir Francis Drake and his band of privateers, returning from a successful raid against the Spanish. They had decided to stop by Roanoke on their way back to England.

On June 10, Lane met with Drake on his flagship. Drake understood the men were desperate. He offered Lane two choices. Drake could provide Lane with men, boats, and enough supplies for thirty days. This would allow him to continue his exploration of Virginia until Grenville arrived with more food. Or Lane and his men could return on Drake's ships back to England. Lane accepted the first offer. He wanted to forge ahead with his mission. Then, a fierce storm struck on June 13, sinking a number of ships in Drake's fleet. Most of the supplies were lost or ruined. Lane saw this as a sign that he was meant to return to England. In his words, "The very hand of God as it seemed, stretched out to take us from there." On June 19, the colonists boarded Drake's ships and set sail for England.

One month later, Sir Richard Grenville finally returned to Roanoke with supplies and reinforcements. When he found the colony deserted, he chose fifteen of his men to hold the fort, and returned to England.

CHAPTER 4

S ir Walter Raleigh must have been extremely disappointed when he learned that Ralph Lane had abandoned the colony. He had invested a considerable amount of his fortune in the colonization effort and had nothing to show for it. Still, his belief in England's destiny to colonize in America could not be shaken.

John White, the artist in Lane's colony, led the effort to organize the third colony, the City of Raleigh. White would also become its governor.

The motivation behind this colony differed from that of the previous effort. Instead of a colony of soldiers, this would be a colony of families who personally invested in the venture. In return for their investment, they would receive a portion of any money made by the colony. Also, unlike the soldiers who were expected to stay at the colony for shifts of a few years, these colonists intended to stay in America permanently. To encourage this, each head of household would receive 500 acres (202 hectares) of land. They were expected to farm the land and be able to support themselves. Ideally, they would also develop products that could be sold for profit in Europe.

John White's Colony

It was difficult for White to find people interested in resettlement. The majority of people were unwilling to live half way across the world in a land inhabited by "savages." In the end, White persuaded 116 colonists to come to America.

Everyone involved in the City of Raleigh agreed that it would have to be established somewhere other than Roanoke Island

John White made this fanciful watercolor painting of several hundred miles of what is now the eastern coast of the United States, including areas around the Chesapeake Bay and northern Florida. Instructed by Sir Walter Raleigh to "draw to life one of each kind of thing that is strange to us in England," White produced accurate and detailed images of plants, animals, fish, and portraits of many of the Native Americans showcasing their customs and dress. Little is known about White, who was ultimately a better artist than governor. Some historians believe that he also accompanied the English explorer Martin Frobisher on his voyage to the Arctic in 1577 prior to joining Raleigh's Roanoke expedition.

since it was unsuitable for ships to approach. Also, there was concern over how receptive the Roanoke Indians would be to another English colony in their territory. The fact that the previous English visitors had killed Wingina and became enemies of the Native Americans worried the new colonists. Would the Roanoke Indians be willing to live peacefully beside them?

The City of Raleigh was instead planned to be established near Chesapeake Bay. Some of Lane's men had visited this area and described it favorably. In the Chesapeake, the water was deeper and would accommodate larger ships. In addition, the bay was somewhat protected from unpredictable and violent weather.

Three ships were ready to leave England on May 8, 1587. Simon Fernandez piloted the flagship, the *Lion*. Of the 117 colonists, nine were children and two were pregnant women.

Eight days later, one of the vessels fell behind and lost contact with the fleet. White blamed Fernandez. He accused Fernandez of intentionally "leaving her [the ship] distressed in the Bay of Portugal." It was the first of many complaints White would have concerning Fernandez's behavior during the voyage.

The remaining ships reached the island of St. Croix on June 22. The colonists left the boats and explored the lush, tropical surroundings that looked nothing like England. Their curiosity, however, would soon get the best of them. According to White,

> At our first landing on this island, some of our women, and men, by eating a small fruit, like green apples, were fearfully troubled with a sudden burning in their mouths, and swelling of their tongues so big, that some of them could not speak.

Later, some of the colonists washed their faces in a pond that turned out to be poisoned. The next morning, according to White's account, "their faces did so burn and swell that their eyes were shut up, and they could not see for five or six days or longer." This must have been a rude awakening for many of the colonists who now realized that danger was everywhere.

Pefe pica.

This image by John White is of one type of fish prevalent in the Northeast. White's drawings remain one of America's best sources of information about conditions in the New World in the late 1500s. White's detailed paintings and maps presented Europeans with the opportunity to view a firsthand account of life on another continent. The images he created of Native Americans, their customs, and the animals of the region helped to inspire Europeans to colonize America in the years that followed.

By July 16, the two ships reached Virginia. White then accused Fernandez of being careless and ignorant after he almost wrecked the *Lion*. Six days later, the colonists arrived at the harbor near Roanoke Island. They had received instructions from Raleigh to check on the men left behind by Grenville, then to continue north to Chesapeake Bay to establish the new colony.

White and forty men boarded the smaller boat called a pinnace in order to reach Roanoke. As they prepared to leave, Fernandez shouted at the crewmen on the boat to not return the colonists to the *Lion*. He intended to take them no farther than Roanoke. According to Fernandez, "The summer was far spent." By this, he meant that he had wasted too much time away from what he really wanted to do—privateering. Fernandez wanted to get rid of the colonists so that he could sail off and steal treasure from the Spanish.

Surely, this must have been a great shock to White, but he was powerless to fight back. Fernandez was the pilot of the ship, and his crew was behind him. If they were determined to leave the colonists at Roanoke, then they could not be stopped.

A greater shock awaited White and his men during their search for the fifteen men left behind by Grenville. White wrote in his journal, "We found none of them, nor any sign that they had been there, saving only we found the bones of one of those fifteen, which the Savages had slain long before."

Despite this grisly discovery, White ordered the colonists to repair the abandoned homes. He also ordered the construction of additional homes to accommodate the colonists. White was attempting to make the best of a bad situation.

Good news finally arrived on July 25 when the vessel that had been abandoned by Fernandez in the Bay of Portugal arrived at Roanoke. Miraculously, its pilot, Edward Spicer, was able to locate Virginia even though he had never been there before. According to White, this was "a great joy and comfort of the whole company." Now all 116 colonists had arrived at the island. Although they were surely disappointed to be dropped off short of their destination, at least they had the comfort of knowing the entire company had arrived safely.

For the first few days on the island, the colonists did not encounter any Native Americans. This may have given the colonists a false sense of security. Soon, however, their vulnerability would be exposed. One of the colonists, George Howe, wandered away. He was wading in shallow water, hunting crabs, when a group of Native Americans attacked. According to White, "they gave him sixteen wounds with their arrows, and after they had slain him with their wooden swords, beat his head in pieces."

After this incident, a group of colonists traveled to a nearby island called Croatoan, which was home to Manteo, the Englishmen's interpreter. Since Manteo was now living with the Englishmen, they hoped the Croatoans would be friendly. In White's words, he was hoping the Native Americans would "accept our friendship . . . and that all unfriendly dealings past on both parties, should be utterly forgiven and forgotten." The Croatoans agreed to gather leaders from the local villages and bring them to Roanoke to discuss the Englishmen's offer of peace.

The Croatoans also revealed to the Englishmen the fate of the fifteen colonists left behind by Grenville. Wingina's tribe ambushed the men shortly after they arrived. One of them was killed immediately, while the others retreated to the fort. The Indians forced the Englishmen out of the fort by setting it on fire. The two groups fought outside of the fort where another Englishman was killed. Then the remaining colonists fled to the water. They rushed into their boat and sailed away, never to be seen again. No one knows if they attempted to return to England, or if they searched for a new place to settle. Either way, they probably died shortly thereafter.

After meeting with the Croatoans, the Englishmen returned to Roanoke. There they waited for the arrival of the Indian leaders for seven days. After the week had passed, the Englishmen interpreted the lack of response as a rejection of their offer

Based on direct observations made by John White in the 1580s, Englishman Theodor de Bry created a series of hand-colored engravings for Thomas Harriot's *A Briefe and True Report of the New Found Land of Virginia* (1590). Among them is the one seen here, called *A Great Lord of Virginia*.

of peace. White then decided to attack the Native Americans at Dasemunkepeuc to avenge the murder of George Howe.

The Englishmen arrived at Dasemunkepeuc on the morning of August 9 and silently approached the village. When they saw a group of Native Americans around an open fire, they attacked without warning. The soldiers shot one of the Indians and pursued the others into the woods. Soon, they realized the Indians were not Wingina's men but Croatoans. They had attacked the only Indians who had remained friendly to them! The Croatoans explained that Wingina's men had fled Dasemunkepeuc soon after Howe's death. They had anticipated the Englishmen would come after them, and had moved deep into their territory for protection. The Croatoans were there to gather the corn left behind by the Roanoke settlers when they fled.

White reported that Manteo grieved over the unfortunate attack on his people, but at the same time blamed them for their misfortune. He told his people that if they would have brought the Indian leaders to Roanoke as promised, the attack would not have happened. It's unclear how the Croatoans felt about Manteo's statements, but most likely they felt betrayed by him.

A few days after the attack, the colonists rewarded Manteo for his loyalty to England. White appointed him as lord of Dasemunkepeuc. The title gave him control of the land previously ruled by Wingina. He was also baptized, making him the first Native American to convert to the Church of England.

On August 18, another landmark event occurred. Eleanor Dare, the daughter of John White, gave birth. Her daughter, Virginia Dare, became the first English person born in America. It must have been a joyous day for White and the colonists. They celebrated the birth of a healthy, beautiful child, and for that day were able to put aside their fears.

But other matters soon surfaced. The colony decided that at least one of the colonists should return to England for supplies. Well aware of the difficulty Lane's colony had in receiving fresh supplies, they wanted a representative at home to ensure that the shipments were sent in a timely manner. Because they had alienated all the local tribes, the grave danger of not receiving food became increasingly obvious to them.

This nineteenth-century image represents one artist's conception of the historical baptism of Virginia Dare, the first baby born to Europeans in the New World. She was born in August 1587 to Eleanor Dare, daughter of John White, and Ananias Dare. Tragically, White never got to know his granddaughter since she disappeared along with all of the Roanoke colonists between 1587 and 1588. White left Roanoke to obtain supplies, but was delayed in England due to the country's war with Spain.

The men came to White and asked him to return to England. At first, he refused. He didn't think it was right for the leader of the colony to abandon it. They still hadn't decided where they should move the colony. White wanted to influence that decision and he feared that he would be judged unfairly in England if he returned and left the colonists behind. Would he look like a coward? In addition, if he returned to England, he wouldn't be there for his daughter and grandchild.

But the colonists returned the next day and asked again. They put their request in writing and signed it. This was important to White, because now he could present this letter to anyone in England who questioned why he would leave his colony behind. Despite his reservations, and the sadness that he must have felt about leaving his daughter and granddaughter behind, White agreed to leave the colony on August 27.

CHAPTER 5

John White nearly didn't make it back to England. Three weeks into his journey, a powerful storm blew his ship back toward America. It took him seven days to return to the spot where he had been struck by the storm. Then his crew became ill and two men died. To make matters worse, their drinking water had become desperately low. White estimated that they had only three gallons (eleven liters) of liquids—beer, wine, and water—to be shared by thirteen men. White wrote in his journal, "We expected nothing but by famine to perish at sea."

The Lost Colony

Remarkably, on October 16, 1587, the men, weak, thirsty, and starving, spotted land. They were lost, however, and not until a boat came out to greet them did they know their location. They had reached Smerwick, in western Ireland. Many of the men remained sick, and shortly after their arrival three more died.

White fared better than his crew. He was well enough to take the first ship out to England. He reached Cornwall, the westernmost county of England, on November 5.

White met with Sir Walter Raleigh. He described the colony's situation and asked for help. Raleigh remained supportive of the colony. He decided to send a small ship immediately with a portion of the needed supplies. Then, he would send a larger relief fleet in the spring of 1588.

Soon it became clear that no ships would set sail for Roanoke in 1587. The Spanish Armada was preparing to attack England to avenge years of raids by English privateers. The king of Spain's plan was to strike back at England with one of the largest fleets

Hendrik Cornelisz Vroom painted this image in oil of a sea battle between the Spanish Armada and the English navy in 1600. The invasion of the Spanish Armada on English shores in 1588 was an attempt by King Phillip of Spain to overthrow England and restore the power of the Catholic Church. Although its navy was greatly outnumbered by the immense Spanish fleet, a combination of trickery and bad weather foiled the Spaniards' attempt to take over the country.

ever assembled. In response, Queen Elizabeth recalled all of England's ships to help defend the country.

Despite this setback, White didn't give up. After much effort, he was given permission to use two smaller ships. Because of their size and poor condition, they would be of no use in the defense against Spain, but acceptable for White's purpose.

The *Brave* and the *Roe* left England on April 22, 1588. They carried supplies and eleven colonists recruited by White. It soon became clear that the captains of these two ships were more interested in privateering than reaching Roanoke. With the coast of England still in sight, they overtook two ships and, in the words of White, "took from them whatsoever we could find worth the taking."

Their success was short-lived. Two French ships began to chase the *Brave* after it had separated from the *Roe*. The French ships were both superior to the *Brave* and had no trouble reaching it. The ships exchanged cannon fire. The *Brave*'s cannon took out its enemy's gunner, but could not stop the ship's approach. One of the French ships made contact with the *Brave*. The Frenchmen swarmed onto the English ship, and a bloody fight ensued. White reported that he was "wounded twice in the head, once with a sword, and another time with a pike, and hurt also in the side of the buttock with a shot." The fight lasted more than an hour until the Frenchmen overwhelmed the *Brave*. The English surrendered. Defenseless and without supplies, the *Brave* was forced to return to England on May 22. A few weeks later, the *Roe* also returned. Both had failed to reach Roanoke.

It wasn't until March 20, 1590, that White would set sail for Roanoke again. Two years and seven months had passed since he had left the island. White probably had mixed feelings about the voyage. Surely he was excited about the possibility of returning to his colony and being reunited with his daughter and granddaughter. At the same time, he likely feared what might have happened in the years since his departure. Because he remembered the attack gone awry at Dasemunkepeuc and the murder of George Howe, he must have been concerned that the colonists were unable to reestablish peace with the Native Americans.

White's fleet consisted of four ships, *Little John*, *Hopewell*, *John Evangelist*, and *Moonlight*. White knew from the outset that this would be a privateering mission first, and a relief mission to Roanoke second. Because of this he was not allowed to bring any colonists on this trip, nor was he able to pack anything beyond a few personal belongings. The fact that he was returning almost three years late, and without any supplies, as promised, must have further torn at his conscience.

The fleet crossed the Atlantic quickly but then spent three full months hunting Spanish ships in the Caribbean. The English overtook numerous Spanish ships, including the *Buen Jesus*, one of the finest ships in the Spanish fleet. From other ships the Englishmen stole cinnamon, wine, ginger, hides, and other commodities that could be sold for a profit back in Europe. Despite a number of English casualties, the voyage was a success. Finally, on July 30, White was able to persuade the captains of the *Hopewell* and the *Moonlight* to advance toward Roanoke.

They arrived at the harbor near Roanoke by mid-August. A column of smoke could be seen rising from the island in the distance. According to White, the smoke "put us in good hope that some of the colony were expecting my return out of England." The next morning, two boats left the anchored ships and headed to shore.

The weather worsened as the men approached Roanoke. A large wave nearly knocked over the lead boat. It managed to reach the beach, but the second boat overturned. Violent waves pounded the men as they struggled. Few could swim. They tried to hold on to the overturned boat, but the sea was too strong. Some drowned. Of the eleven men on the boat, only four survived. After the accident, the men were shaken. White managed

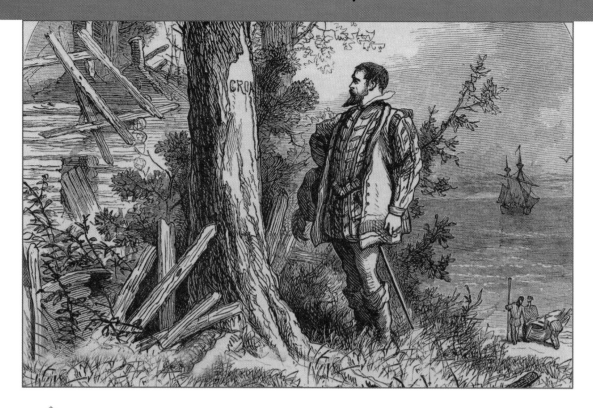

Artist Allen B. Doggett was also intrigued by the mysterious fate of the lost colonists and their settlement on Roanoke Island, as demonstrated by this image that dates from 1895. Throughout the centuries, many artists, writers, historians, and other scholars have tried to piece together information about what resulted with the colonists after they were left on the island by John White in 1587.

to persuade them to continue, but night had arrived, and their mission would have to wait until the next morning.

On August 18, the men reached the spot where White had left the colony. White's heart must have been pounding. His nervous anticipation probably turned to alarm when he saw no signs of the colonists. In the sand, White noticed footprints. Then, he discovered the letters *CRO* carved into a tree. White believed this was a message from the colonists. Before he had left he had instructed them to leave such a message if they ever decided to leave Roanoke. White was comforted that the message did not have a cross carved above it. A cross would have indicated that the colonists had left because they were in danger. But what exactly did the letters *CRO* mean?

As White approached the village, he discovered that the houses had been torn down and removed. The area was over-grown with weeds and grass, indicating that the colonists had left a long time ago. Carved into one of the fence posts on the out-skirts of the village, the men found the word *CROATOAN*. Like the message *CRO* found on the tree near the beach, this message did not have a cross carved above it. To White, this meant that colonists had left Roanoke for Croatoan Island, the home of their interpreter, Manteo. They had probably torn down their houses and taken them with them.

White and his crew returned to the ship anchored off Roanoke. The next morning it was agreed that they should advance to Croatoan Island. They rushed to depart, as they expected another storm. In their haste, the ship was almost run ashore. Two of their anchors got stuck in the sand. Both were cut loose, leaving them with only one. Then, the winds picked up and they were blown away from the shore before they could load their water casks. These events convinced the crew of the *Hopewell* to head for the island of Trinidad in the Caribbean to replenish their supplies instead of Croatoan. They would also be able to resume their raids on the Spanish. The plan was to return to Croatoan in the spring.

Once again, fate turned against White. Strong winds blew the *Hopewell* off course. Instead of spending the winter in the Caribbean, the *Hopewell* sailed back to England.

This is the title page from the third volume of *Principal Navigations, Voyages, and Discoveries of the English Nation*, written by English geographer and writer Richard Hakluyt. First published in 1598, Hakluyt's work details all of the progress made by the English explorers based on geographical region. Basing his writings on the direct observations of explorers, their own writings, ship logs, and other works, Hakluyt was able to reassemble the history of sea exploration from its beginnings until the sixteenth century.

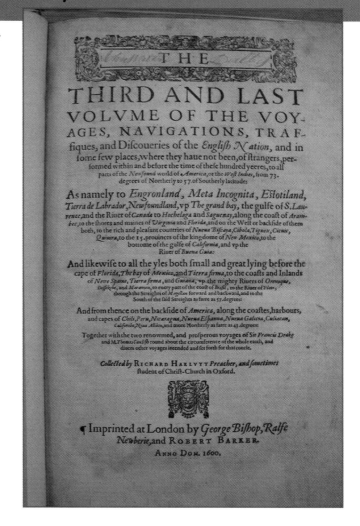

This was White's final attempt to contact the settlers. In 1593, he expressed his thoughts on the fate of the colony in a letter to Richard Hakluyt. He wrote that his colony was left to "the merciful help of the almighty, who I most humbly beseech to help and comfort them according to his most holy will and desire."

CHAPTER 6

A fter the failed relief voyage of 1590, Sir Walter Raleigh shifted his attention away from the Roanoke colony. It wasn't until 1603 that he sponsored another voyage to Virginia. This expedition only searched the area briefly, and found no sign of the colonists.

In 1607, Jamestown was founded on the shore of Chesapeake Bay, about 120 miles (193 km) from Roanoke Island. Unlike Roanoke, this colony would survive to become the first permanent English settlement in America. Their governor, John Smith, sent several expeditions in search of the Roanoke colonists, but no traces of them were found. By 1612, Smith had given up the search.

An Unsolved Mystery

Today, several theories have been proposed to explain what happened at Roanoke. Some historians believe that Spanish soldiers killed the colonists. Others think that they attempted to sail back to England but drowned at sea. Many more believe that Indians either killed all the colonists, or that some of them survived and were welcomed into local tribes.

Most historians believe the first theory can be ruled out. Since there is no account of such an event in any of the Spanish letters, books, or diaries that have survived the period, they believe these killings never took place.

Although the colonists might have attempted to return home, historians believe this, too, seems unlikely. White left a ship with the colonists in 1587, but none of them was experienced enough

This image of an archaeological dig on Roanoke Island was taken by a photographer working for the National Park Service in North Carolina in the 1990s. Over the years, several digs have been conducted with the help of the organization in an effort to locate remains of the 1585 and 1587 settlements, or artifacts from that period. Thus far, the most exciting discovery has been of an earthwork, or fort, which is believed to have been constructed by colonists working under Ralph Lane in 1585 or Richard Grenville in 1586. Artifacts attributed to the settlement were also found: a sickle made of wrought iron; fragments of Spanish pottery (believed to have been acquired by the colonists from Puerto Rico or Haiti on the way to America); and three metal counting devices that date from the sixteenth century and carry symbols from Tudor England.

to sail it. The colonists must have known that any attempt to reach England by boat would have likely failed, and thus avoided it.

Most historians agree that a conflict with local Indians tribes remains the most logical theory. And it is possible that some of the colonists survived and went on to live with local tribes.

This contemporary photograph shows an area where historians believe the lost colony of Roanoke possibly stood. Union soldiers stationed on Roanoke Island during the Civil War spent some of their time treasure hunting. In doing so, one of them unearthed this iron ax head in 1862. It is believed to date from the time of Sir Walter Raleigh's colony and is now part of the collection of East Carolina University. Even though various teams of archaeologists have since completed several excavations on the island, no other tools have been found. This ax head remains one of the best examples of a colonial artifact from the lost colony.

Many historians believe the colonists split into groups. If this happened, the separation may have resulted in different outcomes. For example, historians have theorized that some of the colonists went to Croatoan while others went north to Chesapeake Bay. If this occurred, then it's possible that Chesapeake Bay tribes killed some colonists, while others joined forces with Croatoan tribes.

Still, no one knows for sure what happened at Roanoke. Historians continue to search for clues in primary source documents, while archaeologists dig in the soil of Roanoke Island for artifacts. Each group believes the answers are within reach. Whether the answers can be found within a dusty book, or buried underground, they are certain the truth is out there waiting to be discovered.

TIMELINE

June 11, 1578 — Queen Elizabeth I grants Sir Humphrey Gilbert permission to explore and settle America.

September 9, 1583 — Sir Humphrey Gilbert drowns returning from Newfoundland after an unsuccessful attempt to establish a colony there.

March 25, 1584 — Queen Elizabeth I grants Sir Walter Raleigh permission to explore and settle America.

April 27, 1584 — The scouting expedition led by Philip Amadas and Arthur Barlowe leaves England for North America.

July 4, 1584 — Scouting expedition arrives at the Outer Banks (chain of islands off the coast of present-day North Carolina).

January 6, 1585 — Sir Walter Raleigh is knighted by Queen Elizabeth.

June 22, 1585 — Ralph Lane's military colony arrives at the Outer Banks.

June 19, 1586 — Lane's colonists depart Roanoke for England on Sir Francis Drake's ships.

July 22, 25, 1587 — John White and 116 other colonists arrive at Roanoke.

52

August 18, 1587 — Virginia Dare becomes the first English person born in America.

August 27, 1587 — John White leaves Roanoke to return to England for supplies.

April 22, 1588 — John White departs England for Roanoke aboard the *Brave*.

May 22, 1588 — John White returns to England after an unsuccessful attempt to reach Roanoke aboard the *Brave*.

July 29, 1588 — England confronts the Spanish Armada at the Battle of Gravelines.

August 18, 1590 — White arrives at Roanoke and finds the colonists have disappeared.

PRIMARY SOURCE TRANSCRIPTIONS

Page 19: Excerpt of a transcription of Sir Walter Raleigh's *The Historie of the World*

Transcription

If fortune and chance were not sometimes the causes of good and evil in men, but an idle voice, whereby we express success, how comes it then, that so many worthy and wise men depend upon so many unworthy and empty headed fools; that riches and honor are given to external men, and without kernel: and so many learned, virtuous, and valiant men wear out their lives in poor and dejected estates?

In a word there is no other inferior, or apparent cause, beside the partiality of mans affection, but the fashioning and not fashioning of ourselves according to the nature of the time wherein we live, for whosoever is most able, and best sufficient to discern, and hath with all an honest and open heart and loving truth. If princes, or those that govern, endure no other discourse then their own flatteries, then I say such as one, whose virtue and courage forbid him to be base and a dissembler, shall evermore hang under the wheel, which kind of deserving well and receiving ill, we always falsely charge fortune with all. For whosoever shall tell any great man or magistrate, that he is not just, the general of an army, that he is not valiant, and great ladies that they are not fair, shall never be made a counselor, a captain, or a courtier. Neither is it sufficient to be wise with a wise prince, valiant with a valiant, and just with him that is just, for such a one hath no estate in his prosperity; but he must also change with the successor, if he be of contrary qualities, sail with the tide of the time, and alter form and condition, as the estate or the estates master change: Otherwise how were it possible, that the most base men, and separate from all [omitted word] qualities, could so often attain to honor and riches, but by such an observant slavish course? These men having nothing else to value themselves by, but a counterfeit kind of wondering at other men, and by making them believe that all their vices are virtues, and all their dusty actions crystalline, have yet in all ages prospered equally with the most virtuous, if not exceeded them . . .

Page 22: Title page from Thomas Harriot's *A Briefe and True Report of the New Found Land of Virginia*

Transcription

A brief and true report of the new found land of Virginia, of the commodities and of the nature and manners of the natural inhabitants: Discovered by the English

Colony there seated by Sir Richard Grenville Knight In the year 1585. Which remained under the government of twelve months, At the special charge and direction of the Honorable SIR WALTER RALEIGH Knight, lord Warden of the stannaries who therein hath been favored and authorized by her MAJESTY and her letters patents: This fore book Is made in English By Thomas Harriot; servant to the above named Sir WALTER, a member of the Colony, and there employed in discovering.

Page 27: Transcription of excerpt from Hakluyt's *Discourse of Western Planting*

Transcription

A particular discourse concerning the great necessity and manifold commodities that are like to grow to this Realm of England by the Western discoveries lately attempted, written in the year 1584 by Richard Hakluyt of Oxford at the request and direction of the right worshipful Mr. Walter Raleigh now Knight . . .

That this western discovery will be greatly for the enlargement of the gospel of Christ whereunto the Princes of the reformed religion are chiefly bound among whom her Majesty is principal.

That all other English Trades are grown beggarly or dangerous, especially in all the king of Spain his Dominions, where our men are driven to fling their Bibles and prayer books into the sea, and to forswear and renounce their religion and conscience and consequently their obedience to her Majesty.

That this western voyage will yield unto us all the commodities of Europe, Africa, and Asia, as far as we were wont to travel, and supply the wants of all our decayed trades.

That this enterprise will be for the manifold employment of numbers of idle men, and for breeding of many sufficient, and for utterance of the great quantity of the commodities of our Realm.

That this voyage will be a great bridle to the Indies of the king of Spain and a means that we may arrest at our pleasure for the space of time weeks or three months every year, one or two hundred sail of his subjects ships at the fishing in New found land.

That the riches that the Indian treasure wrought in time of Charles the late Emperor father to the Spanish king, is to be had in consideration of the Q[ueen] most excellent Majesty, least the continual communion of the like treasure from thence to his son, work the unrecoverable annoy of this Realm, whereof already we have had very dangerous experience.

What special means may bring King Phillip from his high Throne, and make him equal to the Princes his neighbors, wherewithal is showed his weakness in the west Indies.

That the limits of the king of Spain's dominions in the west Indies be nothing so large as is generally imagined and surmised, neither those parts which he hold be of any such forces as is falsely given out by the [omitted word] clergy and others his suitors, to terrify the Princes of the Religion and to abuse and blind them.

The Names of the rich towns lined along the sea coast on the north side from the [omitted word] of the main land of America under the king of Spain.

A brief declaration of the chief lands in the Bay of Mexico being under the king of Spain, with their havens and forts, and what commodities they yield.

That the Spaniards have executed most outrageous and more then Turkish cruelties in all the West Indies, whereby they are every where there, become most odious unto them, who would join with us or any other most willingly to shake of their most intolerable yoke, and have begun to do it already in [omitted word] places where they were Lords heretofore.

That the passage in this voyage is easy and short, that it cut not near the trade of any other mighty Princes, nor near their countries, that it is to be performed at all times of the year, and need but one kind of wind, that Ireland being full of good havens on the south and west sides, is the nearest part of Europe to it, which by this trade shall be in more security, and the sooner drawn to more civility.

That hereby the revenues and customs of her Majesty both outwards and inwards shall mightily be enlarged by the toll, excises, and other duties which without oppression may be raised.

That this action will be greatly for the increase, maintenance and safety of our navy, and especially of great shipping which is the strength of our Realm, and for the support of all those occupations that depend upon the same.

That speedy planting in divers fit places is most necessary upon these lucky western discoveries for fear of the danger of being prevented by other nations which have the like intentions, with the order thereof and other reasons there with all alleged.

Means to keep this enterprise from [being] overthrown and the enterprisers from shame and dishonor.

That by these Colonies the Northwest passage to Cathay [Japan] and China may easily quickly and perfectly be searched out as well by river and overland, as by sea, for proof whereof here are quoted and alleged divers rare testimonies out of the three volumes of voyages gathered by Ramses and other grave authors.

That the Queen of England title to all the west Indies, or at the least to as much as is from Florida to the Circle Arctic, is more lawful and right then the Spaniards or any other Christian Princes . . .

GLOSSARY

America Landmass consisting of the present-day continents of South America and North America.

circumnavigate To go completely around.

commodity Something useful or valued, usually meant to be sold.

conspire To secretly agree to do something.

Devonshire A county in southwestern England.

flagship The ship that carries the commander or captain of a fleet and flies the flag that identifies the fleet.

fleet A number of ships sailing together.

mariner A sailor or seaman.

palisade A fence made out of stakes, often used for military purposes.

pike A weapon made of a spearhead attached to a long pole.

pinnace A light sailing ship.

privateer A sailor or ship that is licensed to attack enemy shipping fleets. Also known as a "gentleman pirate."

shoal A sandbank or sandbar below shallow water.

sound Area of water separating the mainland from an island.

Spanish Armada Fleet of 130 Spanish warships carrying 8,000 sailors and 19,000 soldiers sent by King Philip II of Spain to attack England in 1588.

Virginia In colonial times, the territory in America claimed by Sir Walter Raleigh. It included the present-day states of Virginia and North Carolina.

FOR MORE INFORMATION

Fort Raleigh National Historic Site
1401 National Park Drive
Manteo, NC 27954
(252) 473-5772
Web site: http://www.nps.gov/fora

The Lost Colony Symphonic Drama
1409 National Park Drive
Manteo, NC 27954
(800) 488-5012
Web site: http://www.thelostcolony.org

The Museum of the Native American Resource Center
PO Box 1510
Pembroke, NC 28372-1510
(910) 521-6282
Web site: http://www.uncp.edu/nativemuseum

North Carolina Museum of History
4650 Mail Service Center
Raleigh, NC 27699-4650
(919) 715-0200
Web site: http://ncmuseumofhistory.org

Roanoke Colonies Research Office
c/o Department of English
East Carolina University
Greenville, NC 27858-4353
(919) 328-6715
Web site: http://www.ecu.edu/rcro/default.htm

Roanoke Island Festival Park
1 Festival Park
Manteo, NC 27954
(252) 475-1500
Web site: http://www.roanokeisland.com

Web Sites

Due to the changing nature of Internet links, The Rosen Publishing Group, Inc., has developed an online list of Web sites related to the subject of this book. This site is updated regularly. Please use this link to access the list:

http://www.rosenlinks.com/pstc/roan

FOR FURTHER READING

Bosco, Peter I. *Roanoke: The Story of the Lost Colony*. Brookfield, CT: Millbrook, 1992.

Campbell, Elizabeth A. *The Carving on the Tree*. Boston, MA: Little, Brown, and Company, 1968.

Dolan, Edward F. *The Lost Colony of Roanoke*. New York, NY: Marshall Cavendish, 2002.

Fradin, Dennis Brindell. *The North Carolina Colony*. Chicago, IL: Children's Press, 1991.

Hilliam, Paul. *Elizabeth I: Queen of England's Golden Age*. New York, NY: Rosen, 2005.

Kent, Zachary. *The Mysterious Disappearance of Roanoke Colony in American History*. Berkeley Heights, NJ: Enslow Publishers, 2004.

Korman, Susan. *Sir Walter Raleigh: English Explorer and Author*. Philadelphia, PA: Chelsea House, 2001.

Marrin, Albert. *The Sea King: Sir Francis Drake and His Times*. New York, NY: Atheneum, 1995.

McCarthy, Shaun. *Sir Walter Raleigh*. Chicago, IL: Heinemann Library, 2002.

Rossi, Ann. *Cultures Collide: Native American and Europeans 1492-1700*. Washington, DC: National Geographic, 2004.

Staiger, Ralph C. *Thomas Harriot: Science Pioneer*. New York, NY: Clarion Books, 1998.

BIBLIOGRAPHY

Blacker, Irwin R., ed. *Hakluyt's Voyages*. New York, NY: Viking, 1965.

Conlin, Joseph R. *The American Past: A Survey of American History to 1877*. Fort Worth, TX: Harcourt Brace, 1997.

Harriot, Thomas. *A Briefe and True Report of the New Found Land of Virginia*. New York, NY: Dover, 1972.

Hulton, Paul. *America 1585: The Complete Drawings of John White*. Chapel Hill, NC: University of North Carolina Press, 1984.

Hume, Ivor Noel. *The Virginia Adventure*. New York, NY: Knopf, 1994.

Kupperman, Karen Ordahl. *Roanoke: The Abandoned Colony*. Totowa, NJ: Rowman and Allanheld, 1984.

Mancall, Peter C., ed. *Envisioning America*. Boston, MA: Bedford, 1995.

Miller, Lee. *Roanoke: Solving the Mystery of the Lost Colony*. New York, NY: Arcade, 2001.

Quinn, David B. and Alison M. Quinn, eds. *Virginia Voyages from Hakluyt*. London, UK: Oxford University Press, 1973.

Quinn, David B. *North America from Earliest Discovery to First Settlements*. New York, NY: Harper & Row, 1977.

Quinn, David B. *Set Fair for Roanoke*. Chapel Hill, NC: University of North Carolina Press, 1985.

Stick, David. *Roanoke Island: The Beginnings of English America*. Chapel Hill, NC: University of North Carolina Press, 1983.

Trevelyan, Raleigh. *Sir Walter Raleigh*. New York, NY: Holt, 2004.

Williams, Neville. *The Sea Dogs: Privateers, Plunder, and Piracy in the Elizabethan Age*. New York, NY: Macmillan, 1975.

PRIMARY SOURCE IMAGE LIST

Page 7: Hans Holbein the Younger painted this portrait of King Henry VIII in 1540 during Henry's reign. It is housed at the Palazzo Barberini at the National Gallery of Art in Rome, Italy. The adjacent sixteenth-century portrait of Queen Elizabeth, painted by an anonymous artist, is housed at the Galleria Palatina, Palazzo Pitti, in Florence, Italy.

Page 9: The sixteenth-century map of the world on this page traces Francis Drake's famous voyage around the world. It is housed at the British Library in London, England.

Page 14: John White painted this watercolor between 1570 and 1593. Like other studies of Native Americans, White was careful to observe and re-create their farming and fishing practices as accurately as possible. This image is housed at the British Museum in London, England.

Page 17: This lithograph (*Map of Raleigh's Virginia*) is a copy of a painting by John White of a map of the Virginia coastline and Chesapeake Bay. It was created sometime between 1570 and 1593.

Page 19: Simon de Passe drew this image of Sir Walter Raleigh for the title page of Raleigh's *The Historie of the World*, an account of his experiences in the New World first published in London, England, in 1614.

Page 22: This anonymous portrait (*left*) is believed to be of Thomas Harriot (also spelled Hariot) holding a spiced orange, common during Elizabethan times. It is located at Trinity College in Oxford, England. The title page of Thomas Harriot's book, *A Briefe and True Report of the New Found Land of Virginia*, is also pictured. It was first published in 1590.

Page 24: Theodor de Bry created this hand-colored engraving in 1590 based on observational drawings by John White. The de Bry engraving was then printed in Harriot's *Briefe and True Report*.

Page 27: A page from Richard Hakluyt's *Discourse of Western Planting*, a book printed in 1584 that detailed arguments for England to continually fund expeditions to colonize the New World.

Page 32: John White created this watercolor map of the eastern coastline of the United States in the 1580s.

Page 34: John White painted this image of a fish during the 1585 expedition to Roanoke.

Page 37: Theodor de Bry created this hand-colored engraving, *A Great Lord of Virginia* in 1590. It is based on a drawing done in the 1580s by John White. De Bry's engraving was printed in Thomas Harriot's *A Briefe and True Report of the New Found Land of Virginia* in 1590.

Page 42: Hendrik Cornelisz Vroom made this oil painting of a sea battle between the Spanish Armada and the English navy in 1600. It is housed at the Landes Museum Ferdinandeum in Innsbruck, Austria.

Page 47: The title page from the third volume of Richard Hakluyt's book, *Principal Navigations, Voyages, and Discoveries of the English Nation*, circa 1598. This title page is from a later edition.

Page 50: In 1862, Union soldiers unearthed this ax head, believed to be a tool used during the time of Walter Raleigh's colony. It is housed at East Carolina University.

INDEX

About the Author

Brian Belval is an editor of young adult nonfiction in New York City. His work on *The Lost Colony of Roanoke* has resulted in a continuing interest in early American history and English exploration of the New World. Recently, he has begun to research the life of Sir Francis Drake, one of England's legendary "sea dogs."

Photo Credits

Cover, p. 24 The New York Public Library/Art Resource, NY; p. 1 Library of Congress Prints and Photographs Division; p. 5 The Mariners' Museum, Newport News, VA; p. 7 (left) Palazzo Barberini, Rome, Italy/Bridgeman Art Library; p. 7 (right) Scala/Art Resource, NY; pp. 8–9 Library of Congress Rare Book and Special Collections Division; p. 13 © Guildhall Art Gallery, London, Great Britain/HIP/Art Resource, NY; pp. 14, 17, 19 Private Collection/Bridgeman Art Library; p. 18 Library of Congress, Washington D.C., USA/Bridgeman Art Library; p. 22 (left) Property of the President and Fellows of Trinity College, Oxford. Used with permission; p. 22 (right) Beinecke Rare Book and Manuscript Library, Yale University; p. 27 George A. Arents Collection, The New York Public Library, Astor, Lenox and Tilden Foundation; p. 29 © North Wind Picture Archives; p. 32 Art Resource, NY; p. 34 British Museum, London, UK/Bridgeman Art Library; p. 37 Service Historique de la Marine, Vincennes, France/Bridgeman Art Library; p. 39 © Bettmann/Corbis; p. 42 Erich Lessing / Art Resource, NY; p. 45 Picture Collection, The Branch Libraries, The New York Public Library, Astor, Lenox and Tilden Foundations; p. 47 Rare Books Division, The New York Public Library, Astor, Lenox and Tilden Foundation; p. 49 National Park Service, Fort Raleigh National Historic Site; p. 50 (top) © Raymond Gehman/ Corbis; p. 50 (bottom) Collection of East Carolina University, photo courtesy of the National Parks Service, used by permission of Charles R. Ewen, PhD.

Editor: Joann Jovinelly; **Photo Researcher:** Sherri Liberman